Sunset

BASIC
GARDENING
ILLUSTRATED

BY CAROL MOHOLT, JANET SANCHEZ
AND THE EDITORS OF SUNSET BOOKS

SUNSET BOOKS · MENLO PARK,

THE GARDENER'S GUIDEBOOK

Welcome to the world of gardening-a world full of variety, wonder, and ongoing delight. Whether you want a garden filled with bright flowers, a sweep of distinctive shrubs and trees, a cornucopia of vegetables and fruits—or all of these, plus a verdant lawn as well!—this book will give you the hands-on advice to help you reach your goal.

There's really no mystery to creating a satisfying garden. As is true for other endeavors, success in gardening involves understanding some basic principles. In the first part of this book, "Gardening Basics," you'll find complete information and step-by step guidance on everything from soil preparation and watering to pruning, propagation, and pest control. In the second section, "A Primer of Garden Plants," you'll find information on choosing and caring for a wide variety of plants: trees, shrubs, lawns, ground covers, vines, flowering perennials and annuals, and all sorts of delicious edibles.

Let this book make gardening a rewarding, enjoyable, and satisfying part of your life, a hobby that will bring you joy well beyond the effort involved.

SUNSET BOOKS

Vice President, Sales: Richard A. Smeby
Editorial Director: Bob Doyle
Production Director: Lory Day
Art Director: Vasken Guiragossian

Staff for this book:

Managing Editor: Suzanne Normand Eyre
Copy Editor and Indexer: Rebecca LaBrum
Photo Researcher: Tishana Peebles
Contributing Editors: Philip Edinger, Susan Lang
Production Coordinator: Patricia S. Williams
Special Contributors: Lisa Anderson, Jean Warboy

Art Director: Alice Rogers
Principal Illustrators: Erin O'Toole, Jenny Speckels
Additional Illustrations: Lois Lovejoy, Jane McCreary, Rik Olson, Mimi Osborne, Lucy Sargeant, Wendy Smith-Griswold, Catherine M. Watters
Map Design and Cartography: Reineck & Reineck, San Francisco
Computer Production: Joan Olson, Fog Press

Cover: Photography by Glenn Cormier.
Border photograph by David McDonald.

First printing January 1999
Copyright © 1999 Sunset Publishing Corporation, Menlo Park, CA 94025.
Fourth edition. All rights reserved, including the right of reproduction in whole or in part in any form. Library of Congress Catalog Card Number: 98-86300.
ISBN 0-376-03079-8

Printed in the United States

For additional copies of *Basic Gardening Illustrated* or any other *Sunset* book, call our distribution partners at Leisure Arts, 1-800-526-5111.

CONTENTS

Behind every successful garden is a gardener who has come to understand certain basic gardening procedures and the ideas behind them. In the next 88 pages, we review these procedures and show you how to implement them.

GARDENING
BASICS

You'll first find a discussion of the importance of climate, followed by descriptions and a map of the 45 Sunset garden climate zones of North America. Next, "How Plants Grow" gives you an overview of the interrelated functions of seeds, roots, stems, leaves, flowers, and fruits.

Sections on soil management and fertilizing provide information on these fundamental aspects of gardening. You'll then learn how to plant seedlings and larger plants, and when and how to water them. The next section offers advice on pruning plants properly to keep them at their best and "Propagating Plants" gives you the skills you need to start your own plants from seeds, cuttings, and layering.

At some point, most gardeners encounter problems of one kind or another. Look to pages 62–88 for help in preventing, identifying, and managing pests, diseases, and weeds.

Finally, "Modifying Climate" gives tips on protecting plants from extremes of heat and cold.

Making compost gives your garden new life from old by recycling fallen leaves, grass clippings, and other organic materials into an ideal soil amendment.

C LIMATE

Of all the factors affecting our gardens, we have the least control over climate. The best we can do is understand the local climate, then choose the plants most likely to flourish under these conditions.

When you're trying to decide if a certain plant will grow in your garden, you often begin by thinking about your typical winter and summer temperatures. Will the plant freeze in January? Will it bake and shrivel come August? But while summer heat and winter cold are crucial considerations, other climatic features are just as important. Do you garden in a humid region or in one that's very dry? Is your weather windy all the time, or is it typically calm? Perhaps you're living in a sunny area where rain is the exception; perhaps you garden in frequently overcast conditions where rain comes year-round. All these factors play a role in determining the success or failure of the plants you want to grow.

Latitude, elevation, and the jet streams (see facing page) are the three general factors determining climate. Several other factors play a role, as well: amount of wind, timing and amount of annual rainfall, location of mountain ranges (which, in turn, has some influence on the preceding two factors), and the proximity of large bodies of water.

WINDY OR CALM CONDITIONS

Some areas are perpetually windy; in others, windy weather is associated only with certain seasons. Wind dries out plants and soil, and it's hard on plants with delicate foliage and flowers. You may be able to compensate by providing windbreaks and extra water, and by choosing plants that withstand wind successfully.

TIMING AND AMOUNT OF RAINFALL

Many plants are accustomed to receiving a certain amount of rain at a particular time of year, depending on the conditions prevailing in their native regions. In general, the eastern half of the United States has rainy summers, while summers in the West are dry (though early summer can be wet in the Pacific Northwest). Many plants native to the

WHAT IS A MICROCLIMATE?

First off, there's a difference between a climate zone change and a microclimate. Gardeners living on or near the border of two climate zones deal with adjacent yet different climates—and they sometimes think of these as microclimates. For example, greater Seattle straddles *Sunset* Zones 4 and 5; tender plants that thrive in marine-influenced Zone 5 will freeze if moved into a Zone 4 neighborhood a few blocks away.

Used in its correct sense, though, "microclimate" refers to local conditions resulting in a different climates within a single garden or slightly larger area in a neighborhood—all within *one* climate zone. For instance, south-facing portions of a garden are typically warmer than those facing north, and areas near walls and fences tend to be drier than those in the middle of a garden bed. Look for the following microclimates:

Enclosed on all sides, this narrow courtyard garden has its own warm, wind-protected microclimate, where heat-loving plants thrive.

East require extra summer water if planted in the West; conversely, some western natives will die in eastern gardens, drowning in the summer rain. Be sure the rainfall where you live suits the plants you choose.

LOCATION OF MOUNTAIN RANGES

Mountains interfere with basic wind patterns and the movement of air masses: depending on their height and alignment, they either block the wind's progress or direct it. They also cause moist air to rise and cool, so that more rain is deposited on one side of a mountain than on the other. If you live near hills or mountains, your climate may differ from that of a neighbor living on the opposite slope: you may live on the west side of a mountain and receive 40 inches of rain per year, for example, while someone on the eastern side, just 20 miles away, gets only 12 inches.

INFLUENCE OF WATER

If you live near the ocean or a large inland body of water, your climate will differ from the climate at the same latitude some miles inland. In Buffalo, New York, for example, the nearby Great Lakes produce extremely snowy winters. In San Francisco, California, the Pacific Ocean makes for cool, overcast summers. You'll need to account for these conditions in choosing plants for such ocean- or lakeside regions.

UNUSUALLY WARM SECTIONS. A courtyard that receives full afternoon sun and is surrounded by high walls on all four sides will be a garden hot spot. Even a single cement or stucco wall may warm part of a garden if it receives several hours of afternoon sun each day—the wall absorbs heat during the day, then gradually releases it during the cooler hours. Avoid creating hot spots if your overall climate is already a warm one and you want to grow more than just heat-loving plants.

COOL POCKETS. Because cool air travels downward, the bottom of a slope is colder than the top—so the base of a hill isn't the place for heat-loving summer vegetables. A cold air pocket may also develop halfway down a slope if a hedge or wall impedes airflow. If you garden in a northern latitude or a mountainous region with many frosty days and nights each year, be particularly careful not to plant tender plants or vegetables in such cool pockets.

WINDY AREAS. The placement of buildings on your property can generate a local wind tunnel. Even if the enhanced wind isn't especially severe, it can still damage the leaves of sensitive plants and dry out the soil, resulting in a need for extra water. To neutralize a wind tunnel, you can plant fast-growing trees or shrubs facing into the wind. Don't construct a solid wall; it will simply deflect the wind briefly, then drop it back into the garden a few feet away.

LATITUDE, ELEVATION, AND JET STREAMS

Three factors have the most general effects on climate.

LATITUDE

The farther north of the equator a place is, the colder its winters are likely to be, and the longer the wintry weather is likely to last. Winter may arrive early, too—as shown in the photo at right.

A yet-to-be-picked autumn apple crop in a Massachusetts garden glows through the frosty cloak of an early snow.

ELEVATION

The higher your elevation, the cooler the temperatures will be, in both winter and summer. The growing season is usually shorter, as well.

JET STREAMS

The strong, fast high-altitude air currents known as jet streams affect climate by picking up air of all types—moist, dry, warm, cold—and carrying it to other areas. The jet streams tend to dip farther south in winter and move more to the north in summer, following the movement of the sun. The predictable storms that follow the jet streams' path are largely responsible for the rainy and dry seasons we experience.

At an altitude of 7,000 feet, this Colorado garden enjoys only a brief growing season—but it's lush with summer color nonetheless.

SUNSET'S GARDEN CLIMATE ZONES

A plant's performance is governed by the total climate: length of growing season, timing and amount of rainfall, winter lows, summer highs, humidity. *Sunset*'s climate zone maps take all these factors into account—unlike the familiar hardiness zone maps devised by the U.S. Department of Agriculture, which divide the U.S. and Canada into zones based strictly on winter lows. The U.S.D.A. maps tell you only where a plant may survive the winter; our climate zone maps let you see where that plant will thrive year-round. Below are brief descriptions of the 45 zones illustrated on the map on pages 10–11. For more information, consult *Sunset*'s *National Garden Book* and *Western Garden Book*.

ZONE 1. Coldest Winters in the West and Western Prairie States

Growing season: early June through Aug., but with some variation—the longest seasons are usually found near this zone's large bodies of water. Frost can come any night of the year. Winters are snowy and intensely cold, due to latitude, elevation, and/or influence of continental air mass. There's some summer rainfall.

ZONE 2. Second-coldest Western Climate

Growing season: early May through Sept. Winters are cold (lows run from −3° to −34°F/−19° to −37°C), but less so than in Zone 1. In northern and interior areas, lower elevations fall into Zone 2, higher areas into Zone 1.

ZONE 3. West's Mildest High-elevation and Interior Regions

Growing season: early May to late Sept.—shorter than in Zone 2, but offset by milder winters (lows from 13° to −24°F/−11° to −31°C). This is fine territory for plants needing winter chill and dry, hot summers.

ZONE 4. Cold-winter Western Washington and British Columbia

Growing season: early May to early Oct. Summers are cool, thanks to ocean influence; chilly winters (19° to −7°F/−7° to −22°C) result from elevation, influence of continental air mass, or both. Coolness, ample rain suit many perennials and bulbs.

ZONE 5. Ocean-influenced Northwest Coast and Puget Sound

Growing season: mid-April to Nov., typically with cool temperatures throughout. Less rain falls here than in Zone 4; winter lows range from 28° to 1°F/−2° to −17°C. This "English garden" climate is ideal for rhododendrons and many rock garden plants.

ZONE 6. Oregon's Willamette Valley

Growing season: mid-Mar. to mid-Nov., with somewhat warmer temperatures than in Zone 5. Ocean influence keeps winter lows about the same as in Zone 5. Climate suits all but tender plants and those needing hot or dry summers.

ZONE 7. Oregon's Rogue River Valley, California's High Foothills

Growing season: May to early Oct. Summers are hot and dry; typical winter lows run from 23° to 9°F/−5° to −13°C. The summer-winter contrast suits plants that need dry, hot summers and moist, only moderately cold winters.

ZONE 8. Cold-air Basins of California's Central Valley

Growing season: mid-Feb. through Nov. This is a valley floor with no maritime influence. Summers are hot; winter lows range from 29° to 13°F/−2° to −11°C. Rain comes in the cooler months, covering just the early part of the growing season.

ZONE 9. Thermal Belts of California's Central Valley

Growing season: late Feb. through Dec. Zone 9 is located in the higher elevations around Zone 8, but its summers are just as hot; its winter lows are slightly higher (temperatures range from 28° to 18°F/−2° to −8°C). Rainfall pattern is the same as in Zone 8.

ZONE 10. High Desert Areas of Arizona, New Mexico, West Texas, Oklahoma Panhandle, and Southwest Kansas

Growing season: April to early Nov. Chilly (even snow-dusted) weather rules from late Nov. through Feb., with lows from 31° to 24°F/−1° to −4°C. Rain comes in summer as well as in the cooler seasons.

ZONE 11. Medium to High Desert of California and Southern Nevada

Growing season: early April to late Oct. Summers are sizzling, with 110 days above 90°F/32°C. Balancing this is a 3½-month winter, with 85 nights below freezing and lows from 11° to 0°F/−12° to −18°C. Scant rainfall comes in winter.

ZONE 12. Arizona's Intermediate Desert

Growing season: mid-Mar. to late Nov., with scorching midsummer heat. Compared to Zone 13, this region has harder frosts; record low is 6°F/−14°C. Rains come in summer and winter.

ZONE 13. Low or Subtropical Desert

Growing season: mid-Feb. through Nov., interrupted by nearly 3 months of incandescent, growth-stopping summer heat. Most frosts are light (record lows run from 19° to 13°F/−17° to −11°C); scant rain comes in summer and winter.

ZONE 14. Inland Northern and Central California with Some Ocean Influence

Growing season: early Mar. to mid-Nov., with rain coming in the remaining months. Periodic intrusions of marine air temper summer heat and winter cold (lows run from 26° to 16°F/−3° to −9°C). Mediterranean-climate plants are at home here.

ZONE 15. Northern and Central California's Chilly-winter Coast-influenced Areas

Growing season: Mar. to Dec. Rain comes from fall through winter. Typical winter lows range from 28° to 21°F/−2° to −6°C. Maritime air influences the zone much of the time, giving it cooler, moister summers than Zone 14.

ZONE 16. Northern and Central California Coast Range Thermal Belts

Growing season: late Feb. to late Nov. With cold air draining to lower elevations, winter lows typically run from 32° to 19°F/0° to −7°C. Like Zone 15, this region is dominated by maritime air, but its winters are milder on average.

ZONE 17. Oceanside Northern and Central California and Southernmost Oregon

Growing season: late Feb. to early Dec. Coolness and fog are hallmarks; summer highs seldom top 75°F/24°C, while winter lows run from 36° to 23°F/2° to −5°C. Heat-loving plants disappoint or dwindle here.

ZONE 18. Hilltops and Valley Floors of Interior Southern California

Growing season: mid-Mar. through late Nov. Summers are hot and dry; rain comes in winter, when lows reach 28° to 10°F/−2° to −12°C. Plants from the Mediterranean and Near Eastern regions thrive here.

ZONE 19. Thermal Belts around Southern California's Interior Valleys

Growing season: early Mar. through Nov. As in Zone 18, rainy winters and hot, dry summers are the norm—but here, winter lows dip only to 27° to 22°F/−3° to −6°C, allowing some tender evergreen plants to grow outdoors with protection.

ZONE 20. Hilltops and Valley Floors of Ocean-influenced Inland Southern California

Growing season: late Mar. to late Nov.—but fairly mild winters (lows of 28° to 23°F/−2° to −5°C) allow gardening through much of the year. Cool and moist maritime influence alternates with hot, dry interior air.

ZONE 21. Thermal Belts around Southern California's Ocean-influenced Interior Valleys

Growing season: early Mar. to early Dec., with the same tradeoff of oceanic and interior influence as in Zone 20. During the winter rainy season, lows range from 36° to 23°F/2° to −5°C—warmer than in Zone 20, since the colder air drains to the valleys.

ZONE 22. Colder-winter Parts of Southern California's Coastal Region

Growing season: Mar. to early Dec. Winter lows seldom fall below 28°F/–2°C (records are around 21°F/–6°C), though colder air sinks to this zone from Zone 23. Summers are warm; rain comes in winter. Climate here is largely oceanic.

ZONE 23. Thermal Belts of Southern California's Coastal Region

Growing season: almost year-round (all but first half of Jan.). Rain comes in winter. Reliable ocean influence keeps summers mild (except when hot Santa Ana winds come from inland), frosts negligible; 23°F/–5°C is the record low.

ZONE 24. Marine-dominated Southern California Coast

Growing season: all year, but periodic freezes have dramatic effects (record lows are 33° to 20°F/1° to –7°C). Climate here is oceanic (but warmer than oceanic Zone 17), with cool summers, mild winters. Subtropical plants thrive.

ZONE 25. South Florida and the Keys

Growing season: all year. Add ample year-round rainfall (least in Dec. through Mar.), high humidity, and overall warmth, and you have a near-tropical climate. The Keys are frost-free; winter lows elsewhere run from 40° to 25°F/4° to –4°C.

ZONE 26. Central and Interior Florida

Growing season: early Feb. to late Dec., with typically humid, warm to hot weather. Rain is plentiful all year, heaviest in summer and early fall. Lows range from 15°F/–9°C in the north to 27°F/–3°C in the south; arctic air brings periodic hard freezes.

ZONE 27. Lower Rio Grande Valley

Growing season: early Mar. to mid-Dec.. Summers are hot and humid; winter lows only rarely dip below freezing. Many plants from tropical and subtropical Africa and South America are well adapted here.

ZONE 28. Gulf Coast, North Florida, Atlantic Coast to Charleston

Growing season: mid-Mar. to early Dec. Humidity and rainfall are year-round phenomena; summers are hot, winters virtually frostless but subject to periodic invasions by frigid arctic air. Azaleas, camellias, many subtropicals flourish.

ZONE 29. Interior Plains of South Texas

Growing season: mid-Mar. through Nov. Moderate rainfall (to 25" annually) comes year-round. Summers are hot. Winter lows can dip to 26°F/–3°C, with occasional arctic freezes bringing much lower readings.

ZONE 30. Hill Country of Central Texas

Growing season: mid-Mar. through Nov. Zone 30 has higher annual rainfall than Zone 29 (to 35") and lower winter temperatures, normally to around 20°F/–7°C. Seasonal variations favor many fruit crops, perennials.

ZONE 31. Interior Plains of Gulf Coast and Coastal Southeast

Growing season: mid-Mar. to early Nov. In this extensive east-west zone, hot and sticky summers contrast with chilly winters (record low temperatures are 7° to 0°F/–14° to –18°C). There's rain all year (an annual average of 50"), with the least falling in Oct.

ZONE 32. Interior Plains of Mid-Atlantic States; Chesapeake Bay, Southeastern Pennsylvania, Southern New Jersey

Growing season: late Mar. to early Nov. Rain falls year-round (40" to 50" annually); winter lows (moving through the zone from south to north) are 30° to 20°F/–1° to –7°C. Humidity is less oppressive here than in Zone 31.

ZONE 33. North-Central Texas and Oklahoma Eastward to the Appalachian Foothills

Growing season: mid-April through Oct. Warm Gulf Coast air and colder continental/arctic fronts both play a role; their unpredictable interplay results in a wide range in annual rainfall (22" to 52") and winter lows (20° to 0°F/–7° to –18°C). Summers are muggy and warm to hot.

ZONE 34. Lowlands and Coast from Gettysburg to North of Boston

Growing season: late April to late Oct. Ample rainfall and humid summers are the norm. Winters are variable—typically fairly mild (around 20°F/–7°C), but with lows down to –3° to –22°F/–19° to –30°C if arctic air swoops in.

ZONE 35. Ouachita Mountains, Northern Oklahoma and Arkansas, Southern Kansas to North-Central Kentucky and Southern Ohio

Growing season: late April to late Oct. Rain comes in all seasons. Summers can be truly hot and humid. Without arctic fronts, winter lows are around 18°F/–8°C; with them, the coldest weather may bring lows of –20°F/–29°C.

ZONE 36. Appalachian Mountains

Growing season: May to late Oct. Thanks to greater elevation, summers are cooler and less humid, winters colder (0° to –20°F/–18° to –29°C) than in adjacent, lower zones. Rain comes all year (heaviest in spring). Late frosts are common.

ZONE 37. Hudson Valley and Appalachian Plateau

Growing season: May to mid-Oct., with rainfall throughout. Lower in elevation than neighboring Zone 42, with warmer winters: lows are 0° to –5°F/–18° to –21°C, unless arctic air moves in. Summer is warm to hot, humid.

ZONE 38. New England Interior and Lowland Maine

Growing season: May to early Oct. Summers feature reliable rainfall and lack oppressive humidity of lower-elevation, more southerly areas. Winter lows dip to –10° to –20°F/–23° to –29°C, with periodic colder temperatures due to influxes of arctic air.

ZONE 39. Shoreline Regions of the Great Lakes

Growing season: early May to early Oct. Springs and summers are cooler here, autumns milder than in areas farther from the lakes. Southeast lakeshores get the heaviest snowfalls. Lows reach 0° to –10°F/–18° to –23°C.

ZONE 40. Inland Plains of Lake Erie and Lake Ontario

Growing season: mid-May to mid-Sept., with rainy, warm, variably humid weather. The lakes help moderate winter lows; temperatures typically range from –10° to –20°F/–23° to –29°C, with occasional colder readings when arctic fronts rush through.

ZONE 41. Northeast Kansas and Southeast Nebraska to Northern Illinois and Indiana, Southeast Wisconsin, Michigan, Northern Ohio

Growing season: early May to early Oct. Winter brings average lows of –11° to –20°F/–23° to –29°C. Summers in this zone are hotter and longer west of the Mississippi, cooler and shorter nearer the Great Lakes; summer rainfall increases in the same west-to-east direction.

ZONE 42. Interior Pennsylvania and New York; St. Lawrence Valley

Growing season: late May to late Sept. This zone's elevation gives it colder winters than surrounding zones: lows range from –20° to –40°F/–29° to –40°C, with the colder readings coming in zone's Canadian portion. Summers are humid, rainy.

ZONE 43. Upper Mississippi Valley, Upper Michigan, Southern Ontario and Quebec

Growing season: late May to mid-Sept. The climate is humid from spring through early fall; summer rains are usually dependable. Arctic air dominates in winter, with lows typically from –20° to –30°F/–29° to –34°C.

ZONE 44. Mountains of New England and Southeastern Quebec

Growing season: June to mid-Sept. Latitude and elevation give fairly cool, rainy summers, cold winters with lows of –20° to –40°F/–29° to –40°C. Choose short-season, low heat-requirement annuals and vegetables.

ZONE 45. Northern Parts of Minnesota and Wisconsin, Eastern Manitoba through Interior Quebec

Growing season: mid-June through Aug., with rain throughout; rainfall (and humidity) are least in zone's western part, greatest in eastern reaches. Winters are frigid (–30° to –40°F/–34° to –40°C), with snow cover, deeply frozen soil.

Sunset's Garden Climate Zones

| Climate Zones | | 1 | 2 | 3 | 4 | 5 | 6 | 7 | 8 | 9 | 10 | 11 | 12 | 13 | 14 | 15 | 16 | 17 | 18 | 19 | 20 | 21 |

James
Bay

ONTARIO

QUÉBEC

NEW
BRUNSWICK

45

45

Lake
Superior

43

Québec

43

Presque
Isle

42

MAINE

44

38

MICHIGAN

MINNESOTA

45

Duluth

Montréal

Ottawa

St. Lawrence River

43

Burlington

VERMONT

Bangor

(95)

(87)

NEW
HAMPSHIRE

38

Portland

Minneapolis

Lake
Huron

(94)

WISCONSIN

43

Lake
Michigan

39

(75)

41

MICHIGAN

Lake
Ontario

Toronto

43

39

42

(81)

(90)

40

(88)

Albany

38

Boston

MASSACHUSETTS

(91)

(94)

(90)

(43)

Milwaukee

Detroit

(94)

39

Lake
Erie

Buffalo

39

(90)

NEW YORK

(87)

34

RHODE ISLAND

CONNECTICUT

34

(80)

Dubuque

(35)

IOWA

Chicago

(80)

39

Cleveland

(80)(90)

(79)

Akron

40

(80)

PENNSYLVANIA

(78)

Newark

(95)

New
York

NEW
JERSEY

(35)

(80)

(74)

41

(69)

(75)

(71)

Pittsburgh

(76)

Philadelphia

(32)

DELAWARE

Des
Moines

(57)

(65)

INDIANA

77

34

Washington,
D.C.

MARYLAND

29

(35)

41

Springfield

(55)

Indianapolis

(70)

(71)

Columbus

OHIO

(70)

Cincinnati

35

WEST
VIRGINIA

36

(66)

(95)

Richmond

(64)

Mississippi River

Missouri River

Kansas
City

(70)

St.
Louis

(70)

(35)

(65)

Louisville

Charleston

(64)

VIRGINIA

32

31

Atlantic
Ocean

MISSOURI

(44)

35

(57)

Ohio River

(65)

KENTUCKY

(75)

(81)

(85)

(95)

(77)

36

Raleigh

NORTH
CAROLINA

(40)

31

ARKANSAS

Nashville

(40)

TENNESSEE

(85)

(40)

33

(24)

(75)

Arkansas River

Little
Rock

(40)

Memphis

32

SOUTH
CAROLINA

(95)

(30)

33

(65)

(59)

(85)

32

Columbia

(26)

35

Mississippi River

(55)

Atlanta

(20)

Birmingham

(59)

GEORGIA

(16)

Savannah

Shreveport

(20)

(59)

MISSISSIPPI

Jackson

(20)

ALABAMA

(85)

(75)

31

LOUISIANA

31

(49)

(59)

(65)

(10)

Mobile

(10)

Jacksonville

28

Lake
Pontchartrain

(75)

(95)

Houston

(10)

28

New
Orleans

FLORIDA

Gulf of
Mexico

Orlando

(4)

Tampa

26

(75)

Lake
Okeechobee

25

Miami

0   100   200   300 miles

| 24 | 25 | 26 | 27 | 28 | 29 | 30 | 31 | 32 | 33 | 34 | 35 | 36 | 37 | 38 | 39 | 40 | 41 | 42 | 43 | 44 | 45 | Climate Zones |

HOW PLANTS GROW

Seeds, roots, stems, leaves, flowers, fruits—if you understand how these basic plant parts function, both individually and together, you'll find all aspects of gardening and plant care more comprehensible, manageable, and enjoyable.

Emerging bean seedlings are nourished by food stored in the fleshy cotyledons (seed leaves). As the true leaves expand, they begin producing food for the plant through photosynthesis; the cotyledons, their food supplies spent, wither away.

SEEDS

Many of the plants we grow begin life as seeds (exceptions are ferns and mosses, which develop from spores, and plants grown from cuttings or by other means of asexual reproduction). A seed is an amazing object, containing within it a rudimentary plant (the embryo) and a supply of food used both to start the embryo growing and to feed the seedling until it can manufacture its own food through photosynthesis. Seeds of some plants are viable (capable of germination) for only a brief time; others remain sound for many years, sometimes even for centuries, helping to ensure the survival of their species.

Seeds cannot germinate until certain favorable environmental conditions are met. These include adequate moisture, a preferred temperature, and, for most species, a loose-textured soil that provides oxygen to the sprouting seed. Gardeners supply these conditions when planting seeds in potting mixes or well-prepared seedbeds.

CLASSIFYING FLOWERING PLANTS

Angiosperms are the large class of flowering plants that bear seeds enclosed within fruits. The seeds of angiosperms contain either one or two *cotyledons* (seed leaves), which provide stored food for the germinating seedling. The majority of garden plants have two seed leaves and are called *dicotyledons* (*dicots* for short). Among the dicots are such diverse plants as maple trees, cabbages, and roses. Numerous other familiar plants have only one cotyledon and are called *monocotyledons (monocots);* among these are lilies, irises, palms, and grasses, including cereal grains such as wheat, oats, and rice.

In contrast to angiosperms are *gymnosperms,* the class including conifers and cycads. Gymnosperms do not bear flowers, and their seeds are naked—that is, not enclosed within fruits. They have many seed leaves.

Some seeds have additional requirements for germination. For example, seedlings of plants from cold-winter areas are most likely to survive if they sprout in spring, after winter is past: were the seeds to sprout immediately after ripening in fall, the seedlings would be killed by freezing weather. To ensure the necessary delay in germination, such seeds will sprout only after they are first moistened by fall rains, then exposed to a period of low temperatures. Called *stratification,* this process occurs naturally outdoors—but gardeners can mimic it by placing the seeds between layers of damp paper towels in a plastic bag and storing them in the refrigerator for a month or two. Other kinds of seeds may require nicking, grinding, or scarifying to break their hard seed coats; still others may need light, darkness, or even intense heat to sprout.

Seed size varies with the kind of plant. The range is wide, from the very large seeds of a coconut palm, down through sunflower and mustard seeds, to the very tiny, almost dustlike seeds of begonias. A seed's size is proportional to the amount of stored food it contains and thus to the maximum allowable planting depth. Small seeds, for example, have small food reserves; if planted too deeply, they will use up that food and die before the cotyledons (see "Classifying Flowering Plants," facing page) reach the soil surface. Seed packets give directions on planting depth. As a rule of thumb, it is safest to bury a seed no deeper than its length.

ROOTS

Though hidden below ground and often ignored by gardeners, roots are vital to a plant's survival and growth. They absorb water and nutrients and help transport them throughout the plant; they store food for future use; and they anchor the plant in the soil.

As they seek water and nutrients, roots grow through the soil away from the center of the plant. This growth takes place in the *apical meristem,* a region at the *root tip* where cells are actively dividing and elongating. Just behind the tender root tip, which is protected by the *root cap,* is a zone of cells that produce many tiny projecting *root hairs.* These are in direct contact with the soil and increase the surface area available for absorption of water and nutrients.

If exposed to sunshine or dry air, the root hairs quickly shrivel and die. When plants are dug for transplanting, the root hairs inevitably suffer some exposure, and the plant wilts as a result. Gardeners therefore try to plant and transplant leafy (nondormant) plants quickly, minimizing the contact of roots with air.

Plants are anchored in the soil by fibrous roots, taproots, or (sometimes) a combination of both. A fibrous root system has many branching roots that grow fairly close to the soil surface. The taproots of some large trees and shrubs, in contrast, grow deep into the soil and develop horizontal branches that hold the plant firmly in place.

STEMS

Stems bear a plant's growth buds, leaves, and flowers. Beyond that, they transport water and nutrients, provide support for the plant, and store reserves of food.

When a seedling begins growth, it produces a growing tip, also known as a *terminal (apical) bud.* Like the growing tip of a root, this area contains the actively dividing cells of the *apical meristem*—responsible, in stems, for stem elongation and leaf development. As the stem grows, *lateral (axillary) buds* form. These develop into leaves and branches.

ADVENTITIOUS ROOTS AND STEMS

Adventitious roots are roots that grow in unexpected positions, such as from leaves or the sides of stems; strawberry stems ("runners"), for example, form adventitious roots as they spread across the ground. Propagation by stem or leaf cuttings (see pages 57–60) is based on a plant's ability to form adventitious roots from its stems or leaves. Ground layering (see page 61) is another propagation method that depends on the development of adventitious roots.

Adventitious stems (adventitious shoots) are, likewise, stems growing in an unusual position—from a root, for instance. The suckers formed by raspberry plants are upright adventitious stems arising from horizontal roots. Propagation by root cuttings (see page 60) involves the formation of adventitious stems from pieces of root.

WHERE DO TREE ROOTS GROW?

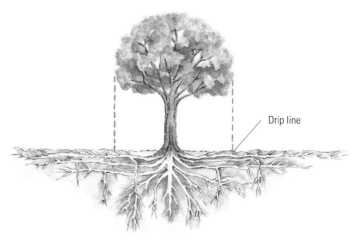

Drip line

A large proportion of a mature tree's roots are in the top 1 to 3 feet of soil, where they have access to oxygen, water, and nutrients. In their search for these essentials of life, the roots may extend horizontally well beyond the drip line at the edge of the tree's canopy.

THREE KINDS OF LEAVES

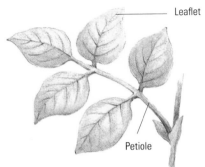

COMPOUND LEAF

Leaflet

Petiole

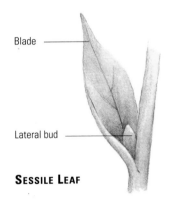

Blade

Lateral bud

SESSILE LEAF

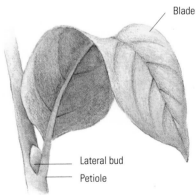

Blade

Lateral bud

Petiole

SIMPLE PETIOLE LEAF

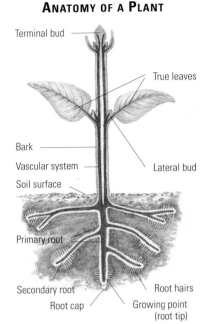

Terminal bud

True leaves

Bark

Vascular system

Lateral bud

Soil surface

Primary root

Secondary root

Root hairs

Root cap

Growing point
(root tip)

When stems are pruned or pinched back, the growth pattern of the plant is affected. If a terminal bud is removed, the growth of lateral buds is stimulated and the plant becomes bushier. But if lateral buds or branches are removed, growth is channeled into the terminal bud and the plant becomes taller or longer.

In some plants, growth buds may remain dormant in the stem (or in the bark covering it) for many years. These *latent buds* begin to grow only after the tissue above them is removed by pruning or injury.

Through their complex vascular system, stems transport the water and nutrients absorbed by the root hairs to the aboveground parts of the plant. They likewise conduct the sugars that are manufactured by photosynthesis in the leaves to other parts of the plant.

Stems are also support structures. They are often quite rigid, with cell walls stiffened by cellulose, lignin, or similar substances. In trees and shrubs, the interior dense heartwood serves solely for support, having outlived its former conductive or storage functions. In vining plants, the stems are so long and thin that not even woody tissue can hold them erect. Such plants have developed twining stems, tendrils, coiling leafstalks, or suction (holdfast) discs that enable them to carry leaves and flowers up to the light. Many herbaceous plants (those with soft, non-woody stems) don't form enough rigid tissue to stand upright and often are staked in gardens to keep them from sprawling on the ground.

Another stem function is to stockpile food that will tide the plant over during dormancy, get growth started in spring, and help seeds develop. Food moves through the plant in the form of sugars; when stored, these are converted to starch. When growth resumes after dormancy, the stored starch is changed back into sugars and once again circulates through the plant.

Many familiar garden plants do not have permanent aboveground stems to store food. Their storage depots are, instead, roots or specialized underground or modified stems such as bulbs, corms, rhizomes, or tubers. (For more on these structures, see pages 164–165.)

LEAVES

Although leaves vary in appearance and structure (a few examples are shown at left), all have as their basic function the manufacture of sugars and other carbohydrates through the complex process of *photosynthesis:* the interaction of light energy with chlorophyll (the green material in leaves), which converts carbon dioxide from the air and water from the soil into sugars and oxygen.

Photosynthesis requires large amounts of water. Once this water is drawn up from the roots through the stems and into the leaves, it encounters carbon dioxide, which has entered the leaf through the *stomata,* minute pores located primarily on the leaf undersides. Besides allowing the inflow of carbon dioxide from the air, the stomata permit the outflow of oxygen, which is a byproduct of photosynthesis, and of excess water vapor (transpiration). Since a leaf's interior tissues must be moist but outside air is often dry, the stomata can close as needed to prevent dehydration. Leaves can be further protected from drying by an outer coat *(epidermis)* that may be hairy, extra thick, or waxy.

Photosynthesis comes to a halt in deciduous plants during their leafless dormant season, and it slows greatly in evergreen plants during their modified dormancy in cold weather. For this reason, most plants require much less water from late fall to early spring, so gardeners can dig and move them with less damage during this time.

Anything that interferes with photosynthesis and the subsequent transfer of sugars throughout the plant can have harmful consequences. For example, if leaves are cut by pruning or chewed by insects, the injured tissue may seal to prevent the loss of moisture—but the leaves will not regrow, and the area available for nutrient manufacture will be decreased. Soot, grime, and dust on leaves can interfere with free air circulation through the stomata and reduce the amount of sunlight available to the leaves. A smothering mat of leaves on a lawn can halt the production of chlorophyll in the grass, causing it to turn yellow and stop growing.

FLOWERS

Gardeners cultivate many plants primarily for their flowers—but to botanists, a flower is simply a plant's reproductive unit.

Most flowering plants bear *perfect* flowers: blossoms containing both male and female reproductive parts. In the minority are plants with separate female and male flowers, borne either on the same plant—as in corn, walnut, and squash—or on separate ones, as in asparagus, holly *(Ilex),* and willow *(Salix).*

Continued >

PARTS OF A COMPLETE FLOWER

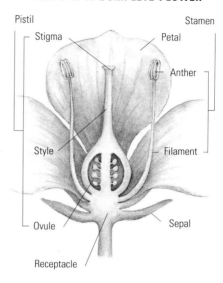

Pistil

Stigma

Style

Ovule

Receptacle

Stamen

Petal

Anther

Filament

Sepal

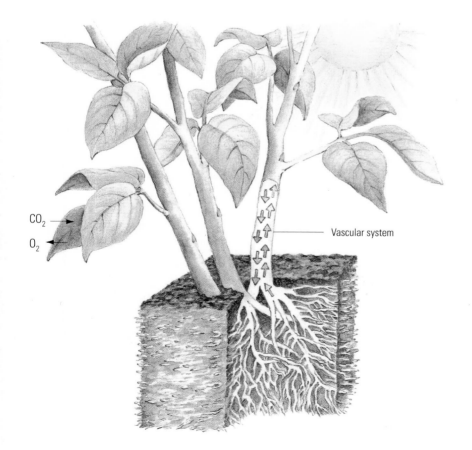

CO_2

O_2

Vascular system

PHOTOSYNTHESIS

SUNLIGHT acts on green chlorophyll in leaves to convert water and carbon dioxide to sugars and oxygen.

LEAVES draw in carbon dioxide from the air and give off oxygen.

THE VASCULAR SYSTEM in stems transports water to leaves from roots and circulates sugars throughout the plant.

Some flowers contain the reproductive structures and nothing more, but many are so-called *complete* flowers: they contain the essential male and female parts as well as accessory structures such as petals and sepals. Though blossom form varies widely among flowering plants, all flowers share a basic structural plan, and the structural elements always appear in the same order.

The *receptacle* is the point at which the floral parts attach to the tip of the specialized stem bearing the flower. The receptacle is often somewhat enlarged.

Sepals make up the outer ring of floral parts; collectively, they are called the *calyx.* They are often green in color, though some flowers (fuchsia and iris, for example) have brightly colored, petal-like sepals.

Petals form the next circle of flower parts, just inward from the sepals. If a blossom is showy, chances are it's the petals you

notice. Petals may be separate, as in camellia and rose, or united in a tubular, cupped, or bell-like shape, as in rhododendron and petunia. Collectively, the petals are called the *corolla;* corolla and calyx together are known as the *perianth.*

Stamens, positioned inward from the petals, contain the male reproductive elements. A typical stamen consists of a slender stalk, the *filament,* topped by an *anther,* which is usually yellow in color. The anther contains grains of *pollen,* the male element needed to fertilize the flower.

Pistils, found in the flower's center, bear the female reproductive parts. Each pistil typically consists of an *ovary* with a stalklike tube (the *style*) rising from it. The style is topped by a *stigma,* which receives the pollen. The ovary contains one or more *ovules;* following pollination and fertilization, these develop into the plant's seeds.

POLLINATION

In many plants, pollination—the transfer of pollen from anther to stigma—is accomplished by insects (including bees, wasps, and butterflies) or birds, especially hummingbirds. These creatures are attracted to a flower by its color and fragrance, and by its nectar, on which they feed. Other plants, such as grasses, oaks, and birches, have inconspicuous flowers whose pollen is spread simply by wind. Wind is also responsible for pollinating gymnosperms, which evolved before the advent of insects.

The production of seed from the union of pollen and egg is called *sexual reproduction.* In nature, sexual reproduction most often occurs between plants of the same species: if pollen from a different species lands on a stigma, pollination often cannot take place. But many kinds of plants have developed ways to prevent *self-pollination*—the pollination of a flower by pollen

from that same flower—and ensure *cross-pollination,* which involves two different parents. For example, some varieties of fruit trees produce sterile pollen; another variety must be present and in bloom at the same time to ensure pollination. Most holly *(Ilex)* plants are either male or female, and both sexes must be present for the female to bear fruit.

Cross-pollination is also possible between species; the resultant offspring are called *hybrids,* and they may or may not resemble either parent.

Because sexual reproduction allows for mixing of genes from different parents, it is important as a source of genetic variation. Such variation can lead to the development of plants better able to survive and adapt to environmental changes.

In contrast to sexual reproduction, *asexual (vegetative) reproduction* yields offspring that are genetically identical to the parent. Examples of asexual reproduction include propagation by cuttings or layering (see pages 57–61) or by division (see pages 155 and 166).

A bee visits coreopsis blossoms (above left). Hummingbirds are attracted to tubular flowers such as fuchsia (above).

Called a *berry* by botanists, the fruit of a tomato contains many seeds.

The succulent fruit of a peach surrounds a hard inner stone or pit. This type of fruit is known as a *drupe*.

The edible part of an apple develops from the greatly enlarged receptacle (rather than from the pericarp, as in most fruits). This is known as a *pome* fruit.

In dry fruits such as the capsule of a poppy, a hard, dry pericarp surrounds the seeds.

FLOWERS OF A GRASS PLANT

Because grasses are pollinated by the wind, they don't need showy flowers to attract pollinating insects and birds.

FERTILIZATION AND DEVELOPMENT OF AN EMBRYO

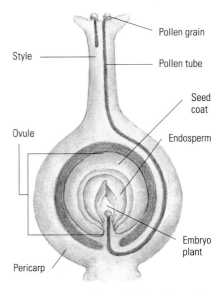

Style

Ovule

Pericarp

Pollen grain

Pollen tube

Seed coat

Endosperm

Embryo plant

After sperm reach the ovule through the pollen tube and fertilization has occurred, the embryo plant develops, surrounded by a seed coat and pericarp.

FRUITS

Fertilization, the process leading to the production of seeds and fruits, occurs after compatible pollen has been transferred to the stigma of a flower. A pollen grain contains two cells. One of these germinates and develops into the *pollen tube,* a structure that quickly grows through the style and enters an ovule. The other pollen cell divides into two *sperm,* which move through the pollen tube. One sperm fertilizes the egg in the ovule; the other unites with another cell in the ovule and develops into the *endosperm,* the food supply which will nourish the developing embryo and, in some plants, the germinating seedling as well.

Fertilization stimulates other changes. A *seed coat* forms around the developing embryo and endosperm, creating the *seed.* Around the seed, the ovary wall forms a layer called the *pericarp,* which in most species develops into the fruit. When the seed is mature—ready for dispersal—the fruit may be fleshy and soft, as in the case of peaches or cherries; or it may be dry, like an acorn or dried pea pod.

The role of a fruit is to protect the seed until maturity; it often helps to spread seeds, as well. For example, the fruits of a maple tree have winglike structures that help them spin through the air; the fruits of a dandelion have a tiny parachute that disperses the seed on the wind. And of course, birds and animals eat many fruits (fleshy and otherwise), scattering the seeds far and wide.

MANAGING SOIL

Plants won't grow well above-ground if their roots don't have favorable conditions below ground. Learning a few basic facts about your soil will let you know what improvements may be needed before you plant—and you'll have a better idea of the right way to water and fertilize your garden, too.

MINERALS, AIR, AND WATER

Any discussion of garden soil starts with some basic geology. Soil includes rock that has been worn down into mineral particles of various sizes. Imagine your garden as a pile of boulders. Now imagine wind and water wearing away at those boulders over a very, very long time—until, eventually, they become the soil in which your plants are growing today.

Though soil may have started out as solid rock, it's usually relatively easy to work by the time we put a shovel to it. That's due both to the small size of the mineral particles and to the air and water contained in the pore spaces between them. In fact, a shovelful of soil is only about half mineral particles; the other half is almost equally divided between air and water. Only a very small amount is organic matter (decaying plant material, for example).

SOIL'S LIVING CREATURES

Besides minerals, air, and water, your garden soil comes complete with living creatures. The most visible one is the familiar earthworm—but besides a few hundred of these, the top several inches of a square yard of soil may include a million mites and mitelike creatures and over 10 million nematodes and protozoans. These creatures all help keep the soil healthy. They process minerals to make them available to plant roots; they keep harmful fungi under control. Their waste products (and later on, their remains) form *humus*, a soft, blackish brown material that improves the structure of any soil.

Turn over a shovelful of garden soil. If you see earthworms, your soil is healthy and "alive." Living creatures add humus to the soil, make nutrients available to plant roots, and help control harmful fungi.

GARDEN SOIL

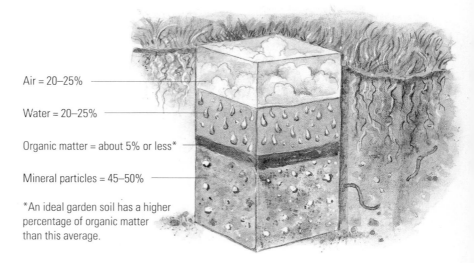

Air = 20–25%

Water = 20–25%

Organic matter = about 5% or less*

Mineral particles = 45–50%

*An ideal garden soil has a higher percentage of organic matter than this average.

Because most of these creatures live in the upper few inches of soil, their habitat is destroyed if this layer has been scraped away (during the construction of a new home, for example) or is constantly worked. If you're starting out with poor or depleted soil, keep in mind that you will need at least a few years to revive it. Part of what happens during this time is that colonies of soil-dwelling organisms become established and begin to flourish.

SOIL TEXTURES

What's the soil like in your garden? You'd probably describe it as sand, clay, loam, or something in between. To soil experts, these are all soil *textures*, determined by the percentage a soil contains of mineral particles of various sizes. Texture, in turn, influences *drainage*, a very important aspect of soil quality. Water applied to the soil surface percolates down through the pore spaces between soil particles. At first, it completely fills the pores. In time, however, it's drawn away—carried downward by gravity, absorbed by plant roots, drawn up from the soil surface and out through foliage. As water leaves the pores, air returns to them, until just a film of water remains on the soil particles.

Clay soil—whether you call it adobe, gumbo, or just plain "heavy" soil—is composed of many flattened, tiny particles packed tightly together to form a dense mass with microscopic pore spaces. (Clay soil can be so dense, in fact, that in some parts of the country it's used to make bricks!) Drainage is slow, since water and nutrients move through the pore spaces slowly. On the plus side, clay's slow drainage lets you water less often. And such soil is better able than others to attract, hold, and release certain nutrients. On the minus side, clay is difficult for plant roots to penetrate, and during rainy periods it can remain saturated and airless to the point of suffocating roots (which need air as well as water to live).

Claylike soils are produced by a number of factors. In parts of California, for instance, the particular series of geological events and climatic changes eventually broke a high proportion of mineral particles down to microscopic size; due to the lack of summer rain, vegetation was sparse, and what there was tended to dry up and blow away rather than decaying to help loosen the soil.

At the opposite end of the spectrum from clay is *sand*, typically found in areas near oceans and rivers and in places where these once existed. Its large, irregularly rounded particles fit loosely together, with large pore spaces between them. Water and nutrients drain through sand quickly—so fast that it can be difficult to keep plants well watered in hot weather. Sand is less fertile than clay, but roots penetrate it easily, growing deeply and rapidly, and it's far easier than clay to work.

A third soil texture, midway between the extremes of sand and clay, is *loam*. This is the excellent soil often found in climates with ample summer rain and cold winters: the rainy summers encourage lush vegetation, while the harsh, freezing winters make for the slow decay of dead plants directly into the soil. This combination of conditions tends to break down mineral particles into a variety of sizes, ranging from quite large (as in sand) to almost microscopic (as in pure clay), with particles of an intermediate size (known as silt) in between. Loam typically contains about 40% sand, 40% silt, and 20% clay. Soil of this texture that also contains a relatively high proportion of organic matter (5% or more of the total volume) is the ideal that gardeners strive to achieve.

To identify the soil texture in your garden, thoroughly wet a patch of soil, then let it dry out for a day. Now pick up a handful of soil and squeeze it firmly in your fist. If it forms a tight ball and has a slightly slippery feel, it's predominantly claylike. If it doesn't hold its shape at all but simply crumbles apart when you open your hand, it's sandy. If it is slightly crumbly but still holds a loose ball, it's close to loam.

SOIL PARTICLES

Clay
Less than $\frac{1}{12,500}$ in.

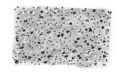

Silt
Up to $\frac{1}{500}$ in.

Fine sand
Up to $\frac{1}{250}$ in.

Medium sand
Up to $\frac{1}{50}$ in.

Coarsest sand
$\frac{1}{12}$ in.

While many plants prefer loam, some come from regions with sandy or claylike soil and thrive in garden soils of the same texture. Shown here is *Rosa rugosa,* native to the ocean shores of temperate-climate Asia. The species and its hybrids thrive in sandy coastal gardens like this one.

Shown below are six organic amendments. From left to right, first two bags hold organic compost; others contain shredded bark, redwood mulch, forest bark, and peat moss.

IMPROVING SOIL STRUCTURE WITH AMENDMENTS

Most gardens have soil that provides something less than the ideal environment for many garden plants. Perhaps it's rocky or scraped bare from new construction; perhaps it's too claylike or too sandy to suit the plants you want to grow. While changing a soil's basic texture is very difficult, you *can* improve its *structure*—making clay more porous, sand more water retentive—by adding amendments.

The best amendment for soil of any texture is organic matter, the decaying remains of plants and animals. As it decomposes, organic matter releases nutrients that are absorbed by soil-dwelling microorganisms and bacteria. The combination of these creatures' waste products and their remains, called humus, binds with soil particles. In clay, it forces the tightly packed particles apart; drainage is improved, and the soil is easier for plant roots to penetrate. In sand, it lodges in the large pore spaces and acts as a sponge, slowing drainage so the soil stays moist longer.

Among available organic amendments are compost, well-rotted manure, and soil conditioners (composed of several ingredients); these and others are sold in bags at many full-service nurseries, or in bulk (by the cubic yard) at supply centers. Byproducts of local industries, such as rice hulls, cocoa bean hulls, or mushroom compost, may also be available.

Finely ground tree trimmings (wood chips) and sawdust are also used, but because they are "fresh" ("green") amendments, they'll use nitrogen as they decompose, taking it from the soil. To make sure your plants aren't deprived of the nitrogen they need, add a fast-acting nitrogen source such as ammonium sulfate along with the amendment (use about 1 pound for each 1-inch layer of wood chips or sawdust spread over 100 square feet of ground).

Though the particular organic amendment you use is often decided simply by what's available at the best price, many experts favor compost over all other choices. Vegetable gardeners in particular prefer compost, and they often also add plenty of well-rotted manure to their planting beds.

ADDING AMENDMENTS: WHEN AND HOW

New beds for landscape plants should be amended before any plants go into the ground. For long-term benefits, choose an amendment that breaks down slowly. Shredded bark and peat moss hold their structure the longest, taking several years to decompose. It's a good idea to include compost in the mix as well; though it breaks down in just a few months, it bolsters the initial nutrient supply available to soil microorganisms—and these will contribute humus to the soil, improve soil aeration, and help protect your new plants from some diseases.

In beds earmarked for vegetables and annual flowers, amend the soil before each new crop is planted. Compost and well-rotted manure are preferred by most gardeners, since they dramatically improve the soil's structure, making it hospitable to the fine, tiny roots of seedlings. Unamended soil may dry into hard clods that small roots cannot penetrate, and plants may grow slowly, be stunted, or die as a result. Manure and compost break down rapidly—manure in a few weeks, compost in several months—so be sure to replenish these amendments before you plant each crop.

To add amendments to unplanted beds like those just discussed, spread the material evenly over the soil, then work it in by hand or with a rototiller to a depth of about 9 inches. If your soil is mostly clay or sand, spread 4 to 5 inches of amendment over it; once this is worked in, the top 9 inches of soil will be about half original soil, half amendment. If the soil is loamy or has been regularly amended each season, add just a 2- to 3-inch layer of amendment; you'll have a top 9-inch layer of about three-quarters original soil, one-quarter amendment.

Permanent or semipermanent plantings of trees, shrubs, or perennials benefit from soil amendment too, but you need to do the job without damaging plant roots. It's often sufficient simply to spread the amendment over the soil surface as a mulch; earthworms, microorganisms, rain, and irrigation water will all carry it downward over time, gradually improving the soil's top layer. If the plant isn't a shallow-rooted type (that is, if it doesn't have many roots concentrated near soil level), you can speed up the improvement process by working the amendment into the top inch or so of soil, using a three-pronged cultivator.

Where the climate is generally mild and winters are rainy, amend the soil in established plantings annually after fall cleanup. In cold-winter regions with spring and summer rainfall, do the job as you begin spring gardening.

MAKING COMPOST

Once your garden is planted, it will generate large amounts of organic waste—material you can easily turn into rich compost and return to the soil. The simplest composting method is the familiar backyard pile, but you can also use various kinds of bins or, if your space is extremely limited, even a box of worms.

A SIMPLE COMPOST PILE

For this method, you'll need a space about 10 feet square. Divide the area roughly in half. On one side, alternate 6-inch-thick layers of "green" and "brown" material. Green material includes grass clippings, soft shrub cuttings (chop up any large pieces), some pulled weeds (see page 81), and the like; brown material includes dry leaves, used potting soil, wood chips, and sawdust. This fifty-fifty green-brown mixture helps maintain the carbon-nitrogen ratio optimal for decomposition. Aim for a pile that's about knee-high. If you're short on green material, add alfalfa pellets; if you're short on brown, add straw (not hay, which contains weed seeds). Both are available at feed stores.

Once a week, mix and turn the pile, moving it to the other side of the space. In about a month, you'll have coarse compost. If you want a finer texture, continue mixing and turning for another month or two. In dry weather, hose the pile down when you turn it; it should be kept as moist as a squeezed-out sponge.

Note that this method requires you to have sufficient material for the entire pile at one time; you can't add new material until the current batch is finished.

Straw and alfalfa pellets are added to garden debris in this simple compost pile.

CLASSIC COMPOSTING SYSTEM

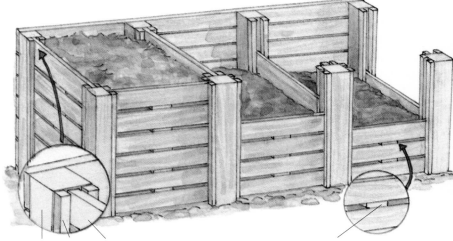

4 by 4   1 by 1   2 by 6   2 by 2 spacer between 2 by 6s

SIMPLE COMPOST BIN

WORM COMPOSTING

Shredded newspaper and kitchen scraps keep the red worms in this worm box happy and productive.

A COMPOST BIN

If you don't have much space available or want a tidier compost-making enterprise, a bin is a good solution. Like the pile just discussed, it relies on you gathering a fair amount of material all at one go.

The simplest bin is a cylindrical wire enclosure, but cylinders made from flexible plastic with many round holes for aeration are becoming increasingly popular. Fill the bin with 6-inch layers of green and brown materials, as described on the preceding page; you may also want to include vegetable and fruit scraps from the kitchen. To speed up decomposition and produce a finer-textured final product, chop all material into 1- to 2-inch pieces.

Once a week, lift off the cylinder. Lift and turn the compost-to-be to aerate it; then fork it back into the cylinder. You'll have finished compost in 3 to 4 weeks.

A CLASSIC COMPOSTING SYSTEM

The classic composting system shown above is a bit more complex than a compost pile or bin, but it's a very practical choice in the long run, since it allows you to add new material as it becomes available. The system has three sections. The left bin holds new green and brown material, the center one contains partially decomposed material, and the right bin holds finished compost. Turn the material in each bin weekly, moving decomposed material to the right. (The last bin will be empty for a few weeks at the very start.)

WORM COMPOSTING

For gardeners with no room for a traditional compost pile or bin, worm composting is a solution. Red worms live in a covered wooden box filled with shredded newspaper. You feed them kitchen scraps, and every few weeks they repay you with a box of rich, fine compost. Worms and supplies are available at many garden supply centers.

SOLVING SPECIAL PROBLEMS

Improving soil structure is important, but you may also need to correct other problems if your garden is to thrive. Soil may drain poorly; it may be too acid or alkaline; it may suffer from chlorosis or excess salts, or be underlain by a cementlike layer of hardpan.

POOR DRAINAGE

Poor drainage causes myriad problems. If water simply stands in the soil's pore spaces rather than draining away, there's not enough air available for roots and beneficial soil-dwelling microorganisms, and both may die. The reduced root structure can't adequately support the plant's leaves and stems, and the resulting stress makes the plant more susceptible to insect infestation or disease. Below ground, molds develop and the normal balance of fungi is disrupted—and the weakened root structure is more prone to invasion by water-mold fungi.

Fortunately, many drainage problems are easily solved once you become aware of them. First, know your soil texture: if the poor drainage is due to heavy clay soil, amend it thoroughly with organic matter. You may also want to mound the amended soil slightly, then grow plants on the mounds (this solution can be pleasing to the eye as well as beneficial to plants).

Many gardens drain poorly only in some spots. To pinpoint problem areas, inspect your garden after a heavy rain to see where water is standing. It may be sufficient simply to slope the soil in those areas so that water drains away from them. If that doesn't do the trick, you may need to dig a sloped trench and install drainage pipe perforated along the top and sides. Then refill the trench; when heavy rain comes, water should flow down through the soil into the pipe and be carried away.

If certain areas in your garden are always slightly boggy and don't lend themselves to structural change, your best tactic is to give in gracefully. Accept the situation and choose water-loving plants for those locations.

ACID OR ALKALINE SOIL: MODIFYING pH

The pH scale indicates acidity or alkalinity. A soil with a pH number below 7 is acid, while one with a pH above 7 is alkaline. Garden plants typically grow best in neutral or slightly acid soil (pH 7 or slightly below; see illustration at right). Most won't thrive in highly acid or highly alkaline soil, though a few have adapted to such extremes. In general, some nutrients cannot be efficiently absorbed by plant roots if soil pH is too high. If it is too low, on the other hand, nutrients may be taken up *too* efficiently: the excess cannot be processed fast enough and overloads a plant's system, causing it to languish and die.

Local climate gives you a clue to the likely soil pH. In high-rainfall areas, soils are often acid. It's in these regions that you tend to find acid-loving plants like azaleas, rhododendrons, camellias, and blueberries. Alkaline soils, in contrast, are typically found in low-rainfall areas. Many of the plants popular for waterwise gardens—sorts that need little water once they are established—do well in soil on the alkaline side. The olive, native to the Mediterranean basin, is one example of a plant that thrives in alkaline soil; oleander *(Nerium oleander)* and pomegranate also perform well.

If you're not sure about your soil's pH, you can test it yourself with one of the inexpensive test kits sold at most garden centers. Such kits can be relied on to tell you whether your soil is basically alkaline, acid, or neutral. If you suspect that your soil is highly alkaline or acid—or if a do-it-yourself kit so indicates—you may want to confirm the diagnosis with a professional soil test. Such tests are analyzed by laboratories; along with the results, you'll normally receive recommendations for correcting the pH of the soil tested.

Lime, available in either ground or powdered form, is often suggested to raise pH. Ground limestone is the slightly less potent of the two and raises pH more slowly. The amount needed depends on the soil texture (more is needed for clay than for sandy soil, for example) and other factors. Wood ashes and oyster shell also make acid soil more neutral.

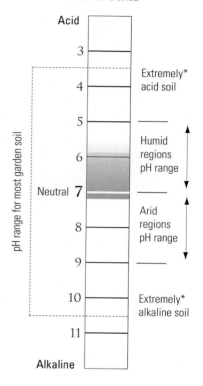

THE pH SCALE

pH range preferred by acid-loving plants

pH range preferred by most garden plants

*Soils nearing extremes require professional intervention to modify pH.

This orange tree is suffering from chlorosis due to a lack of iron. Chelated iron, applied in liquid form to leaves and soil, will quickly return the yellowing leaves to a healthy green.

To lower pH, common sulfur is the least expensive choice, though ferrous sulfate and aluminum sulfate are sometimes recommended instead. Ferrous sulfate, which also adds iron to the soil, is of the most help to plants that show yellow leaves as well as overall poor health. You'll also lower the pH of alkaline soil over time by regularly applying organic amendments such as compost and manure.

To determine how much lime or sulfur to add, follow the advice included with your test results. If your soil is extremely acidic or alkaline and you need to change the level by more than one point on the pH scale, it's best to bring in a professional: he or she can both analyze test results and perform an on-site evaluation to determine whether the soil can be amended successfully and how best to go about it.

If amending the soil just isn't feasible, plant in raised beds filled with problem-free, well-amended topsoil; or choose native plants that thrive in the unamended soil.

IRON CHLOROSIS

Iron chlorosis refers to a loss of green color in leaves due to a lack of iron. Of course, a number of factors cause leaves to yellow—but if chlorosis is the problem, leaves will tend to turn yellow from the edges inwards, with their veins usually remaining green, and new leaves will be affected more than old ones.

While chlorosis may be due to iron-poor soil, it is more likely that iron is present but simply cannot be absorbed by plants. The problem may be alkaline soil, since a high soil pH renders iron insoluble in water. Poorly drained soil that remains soggy for long periods also retards the release of iron from minerals.

To remedy iron chlorosis, check soil drainage and pH and make any necessary corrections. To aid afflicted plants quickly, add chelated iron to the soil or apply it (in spray form) directly to leaves. In this form, the iron will be available to plants at once.

SALTY SOILS

If the soil contains excess salts (whether sodium salts or other kinds), plants typically grow slowly or stop growing completely; they often show yellow leaves as well. Sometimes you'll even see a white, salty deposit on the soil surface.

Salty soils are most often found where rainfall is fairly low and in oceanside regions where salt water has entered the soil or salt spray has been absorbed by plants and soil. But even in inland areas with adequate rainfall, salt can build up in the soil if drainage is poor. Heavy use of fertilizers can also lead to salty soil, as can the salting of roads in winter to dissolve ice.

The way to deal with salty soil depends on what's causing the problem. If you live near the ocean, choose salt-tolerant plants and use windbreaks to protect your garden from sea spray. If poor drainage is the problem, correct it (see page 23). If you suspect that overenthusiastic fertilizing is to blame, consider replacing heavy feeders with plants that require less fertilizer, and choose organic fertilizers that release lower amounts of nutrients at a slower rate.

In low-rainfall regions, water thoroughly and deeply to help leach the salt below the plants' root zone. You may need to increase water by as much as 50% in a season to leach out the salt; you can either forgo planting entirely that season or choose only plants that tolerate ample water. *One caution here:* if the excess salt is in fact sodium, it will bond to the soil particles and cannot be washed away with water alone. Gypsum must be added as well (your Cooperative Extension Office can tell you how much to use). Experts can look at the whitish salt crust on soil and tell at once if it is a sodium salt, but most home gardeners will need to send a sample to a laboratory for identification.

If soil is highly salty, the only successful way to garden may be in high raised beds filled with healthy, well-amended topsoil.

HARDPAN

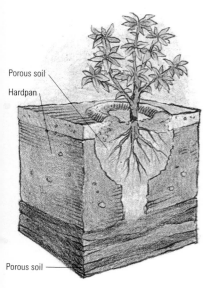

Porous soil

Hardpan

Porous soil

If you know hardpan is present, dig through it when you dig planting holes until you reach the porous soil beneath. Then fill holes with amended soil before planting.

Found anywhere from a few inches to several feet beneath the surface, hardpan is a layer of soil so compacted that neither plant roots nor water can penetrate it. Though typically associated with desert regions, it can be present in other areas, too. In most cases, it results when soil does not break down in the normal fashion and instead forms compound mineral particles that are fused tightly together. Hardpan may be present throughout an entire garden or only in certain parts of it.

You may not know you have a hardpan problem until you try to grow trees and shrubs with deep, extensive root systems. Because the roots cannot penetrate the hardpan, the plants' growth will be slowed, and they'll fail to thrive. Fruit trees will bear small crops. During spells of heavy rain and strong winds, large trees may even topple.

In vegetable and flower gardens, plants may dry out rapidly, since their roots will be confined near the surface. But rot and fungal problems may crop up too: since water cannot drain through the hardpan, it simply pools on top of it, waterlogging nearby roots.

When faced with hardpan, many gardeners despair, believing they must remove the entire hardpan. This isn't necessary! In beds of shallow-rooted plants, you can construct drainage channels to prevent water from pooling and causing root damage. Around established, deep-rooted plants, punch holes through the hardpan at 4-foot intervals; when planting new shrubs and trees, punch a hole through the bottom of the planting hole (see illustration above). Fill the drainage holes thus created with good-quality topsoil. Or simply construct a high raised bed filled with good soil; this is an effective solution if you're growing vegetables or a cutting garden for flowers.

Louisiana iris, thrive in boggy gardens like this one.

SAND AND PEAT MOSS: GOOD AMENDMENTS FOR CLAY SOIL?

Sand is often recommended to lighten clay soil. This seems a practical suggestion: after all, clay is the finest-textured soil and sand the coarsest, so mixing the two should result in just the right blend. It's not that simple, though. The problem is that you must add a great deal of sand to make a difference—at least 4 inches of coarse sand to the top 6 inches of clay soil. Improving even a moderate-size planting bed thus requires a great deal of heavy sand and heavy labor. Many gardeners compromise by simply sprinkling a little sand on top of their clay soil, but such small amounts do no good; in fact, they actually compact the soil further.

Peat moss has long been a favorite soil amendment because it breaks down in the soil more slowly than manure or compost and can thus be replaced less frequently. It is also highly absorbent; it holds water in the soil longer than many other amendments do, making it especially beneficial in sandy soils. But if your soil is naturally claylike and drains slowly, the super-absorbency of peat moss can exacerbate the drainage problem, especially if you have heavy winter rains.

GARDEN BEDS

When you're getting ready to dig, the soil should be neither too wet nor too dry: a handful squeezed in your fist should form a ball that crumbles apart, yet still feels moist. If you dig into soil that's too wet, you'll compact it (making it difficult for air to penetrate throughout the soil once it dries) and destroy beneficial microorganisms. You can't work amendments evenly into wet soil, either.

Garden beds are of two basic types. Some are dug directly in the ground, while others (raised beds) are located in frames that sit on the soil surface.

DIGGING A PLANTING BED IN THE GROUND

When making new in-ground beds, some gardeners always raise them, even if just by a few inches, using decorative stones, bricks, or bender board as an edging. They'll tell you that by time they amend the bed's soil, it's "fluffed up" higher than its original boundaries anyway. The raised soil gives plant roots a few more inches of growing room, and the edging keeps the soil in place.

Other gardeners make mounds as they dig. In this case, the bed's edges are close to the original soil surface, while the center is elevated; plants can grow both on top of the mound and on its sides. You may want to create several mounds, adding large decorative stones for accents; in this case, the mounding forms part of the landscaping. As is true for the slightly raised beds just described, the mounded soil ensures plenty of depth for root growth as well as excellent drainage.

In the vegetable garden, such mounds are convenient for scrambling, vining plants such as melons and squash. You'll also see various types of raised or mounded rows in vegetable gardens; in most, the seedlings are planted at the top to maximize root growth and drainage.

When you dig, start by clearing most of the debris from the soil. Then use a sharp, square-bladed spade or a spading fork to break up the soil to a spade's depth—typically 8 to 12 inches. Don't turn each spadeful completely over; if you do, roots and debris remaining on the soil surface may form a one-spade-deep barrier that cuts off air and water. Instead, turn the loosened spadefuls of soil only onto their sides. Once you've broken up the soil, change to a round-point shovel for mixing in amendments and evening the surface.

If you're digging a large bed, consider using a power-driven rototiller. If the soil hasn't been worked in a long time, go over it first with the blades set to a shallow level. Spread amendments over the surface, then rototill again with the blades set deeper into the soil.

Once a bed is ready for planting, don't walk on it. Following this rule will be simpler if you can easily reach all parts of the bed from its borders; if it must be wider, add board paths or stepping-stones to control foot traffic.

A slightly mounded bed shows off blooming perennials to best advantage—and guarantees good drainage, too.

In hot, dry climates, gardeners sometimes favor sunken beds over raised ones; the sunken planting area holds water more efficiently during irrigation.

Raised beds can be simple or elaborate. In this simple model, sturdy boards are joined loosely at the corners to form the boundaries of a productive garden bed.

MAKING A RAISED BED

Raised beds have many advantages. Their soil warms earlier in the spring and drains well; and because it's usually free from foot traffic, it remains loose and easy for roots, air, and water to penetrate.

Orient raised beds in an east-west direction so they'll receive as much sun as possible. Construct them of wood, cinder blocks, or other materials at least 2 inches thick, and make them 3½ to 4 feet wide; you should easily be able to reach the center of each bed from its edges. The bed's height depends on several factors. If the existing soil is healthy, the bed need be no higher than 8 to 12 inches; deep-rooted plants will grow down into the native soil. If the existing soil is poor, however, you'll probably want to make the bed higher to give roots more room. The maximum height is usually about 1½ feet.

Fill the bed with well-amended soil; you can use soil from another part of the garden or purchased topsoil. Amendments should include well-rotted manure and compost or soil conditioner. The soil surface should be 2 to 4 inches below the rim of the completed bed.

TOOLS FOR MANAGING SOIL

1 Swan-necked hoe
2 Three-pronged cultivator
3 Metal rake
4 Rototiller
5 Round-point shovels
6 Square-bladed spades with long and short handles
7 Spading forks with short and long handles

NUTRIENTS AND FERTILIZING

In order to thrive, plants need light, air, water, and a place for their roots to grow. They also need a continuous supply of nutrients, most of which come from the soil. When the natural supply of nutrients isn't adequate, gardeners add fertilizer to make up the difference.

NUTRIENTS

The nutrients plants need for good health are typically divided into three groups: macronutrients, secondary nutrients, and micronutrients.

MACRONUTRIENTS

The chief plant nutrients are carbon, oxygen, hydrogen, nitrogen, phosphorus, and potassium. Carbon and oxygen are absorbed from the air (the carbon coming from carbon dioxide); hydrogen comes from water. The remaining three nutrients—nitrogen, phosphorus, and potassium—are all absorbed from the soil. Often referred to as "the three major nutrients," these are the elements that must most often be added to garden soil if plants are to thrive.

NITROGEN. Nitrogen is required in large quantities for the synthesis of proteins, chlorophyll, and enzymes. The more rapidly and actively a plant is growing, the more nitrogen it needs.

Plants get their nitrogen naturally through several sources, primarily from decomposing organic matter. Rainfall also carries atmospheric nitrogen into the soil; some ground water contains nitrogen, too. And specialized bacteria living on the roots of certain plants (legumes in particular) can extract nitrogen from the air spaces between soil particles and make it available for absorption.

Because nitrogen is water soluble, it is easily leached from the soil by rain and watering. If plants aren't receiving an adequate supply of nitro-

In plants suffering from nitrogen deficiency, the older, lower leaves turn yellow, while new growth remains green.

gen, they'll look spindly and grow more slowly than they should; older leaves may turn yellow and drop. You can make up a nitrogen deficit in several ways. In beds of ornamentals or vegetables, work compost or well-rotted manure into the soil, or apply nitrogen-containing fertilizers to the soil or to plant foliage (or to both). In vegetable gardens, you can also practice crop rotation, planting legumes such as peas or beans every third year to return nitrogen to the soil.

PHOSPHORUS AND POTASSIUM. While nitrogen is particularly necessary when plants are actively growing, phosphorus and potassium are important when the reproductive phase begins. Both play a role in the development of fruits and seeds. Potassium has another function as well: it is crucial for root formation. A lack of either phosphorus or potassium may result in decreased size or quantity of flowers or fruits. A plant suffering from potassium deficiency also have an overall weak root system (and a decreased yield, if it's a root

Phosphorus and potassium contribute to the development of bountiful crops of fruit.

crop); aboveground symptoms include weak stalks and stems and some curling of older leaves.

Unlike nitrogen, phosphorus and potassium are found in the mineral particles that make up the soil. Over time, they're released into the film of water surrounding the soil particles; from there, they are absorbed by plant roots. Because they do not move readily through the soil in solution (as nitrogen does), they must be applied near plant roots to do the most good. Simply sprinkling them on the soil surface won't have much effect.

In many soils, these elements are naturally present in sufficient quantity to meet the needs of trees, shrubs, and other large plants for many years. Still, gardeners often apply additional phosphorus and potassium to the soil when digging new beds, as part of annual care for heavy feeders such as roses, and to encourage the best performance from annual vegetables and flowers (see "General- and Special-purpose Fertilizers," page 30). Application near the root zone is easy when you're making a new bed. For permanent or semipermanent plantings, you can scratch the supplements into the top inch or two of soil (they'll gradually be carried downward by earthworms, rain, and soil-dwelling microorganisms) or, for a quicker effect, apply them in the form of a liquid fertilizer.

SECONDARY NUTRIENTS

Calcium, magnesium, and sulfur are also important for plant health. They're largely available to plants through minerals in the soil. Calcium plays a fundamental role in cell synthesis and growth; most roots require some calcium right at their growing tips. Magnesium forms the core of every chlorophyll molecule. And sulfur combines with nitrogen in making protoplasm for plant cells.

MICRONUTRIENTS

The micronutrients include copper, iron, manganese, zinc, and other trace minerals. Copper and iron are used in chlorophyll formation. Manganese and zinc seem to function as catalysts in the utilization of other nutrients.

Micronutrients are usually available to plants through minerals in the soil. However, if the soil is highly alkaline (see page 23), plants may be unable to absorb these nutrients in sufficient quantity for good health. Various products can be applied to soil or sprayed on leaves to correct deficiencies. The supplement most commonly needed is chelated iron (for iron-deficiency chlorosis); it can be sprayed directly on leaves and stems.

FERTILIZERS

Fertilizer sections at nurseries, garden centers, and supply stores dazzle the gardener. The shelves are piled with boxes and bottles, the floors covered with bags stacked high. Labels identify the package contents as "rose food" or "vegetable food," "lawn fertilizer" or "general-purpose fertilizer." In some stores, you'll find bins filled with bone meal, blood meal, or hoof-and-horn meal—all labeled "natural fertilizer." Choosing the right products to keep your plants healthy can often be a bit confusing.

UNDERSTANDING N-P-K

Regardless of its type, any fertilizer you buy will come with information about the nutrients it contains. Prominently featured will be the N-P-K ratio, the percentage the product contains by volume of nitrogen (chemical symbol N), phosphorus (P), and potassium (K). A 16-16-16 fertilizer, for example, contains 16% nitrogen, 16% phosphorus, and 16% potassium. A 25-4-2 formulation contains 25% nitrogen, 4% phosphorus, and 2% potassium. All fertilizers contain at least one of these components; if any is missing, the

PLANT NUTRIENTS	
MACRO-NUTRIENTS	**CHEMICAL SYMBOL**
Carbon	C
Oxygen	O
Hydrogen	H
Nitrogen	N
Phosphorus	P
Potassium	K
SECONDARY NUTRIENTS	
Calcium	Ca
Magnesium	Mg
Sulfur	S
MICRONUTRIENTS	
Copper	Cu
Iron	Fe
Manganese	Mn
Zinc	Zn

ratio will show a zero for that nutrient (a 12-0-0 fertilizer contains nitrogen but no phosphorus or potassium, for instance). Boxed, bagged, and bottled products display the N-P-K ratio on the label. For fertilizers sold in bulk from self-serve bins, the ratio is noted on the bin; for future reference, be sure to write the information on the bags you fill and bring home.

The chart on page 29 shows some of the elements you may see listed on fertilizer labels.

COMPLETE AND INCOMPLETE FERTILIZERS

A fertilizer containing all three major nutrients is called a complete fertilizer; a product that supplies only one or two of them is an incomplete fertilizer. Using a complete fertilizer for every garden purpose seems sensible, but in fact it isn't always the best choice. If the soil contains sufficient phosphorus and potassium and is deficient only in nitrogen (as is often the case), you can save money by using an incomplete fertilizer that provides nitrogen alone (ammonium sulfate, for example). In some instances, complete fertilizers can even harm a plant. Exotic, bright-blossomed proteas, for example, will not tolerate excess phosphorus: they "glut" themselves on it and then die.

The inexpensive soil test kits sold at garden centers can give you a rough idea of the nutrients available in various parts of your garden; for a more detailed evaluation, you may want to pay for a professional analysis. By revealing which nutrients may be lacking, such tests can help you choose an appropriate fertilizer.

GENERAL- AND SPECIAL-PURPOSE FERTILIZERS

The various products labeled "general-purpose fertilizers" contain either equal amounts of each major nutrient (N-P-K ratio 12-12-12, for example) or a slightly higher percentage of nitrogen than of phosphorus and potassium (such as a 12-8-6 product). Such fertilizers are intended to meet most plants' general requirements throughout the growing season.

Special-purpose fertilizers, on the other hand, are formulated for specific needs. They're aimed at the gardener who wants a particular combination of nitrogen, phosphorus, and potassium for certain plants or garden situations. These fertilizers are of three general types.

One type, used during the period of active growth, contains largely nitrogen. Such products, with N-P-K ratios such as 16-6-4, are often used in spring, when you want to encourage lush growth or green up your lawn.

Another type is meant to stimulate root growth, stem vigor, and flower and fruit production. Fertilizers of this sort contain little nitrogen and higher levels of phosphorus and potassium; the N-P-K ratio may be 3-20-20, for example. These products are applied at different times and in different ways, depending on what you want to achieve. When you prepare a new planting area, for instance, you'll work a dry granular fertilizer of this sort deeply into the soil, putting the phosphorus and potassium where roots can absorb them. The nutrients help strengthen the new plants' developing stems and encourage the growth of a dense network of roots.

Available dry fertilizers include (clockwise from top left): granules (synthetic), fish meal (organic), and controlled-release granules (synthetic).

When you shop for fertilizer, check the N-P-K ratio on the label to see if the fertilizer is complete or incomplete and to determine the percentage of each major nutrient it contains.

To promote flower production and increase the yields of fruit or vegetable crops, you apply the same sort of fertilizer to established plants after they've completed their first flush of growth. You can use either dry granules, scratching them lightly into the soil, or apply a liquid formula with a watering can or a hose-end applicator.

A third group of fertilizers is designed for use on specific plants. These feature the N-P-K ratios determined to elicit the best performance from the particular plant, as well as other elements proven valuable to that plant. Such fertilizers are named according to the plant they're intended to nourish. Especially useful are formulas for citrus trees and acid-loving plants such as camellia and rhododendron.

Recently, other such plant-specific fertilizers have appeared on nursery shelves, each claiming to be the best choice for a certain plant or group of plants; you may see several sorts of "tomato food" or "flower fertilizer," for example. The jury is still out on the benefit of many of these products, and you will often do just as well to use a general-purpose type. The main distinction is often the price: the "special" formulas are usually costlier than general-purpose kinds.

Rhododendron 'Formosa'

SYNTHETIC AND ORGANIC FERTILIZERS

Some fertilizers are manufactured in the laboratory, while others are derived from natural sources. Each has certain advantages.

SYNTHETIC FERTILIZERS. These products are derived from the chemical sources listed on the product label. They're faster acting than organic kinds and provide nutrients to plants quickly, making them a good choice for aiding plants in severe distress from nutrient deficiencies. Synthetic fertilizers are sold both as dry granules to be applied to the soil and as dry or liquid concentrates to be diluted in water before application. In dry form, they're usually less expensive than their organic counterparts. In some of the dry granular types (those known as controlled-release fertilizers), the fertilizer granules are coated with a permeable substance; with each watering, a bit of fertilizer diffuses through the coating and into the soil. Depending on the particular product, the nutrient release may last anywhere from 3 to 8 months.

Some synthetic products are packaged for special purposes; you'll find spikes and tabs for container plants, for example.

Note that synthetic fertilizers usually do not contain any of the secondary or micronutrients—but in most cases, these nutrients are already present in the soil. If a test indicates that some are missing, look for a fertilizer that provides them.

ORGANIC FERTILIZERS. Organic fertilizers are derived from the remains of living organisms; blood meal, bone meal, cottonseed meal, and fish emulsion are just a few of the many available types. Organic fertilizers release their nutrients slowly: rather than dissolving in water, they're broken down by bacteria in the soil, providing nutrients as they decompose. Because these fertilizers act slowly, it's almost impossible to kill lawns or plants by applying too much (overdosing with synthetics, in contrast, can have potentially fatal results). Some manufacturers combine a variety of organic products in one package, then offer them for general-purpose or specialized use.

Two commonly used soil amendments—compost and manure—have some nutritive value and can be used as part of an organic fertilizing program. The N-P-K ratio of compost varies from 1.5-.5-1 to 3.5-1-2. Chicken manure's N-P-K ratio ranges from 3-2.5-1.5 to 6-4-3; that of steer manure is usually a little less than 1-1-1.

FERTILIZING WITH SEAWEED

Fertilizers containing seaweed are gaining favor with many gardeners. Besides providing nutrients in a form immediately available to plants, seaweed contains mannitol, a compound that enhances absorption of nutrients already in the soil, and various hormones that stimulate plant growth. And the carbohydrates in seaweed break down rapidly, nourishing soil-dwelling bacteria that fix nitrogen and make it available to plant roots.

Mixed with water and sprayed directly on foliage, seaweed-containing fertilizers can have dramatic effects in a matter of days. Plants green up and begin to produce new growth, and those that are weak stemmed and straggly straighten up and become stronger.

Increasingly popular as a fertilizer, seaweed is also an excellent mulch. Here, it blankets the soil of a potato patch. Nutrients gradually move from seaweed to soil during irrigation; after harvest, any remaining mulch can be worked into the bed.

Too much of a good thing? In its native environment, wild lilac *(Ceanothus)* survives with minimal water and grows on rocky slopes. Given rich soil and liberal fertilizer, it responds with fast, lush growth and bloom—but its life cycle speeds up as well, so that it dies at an early age (at 10 years or younger), leaving you with a hole in your garden.

WHEN TO FERTILIZE

To get your plants off to a good start, fertilize when the spring growing season begins. Many gardeners use a general-purpose fertilizer at this time (either an evenly balanced formulation or one slightly higher in nitrogen); others add only nitrogen. How often you fertilize later in the year depends on the plant; you'll find general guidelines for bulbs, lawns, annuals, and many other kinds of plants in Chapter 2 of this book (pages 95–188). As you'll see, nutritional needs differ, so it's important to check the particular requirements of the plants you buy. Some are heavy feeders and benefit from regular applications of general-purpose fertilizers and extra nitrogen throughout the growing season. Others—often those that evolved in nutrient-poor environments—may need only one annual feeding with a general-purpose fertilizer (or they may flourish with no feeding at all).

TIP: Don't apply liquid fertilizer at the same time you plant. No matter how carefully you remove plants from their containers and place them in the ground, some root hairs will break. The fertilizer will reach the roots immediately and enter them at the broken points, "burning" them and causing further dieback. Wait 2 to 3 weeks after planting before you fertilize; by then, the newly set-out plants should have recovered from any root damage.

APPLYING FERTILIZERS

Use a spading fork to work a dry granular fertilizer into a new garden bed. This technique puts phosphorus and potassium at the level where they can best be absorbed by plant roots. Water thoroughly after incorporating the fertilizer.

Using a cultivator, gently scratch the soil beneath plants with roots growing close to the surface. Apply a dry granular fertilizer and water thoroughly. Because roots may extend several feet beyond the drip line, be sure to spread fertilizer out wide enough to reach all the roots.

Liquid fertilizers can be applied with a watering can. You can also use an injector device to run the fertilizer through your watering system. A simple siphon attachment (above) draws a measured amount of fertilizer into a hose from concentrate in a pail.

FERTILIZERS CAN POLLUTE, TOO

While many gardeners are aware that improper use of pesticides can harm the environment, they may not realize that fertilizers pose some of the same risks. Plants can only absorb a certain amount of nitrogen at one time; when you fertilize with synthetic nitrogen fertilizers, excess nitrates remain in the ground to be washed away by rain or watering. They drain into rivers, lakes, and bays, either directly (through runoff) or indirectly (by penetrating the aquifer— the ground water—deep beneath the soil). They increase algal growth in the water, disrupting the ecosystem.

To make sure you don't unintentionally contaminate water sources, determine how much nitrogen is actually needed to keep plants and lawns healthy. Start out by using a low-nitrogen fertilizer, then gradually increase the percentage of nitrogen until you see satisfactory growth. You might consider switching to organic fertilizers only: with the exception of blood meal, these typically have low percentages of nitrogen, and their nitrogen is released slowly, more closely matching the plants' needs and leaving little excess to be washed away.

TOOLS FOR FERTILIZING

1 Short-handled spading fork
2 Push-type drop spreader
3 Hand spreader
4 Hose-end applicator
5 Watering can with measuring spoons
6 Short-handled cultivator

PLANTING

Select your plants wisely and plant them correctly, and you'll be on your way to a successful garden. Many kinds of plants—annuals, vegetables, and some perennials and ground covers—are sold as seedlings in small containers or in flats during the growing season. Larger plants, such as shrubs, trees, and certain vines and perennials, are offered in various ways: as bare-root plants during the dormant season; in 1-gallon, 5-gallon, or larger containers at any time during the growing season; or with the root ball enclosed in burlap from late fall to early spring. In the following pages, you'll learn how to choose and plant each type. For information on starting your own seedlings, see page 54; for tips on planting bulbs, see page 165.

PLANTING ANNUALS AND PERENNIALS

Nurseries offer young seedlings of both annuals and perennials, giving you a head start over sowing seeds yourself. Frost-tender summer annuals, such as marigold *(Tagetes)* and petunia, and warm-season vegetables (tomatoes and peppers, for example) should be planted after the last spring frost in your area. Hardy annuals, including pansy *(Viola)* and calendula, and cool-season vegetables like lettuce and broccoli can be set out 3 to 4 weeks before the last-frost date. They also can be planted in late summer, for flowers and vegetables in fall or (in mild climates) in winter. Plant perennials purchased in pots or cell-packs in spring or early fall.

At the nursery, choose stocky plants with good leaf color. It may be tempting to buy plants already in bloom, but younger ones perform better in the long run. Be sure to keep the plants moist until you're ready to set them out. Prepare the soil as you would for sowing seeds (see page 54); at planting time, it should be moist but not soggy. The illustrations on the facing page show how to remove plants from various containers.

Note that plants in peat pots receive a slightly different treatment. They are not removed from their pots, but go into the ground pot and all; the roots then grow through the pot into the soil, while the pot ultimately decomposes and disappears. Make sure the pots are moist before planting by letting them stand in a shallow container of water for several minutes. If they're dry, they'll absorb moisture too slowly from the soil and the roots may be slow to break through them, resulting in a stunted plant. It's also important to cover the tops of the pots with soil, since exposed peat acts as a wick to draw moisture from the soil. If covering the pot would bury the plant too deeply, break off the rim to slightly below the soil level inside the pot.

PLANTING ANNUALS AND PERENNIALS

1 Dig a hole for each plant, making it the same depth as the container and an inch or two wider.

2 With your fingers, lightly separate matted roots. If there's a pad of coiled white roots at the pot bottom, cut or pull it off so that new roots will form and grow into the soil.

3 Place each plant in its hole so that the top of the root ball is even with the soil surface. Firm soil around the roots; then water each plant with a gentle flow that won't disturb soil or roots.

REMOVING PLANTS FROM SMALL CONTAINERS

From cell-packs. Turn the cell-pack upside down and poke plants out by pushing with your thumbs on the bottom of each cell.

From pots. Turn individual pots upside down, holding the plant between your fingers. The plant should slip out easily.

From flats. Use a putty knife to separate the plants in the flat by cutting straight down around each one.

TOOLS FOR PLANTING

1 ROUND-POINT SHOVELS
2 LONG-HANDLED SPADING FORK
3 RULER OR YARDSTICK
4 PUTTY KNIFE
5 TROWEL
6 KNIFE, SUCH AS A LARGE JACKKNIFE
7 CLIPPERS OR BYPASS PRUNERS

THE PLANTING HOLE

To plant trees and shrubs, dig a planting hole with sides that taper outward into the soil. Make the hole at least twice as wide as the roots of the plant. Roughen the sides with a spading fork; if the sides are smooth, it can be difficult for roots to penetrate the soil. To keep the plant from settling too much after planting and watering, make the hole a bit shallower than the root ball or root system, then dig deeper around the edges of the hole's bottom. This leaves a firm plateau of undug soil to support the plant at the proper depth.

PLANTING BARE-ROOT SHRUBS AND TREES

Bare-root plants are sold in late winter and early spring by retail nurseries and mail-order companies. Many deciduous plants are available this way, including fruit and shade trees, flowering shrubs, roses, grapes, and cane fruits.

Though venturing out in the cold and wet of winter to set out bare-root plants takes a certain amount of determination and effort, it's a worthwhile endeavor. Bare-root plants typically cost only 40 to 70% as much as the same plants purchased in containers later in the year; beyond that, they usually establish more quickly and grow better initially than containerized plants. This faster growth is in part due to the fact that, when you set out a bare-root plant, you refill the planting hole with soil dug from that hole—and the plant's roots thus grow in just one kind of soil. When you plant a containerized or balled-and-burlapped plant, on the other hand, you put two soils, usually with different textures, in contact with each other. The presence of two differing soil types side by side can make it difficult for water to penetrate uniformly into the rooting area.

If you're buying from a local nursery, select bare-root shrubs or trees with strong stems and fresh-looking, well-formed root systems. Avoid those with slimy roots or dry, withered ones; also reject any that have already leafed out.

It's best to plant bare-root plants as soon as possible after purchase. If bad weather prevents immediate planting, heel in the plants by laying them in a temporary trench dug in a shady spot in the garden and covering the roots with moist soil. Before planting, soak the roots overnight in a bucket of water. Just before planting, cut off any damaged roots.

Dig a planting hole as shown at left. In areas with heavy clay soil or hardpan (see page 25), a wider hole will give the roots more growing space. Once the hole is dug, set in the plant as illustrated below.

PLANTING BARE-ROOT PLANTS

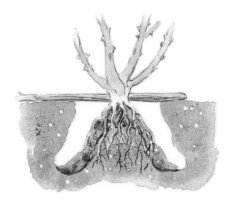
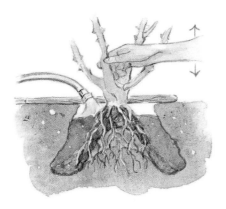

1 Make a firm cone of soil in the planting hole. Spread the roots over the cone, positioning the plant at the same depth as (or slightly higher than) it was in the growing field. Use a shovel handle or yardstick to check the depth.

2 Hold the plant upright as you firm soil around its roots. When backfilling is almost complete, add water. This settles the soil around the roots, eliminating any air pockets. If the plant settles below the level of the surrounding soil, pump it up and down while the soil is saturated to raise it to the proper level.

3 Finish filling the hole with soil; then water again. Take care not to overwater while the plant is still dormant, since soggy soil may inhibit the formation of new roots. When the growing season begins, make a ridge of soil around the hole to form a watering basin; water when the top 2 inches of soil are dry.

1 Dig a hole as shown on facing page. Spread roots out over the central plateau of firm soil. The top of the root ball should be 1 to 2 inches above surrounding soil.

2 Backfill with the unamended soil you dug from the hole, adding the soil in stages and firming it around the roots with your hands as you work.

3 Make a berm of soil to form a watering basin. Irrigate gently, keeping the stem or trunk and crown of the plant dry to prevent fungal infections. Spread a layer of mulch around the plant, keeping it several inches away from the stem or trunk.

SETTING OUT PLANTS FROM CONTAINERS

Containerized plants are popular and convenient—and in fact, many kinds of shrubs and trees are sold only in containers. Such plants offer certain advantages. They are sold throughout the growing season; they are relatively easy to transport; and, unlike bare-root and balled-and-burlapped plants, they don't have to be planted immediately. Furthermore, these plants can be purchased with flowers, fruit, or autumn leaf color on display, letting you see exactly what you're getting.

When selecting container-grown plants, look for healthy foliage and strong shoots. Check the leaves and stems to be sure no insects are present. Inspecting the root system is more difficult, but healthy roots are vital to successful establishment of container plants. A relatively small plant in a 5-gallon container may not be well rooted, usually because it has recently been moved to the larger container from a 1-gallon pot. (If you buy such a plant, it's wise to keep it growing in the container until it develops a good root system.) On the other hand, if a containerized plant has been in its pot for too long, it may be rootbound, with tangled and matted roots that coil around the inside of the pot. If you see roots protruding above soil level or husky roots growing through the container's drainage holes, the plant is rootbound. A plant that looks large for the size of its pot is often rootbound as well. It's best to avoid rootbound plants—but if you do buy one, be sure to loosen the roots before planting (see page 38).

Continued >

REMOVING PLANTS FROM CONTAINERS

1 **Plastic containers and metal cans.** Tap sharply on the bottom and sides to loosen the root ball. The plant should slide out easily. If it doesn't, cut plastic containers down both sides with bypass pruners. To cut metal cans, use tin snips (watch out for sharp edges).

2 **Pulp pots.** Tear the pot away from the root ball, taking care not to damage the roots.

DEALING WITH ROOTBOUND PLANTS

Overgrown plants

Young plants

Choose young plants, above right, with good leaf color and a root ball that holds together but is not tangled or matted. Avoid overgrown, rootbound plants, left. Though you can cut or loosen coiled roots, such plants don't grow as well as younger ones.

1 It is important to loosen coiled roots before planting so they will grow into the soil. With your hands, tease the roots apart. Then cut off any extra-long roots with clippers.

2 Another method is to spray the soil away from the root ball with a strong jet of water, then loosen and uncoil the roots.

3 A third—and more drastic—method is to make several vertical slits in the root ball with a knife to stimulate new root growth.

Plants in containers are available in several sizes. One- and 5-gallon pots are the most common; which of these you buy will depend on how much immediate impact you want the plant to have and on how long you're willing to wait for it to grow. Keep in mind, though, that smaller plants grow quickly; within 3 years of planting, a 1-gallon plant will usually have reached the same size as a 5-gallon one set out at the same time.

PLANTING BALLED-AND-BURLAPPED SHRUBS AND TREES

Some kinds of woody plants have root systems that won't survive bare-root transplanting; some are evergreen and cannot be bare-rooted. Instead, such plants are dug from the growing field with a ball of soil around their roots, and the soil ball is then wrapped in burlap or a synthetic material and tied with twine or wire. These are called balled-and-burlapped plants (B-and-B plants for short). Some deciduous trees and shrubs (large specimens, in particular), evergreen shrubs such as rhododendrons and azaleas, and various conifers are sold this way in fall and early spring.

When buying B-and-B plants, look for healthy foliage and an even branching structure. The covering should be intact so the roots are not exposed, and the root ball should feel firm and moist. If you have any doubts about the condition of the root ball, untie the covering and check for healthy roots and a solid, uncracked root ball.

B-and-B plants can be damaged if handled roughly. Always support the bottom of the root ball when moving the plant; don't pick the plant up by the trunk or drop it, which might shatter the root ball. Because a B-and-B plant is usually quite heavy, it's a good idea to have the nursery deliver it to you or to have a friend help you move it to and from your vehicle in a sling of stout canvas. Once home, you can move the plant by sliding it onto a piece of plywood and pulling it to the planting spot.

To plant a B-and-B plant, dig a hole as shown on page 36. Then follow the steps shown on the facing page.

PLANTING BALLED-AND-BURLAPPED PLANTS

1 Measure the root ball from top to bottom. The hole should be a bit shallower than this distance, so that the top of the root ball is about 2 inches above the surrounding soil. Adjust the hole to the proper depth; then set in the plant.

2 Untie the covering. If it's burlap, it will eventually rot and need not be completely removed; just spread it out to uncover about half the root ball. If the covering is a synthetic material, remove it entirely. If you are planting in a windy site, drive a stake in alongside the root ball. Fill the hole to within 4 inches of the top and water gently.

3 Continue to fill the hole, firming the soil as you go. Make a berm of soil to form a watering basin; then water the plant. If you staked the plant, loosely tie it to the stake. As the plant becomes established, keep the soil moist but not soggy.

SOIL TEXTURE AND BALLED-AND-BURLAPPED PLANTS

While most shrubs and trees grow best if planted in the soil native to your garden, B-and-B plants are sometimes an exception. They are generally grown in clay or heavy soil that holds together well when the plants are dug up and wrapped. If you have medium- to heavy-textured garden soil (such as fairly heavy loam or clay), there's no need to amend the soil you return to the planting hole. But if the B-and-B soil is denser than that in your garden,

the plant may have a hard time getting established, since the dense soil around its roots will absorb water more slowly than the surrounding garden soil: the B-and-B's soil can be dry even if the garden soil is kept moist. To avoid this problem, mix an organic amendment such as peat moss, ground bark, or nitrogen-fortified sawdust into the soil removed from the planting hole, using about one shovelful of amendment for every three shovelfuls of soil. Use this blend to fill in around the roots.

WATERING

How much water do my plants need? How often should I water, and what's the best way to do it? How can I conserve water? These and other important—and often perplexing—questions are addressed in the following pages.

WATERING GUIDELINES

Plants, like animals, need water to live. A seed must absorb water before it can germinate. Roots can take up nutrients only when water is present in the soil; water transports nutrients throughout plants. And water is essential to photosynthesis.

However, how much water your plants need and how frequently they need it depend on a number of interrelated factors, including soil texture, the plants themselves and their age, and the weather.

Your soil's ability to absorb and retain water is closely related to its composition. Clay soils absorb water slowly and drain slowly as well, retaining water longer than other soils. Sandy soils, in contrast, absorb water quickly and drain just as quickly. Loam soils absorb water fairly rapidly and drain well, but not too fast. You can work in organic amendments to help clay soils absorb water faster and drain better and to make sandy soils more moisture retentive. For more on soil texture and organic amendments, see pages 19–20.

Once their roots are established, different sorts of plants have widely differing water needs. Plants native to semiarid and arid climates, called *xerophytes,* have evolved features that allow them to survive with little water and low relative humidity. They may have deep root systems, for example, or leaves that are small, hairy, or waxy. The majority of familiar garden plants, however, are adapted to moist soil and high relative humidity. Called *mesophytes,* they usually have broad, thin leaves. Keep in mind that all young plants, including xerophytes, require more frequent watering than mature plants until their root systems become well established. And many annuals and vegetables require regular moisture throughout the growing season if they are to bloom well or produce a good crop.

Weather affects water needs as well. When it's hot, dry, and windy, plants use water very rapidly, and young or shallow-rooted ones sometimes cannot absorb water fast enough to keep foliage from wilting. Such plants need frequent watering to keep moisture around their roots at all times. During cool, damp weather, on the other hand, plants require much less water. Water needs are lower during winter as well, when the days are short and the sun is low on the horizon.

Because the above factors—soil texture, plant type and age, and weather—are all variable, following a fixed watering schedule year-round (or even all summer) isn't the most efficient way to meet your plants' needs. Always test your soil for moisture and look

SOIL TEXTURE AND WATER PENETRATION

Applied to sand (left), 1 inch of water penetrates about 12 inches. Applied to loam (center), 1 inch of water reaches about 7 inches. Applied to clay (right), 1 inch of water soaks only 4 to 5 inches.

at your plants before you water. To check the soil around new transplants and in vegetable and flower beds, dig down a few inches with your fingers or a trowel; if the top 1 to 2 inches are dry, you probably need to water. In lawns or around established trees and shrubs, a soil sampling tube (shown at right) is useful: it allows you to test moisture at deeper levels without digging a hole that could disturb roots. Leaves can also can tell you when it's time to water. Most will look dull or roll in at the edges just before they wilt.

When you do water, aim to soak the root zone of your plants. As a general guideline, the roots of lawn grasses grow about 1 foot deep; roots of small shrubs and other plants reach 1 to 2 feet deep. While the taproots of some trees and shrubs may grow more deeply into the soil, most roots tend to concentrate in the top 2 to 3 feet. Watering below the root zone only wastes water.

To check how far water penetrates in your soil, water for a set amount of time (say, 30 minutes). Wait for 24 hours, then use a soil sampling tube or dig a hole to check for moisture. You'll soon learn to judge how long to water each plant to soak its root zone thoroughly.

WATERING METHODS

Methods for applying water range from simple hand-held sprayers to hose-end sprinklers to more complex drip systems and underground rigid-pipe systems. The method or methods appropriate for you depend on how often you need to water the size of your garden, and how much equipment you want to buy.

SPRINKLING

Watering with a hand-held nozzle or fan may be enjoyable for you, but it's usually inadequate for plants—it takes too long to truly soak the soil. Hand watering is, however, useful for new transplants, seedlings, and container plants, since you can apply the water gently and exactly where it's needed.

Sprinklers, which essentially produce artificial rainfall, offer the simplest way to apply water over a large surface. Many plants, particularly those that like a cool, humid atmosphere, thrive with overhead sprinkling. And this method rinses dust from foliage and discourages certain pests, especially spider mites. But sprinkling has some negative aspects as well. First, it's wasteful: wind can carry off some water before it even reaches the ground, and water that falls or runs off onto

A sprinkler with an adjustable watering pattern lets you select the shape of the area to be covered, from a rectangular to an almost square plot. Some sprinklers have built-in timers, which can be set to turn off the water automatically .

pavement is lost too. In humid climates, sprinkling encourages some foliage diseases such as black spot and rust (though you can minimize this risk by sprinkling early in the morning, so that leaves dry quickly as the day warms). Another potential drawback is that plants with weak stems and/or heavy flowers bend and can break under a heavy load of water.

USING A SOIL SAMPLING TUBE

This device allows you to check soil moisture at deeper levels than you can reach with a trowel, without disturbing plant roots too much. Push the tube into the ground, pull it out, and examine the soil in the sample. If it is dry or only slightly moist, it's time to water. If the top layer is damp and the rest is dry, you need to water longer to ensure deeper penetration. A soil sampling tube is also useful for detecting compacted layers of soil and checking how deeply roots penetrate.

OVERWATERING

Giving plants too much water, especially in clay soils, can cause as many problems as supplying too little. Roots absorb oxygen from the air found in pore spaces between soil particles. During irrigation or rainfall, water displaces the air in these spaces; then, as the water drains away, evaporates, and is taken up by roots, the pore spaces fill with air again. But if water is applied too often, the pore spaces never have a chance to drain. They remain filled with water, and air is not available to the roots. The lack of oxygen makes roots susceptible to various water-mold fungi, which in turn can lead to rot. Overwatering also compacts the soil and literally washes some nutrients beyond the reach of roots.

Check sprinkler's delivery rate and pattern by placing equal-size containers at regular distances from the sprinkler.

USING A ROOT IRRIGATOR

The needlelike probe on the end of this tool injects water into the root zone of trees and large shrubs. Insert it into the ground slowly, holding it at an angle so the top layer of soil gets wet. Don't go deeper than 1 to 1½ feet or stay in one spot for more than a few minutes. Work in concentric circles around the trunk, gradually moving outward just past the drip line and using the injector about every 3 feet.

SPRINKLER APPLICATION RATES. To sprinkle effectively, you need to know how fast water penetrates your soil and the delivery rate of your sprinklers. As the chart on page 40 shows, 1 inch of water (from sprinkling or rainfall) moistens about 12 inches in sandy soil, 7 inches in loam, and 4 to 5 inches in clay. Thus, if you want to water to a depth of 12 inches, you'll need to apply about an inch of water to sandy soil, 2½ to 3 inches to clay soil.

To determine delivery rate, place a number of equal-size containers (straight-sided coffee cups, for example) at regular intervals outward from the sprinkler, as shown above. Then turn on the water and note how long it takes to fill a container with an inch of water. This test will also show you the delivery pattern: that is, the containers will typically fill at different rates. To ensure that every area ultimately receives the same amount of water, you'll need to move the sprinklers so that the coverage overlaps.

SOIL SOAKER HOSES

Soaker hoses, the forerunners of drip irrigation systems, are still quite useful for slow, steady water delivery to plants in rows. They're long tubes made of perforated or porous plastic or rubber, with hose fittings at one or both ends. When you attach a soaker to a regular hose and turn on the water supply, water seeps or sprinkles from the soaker along its entire length. You also can water wide beds by snaking soakers back and forth around the plants; trees and shrubs can be watered with a soaker coiled in a circle around the plant. You'll probably need to leave soakers on longer than you would sprinklers; check water penetration with a trowel or soil sampling tube.

WATERING IN FURROWS AND BASINS

Furrows 3 to 6 inches deep help irrigate straight rows on level ground. Bubbler on hose end softens flow of water to prevent erosion. This method is good for crops that don't appreciate overhead watering. It works poorly in very sandy soils, however.

Basins with sides 3 inches high hold water around large plants, such as tomatoes and peppers. On level ground, link basins to make watering easier.

ACCESSORIES FOR HAND WATERING

Brass nozzle

Metal lever sprayer

Seedling nozzle

FLOODING

Flooding (soaking) is an effective way to supply sufficient water to the extensive, deep root systems of large shrubs and trees. Make a level basin for the plant by forming a ridge of soil several inches high around its drip line. You'll usually need to fill the basin more than once to ensure that water penetrates throughout the entire root zone. If the soil in the basin hasn't absorbed all the water within a few hours, make a channel in the ridge around it to let the excess drain away.

If you grow vegetables or flowers in rows, you can build adjoining basins for large plants like squash or make furrows between rows (see illustrations above). To minimize damage to roots, it's best to construct the furrows when the plants are young, before their root systems have spread. Broad, shallow furrows are generally better than deep, narrow ones: the wider the furrow, the wider the root area you can soak, since water moves primarily downward rather than laterally. And a shallow furrow is safer for plants—nearby roots are less likely to be disturbed when you scoop out the furrow, and they're likewise less apt to be exposed by a strong flow of water through it.

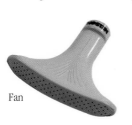

Watering wand with nozzle

Fan

Brass nozzle with adjustable spray pattern

An unreinforced hose (left) is made of a less flexible vinyl that kinks when bent. A reinforced hose (right) bends without kinking.

A SAMPLE DRIP SYSTEM

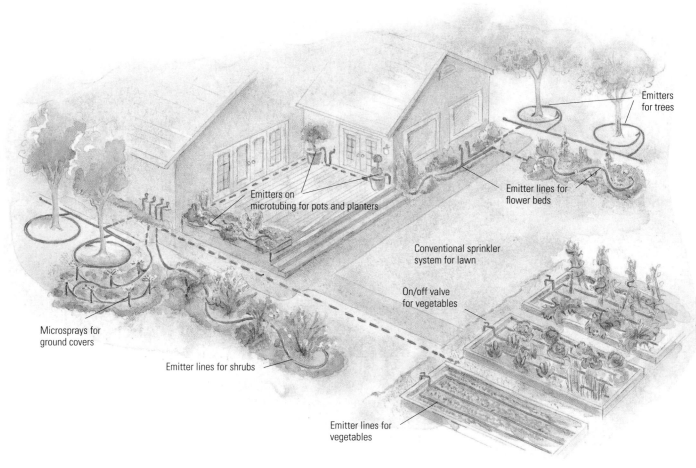

Emitters for trees

Emitter lines for flower beds

Emitters on microtubing for pots and planters

Conventional sprinkler system for lawn

On/off valve for vegetables

Microsprays for ground covers

Emitter lines for shrubs

Emitter lines for vegetables

DRIP IRRIGATION

The term "drip irrigation" describes the application of water not only by drip emitters but also by microsprays. Both of these have two traits in common: they operate at low pressure, and they deliver a low volume of water compared to standard sprinklers. Because the water is applied slowly on or near the ground, there should be no waste from runoff and little or no loss to evaporation. You position the emitters to deliver water just where the plants need it; you control penetration by varying the time the system runs and/or the emitters' delivery capacity (rated in gallons per hour—gph). You can also regulate the volume of water delivered to each plant by varying the type and number of emitters you set up for each.

Besides water conservation, the chief advantage of drip systems is flexibility. You can tailor them to water individual plants by providing each with its own emitter(s); or you can distribute water over larger areas with microsprays. A standard layout might include hookups to two or more valves and many kinds of parts (see illustrations above). Because the lines are aboveground (they're easily concealed with mulch) and are made of limber plastic, changing the system is simple: just add or subtract lines and emitters as needed.

Your drip system can be simply attached to a hose end or screwed into a hose bibb. Or, if you prefer, you can connect it permanently to your main water source.

TOP: Microsprays water a narrow bed of lettuce.

BOTTOM: Emitter lines attached to ½-inch tubing bring water to rows of garlic plants.

EMITTERS FOR DRIP SYSTEMS. Emitters vary in shape, size, and internal mechanism, but all operate on the principle of dispensing water slowly; flow rates range from ½ to 2 gph. You insert the emitters directly into ½- or ⅜-inch drip irrigation tubing or into thinner microtubing positioned to run from the larger tubing to each plant. Non-pressure-compensating emitters (the standard kind) work well on flat or relatively level ground and with lines less than 200 feet long. But when water pressure will be lowered by gravity or friction (on hillsides or with long lines), opt for pressure-compensating emitters. These deliver the same amount of water throughout the system.

Emitters also come factory-installed in polyethylene tubing; these are often referred to as "in-line" emitters or emitter lines. Spaced 12, 18, 24, or 36 inches apart, they deliver ½, 1, or 2 gph and are available in non-pressure-compensating and pressure-compensating versions. Some emitter lines are infused with a small amount of herbicide to prevent root intrusion; these can be buried and used to water lawns.

The standard emitters simply drip, but sorts that deliver water in other ways are available as well. Misters produce a fine spray—a good way to increase humidity for plants like fuchsia and tuberous begonia. Microsprays are low-volume equivalents of standard sprinklers.

THE DRIP LINE

This term does not refer to drip irrigation, but rather to the circle you'd draw on the soil around a tree or shrub directly beneath its outermost branch tips. Rainwater tends to drip from the leaves at this point. When watering young trees and shrubs, you can water up to and just beyond the drip line. As these plants mature, however, their roots usually grow farther out into the soil, eventually extending well beyond the canopy (roots grow wider in sandy soil). To water such plants adequately, you'll need to make a wider basin (for flood irrigation) or move sprinklers, soaker hoses, or drip emitters outward.

DRIP IRRIGATION COMPONENTS

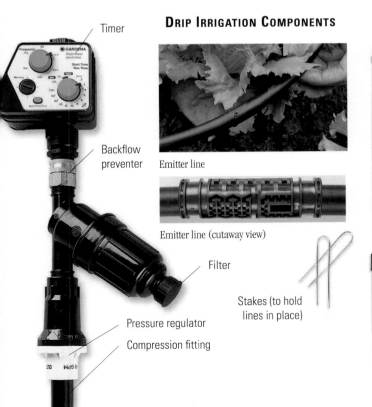

Timer

Backflow preventer

Emitter line

Emitter line (cutaway view)

Filter

Stakes (to hold lines in place)

Pressure regulator

Compression fitting

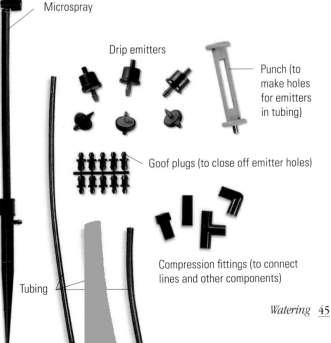

Microspray

Drip emitters

Punch (to make holes for emitters in tubing)

Goof plugs (to close off emitter holes)

Tubing

Compression fittings (to connect lines and other components)

You can conserve water—and create a pleasing and useful landscape—but replacing some of your lawn with ground covers, mulched areas, and/or a hard surface such as a deck or patio.

CONSERVING WATER

Water is a limited resource everywhere. Though the eastern half of the United States typically receives enough (or sometimes too much) precipitation, droughts do occur, and parts of this area sometimes go for several years without enough water to meet the needs of the local population. Most low-elevation areas of the western United States have low rainfall rates and a long dry season—and though the overall western water supply remains virtually fixed, ever more people are putting demands on it. Thus, conserving water is (or should be) a concern everywhere. Here are a few tips for waterwise gardening.

Locate plants wisely. Group plants with similar water needs together. They can then be irrigated together, and no plant will receive too much or too little water. This concept is called hydrozoning. To cut water use on plants that need regular moisture, site the "thirsty" individuals in a spot shielded from drying summer winds.

Reconsider your lawn. Of all the components of a typical garden, the lawn consumes the most water per square foot. Consider eliminating it entirely and replacing it with unthirsty ground covers such as juniper, coyote brush *(Baccharis),* or ivy *(Hedera);* for more on ground covers, turn to page 132. Or install gravel, a hard surface like brick, other paving, or a wooden deck. If you don't want to part with your lawn completely, consider minimizing its size. When planting a lawn, choose a grass or grass blend adapted to your climate (see pages 122–123).

Mulch your plantings. An organic mulch spread several inches thick over the soil acts as an insulating blanket, slowing evaporation from the soil and keeping it cooler than it would be if unprotected. Rocks and gravel also do the job. Black plastic sheeting, sold in rolls, conserves moisture and suppresses weeds. You can also buy rolls of various plastic materials known collectively as landscape fabrics. Permeable to water and air, these are manufactured expressly for use as a mulch. See pages 82–83 for more on mulches.

Soaker hoses deliver water to a rose bed. Mulch hides the hoses (but doesn't interfere with water delivery), aids moisture retention, and helps prevent the growth of weeds.

Eliminate runoff. Don't waste water by irrigating paved surfaces. If your sprinkler system showers water over sidewalks, patios, or driveways, replace the heads with a model that delivers water where it is needed. Or redesign the system.

Sloping land and heavy clay soils invite runoff—due to gravity in the first case, due to slow water penetration in the second. To solve the problem, adjust the rate at which water is applied. If you use sprinklers, you can improve penetration by watering in several successive short intervals, allowing time for water to soak in between each spell of sprinkling. Terraces and basins can also help prevent runoff on slopes; see below.

Use low-volume watering devices. Soil soaker hoses are effective and easy to install. Drip irrigation (see pages 44–45) offers an excellent way to reduce water use. You can also upgrade an existing underground sprinkler system by installing low-volume sprinkler heads; or convert it entirely to a drip system, using parts and kits available at hardware stores.

Use timers. With the simplest timers, you set the dial for the length of time you want the water to run or the number of gallons of water you want to apply; then you turn on the water. The timer turns off the faucet for you.

More sophisticated timers operate on batteries or household current. You set them to a schedule; they turn the water on and off as programmed. Such timers assure that your garden will be watered whether you're at home or away. What's more, you can select a schedule that will give your plants no less and no more water than they need to thrive.

The flaw of automatic controllers is that they follow your schedule regardless of weather: they'll turn on the water during a deluge or apply amounts of water appropriate for hot summer temperatures on a cool fall day. To solve this problem, reset the controller to take seasonal rainfall and weather conditions into account. Or use electronic attachments that function as weather sensors. By linking a soil moisture sensor to the controller, for example, you can trigger the sprinklers to turn on only when the sensor indicates that soil moisture has dropped to the point where water is needed. Another useful attachment is a rain shutoff device; it accumulates rainwater in a special collector pan, turning off the controller when the pan is filled to a prescribed depth and triggering it to resume watering when the collected water has evaporated. Before installing either of these sensors, be sure they are compatible with your controller.

An electronic controller can be programmed to activate your watering system automatically, according to the schedule you select. Be sure to reprogram the controller as needed to take into account seasonal rainfall and weather conditions.

CONSERVING WATER ON SLOPES

Plants on slopes are often challenging to irrigate, since water can run downhill faster than it can seep into the root zone. To prevent wasteful runoff, make basins or terracing to channel water directly to plant roots, as shown below.

Individual basin. Make a wide basin. Build up on the low side to increase water-holding capacity.

Terracing. Headers help control runoff. Because surface reservoir is small, water must be applied slowly.

PRUNING

In a well-planned, well-pruned garden, you're rarely aware of the pruning. Trees and shrubs grow in perfect proportion to each other; they complement houses and other structures rather than overwhelming them. In fact, most of us notice pruning only when it's badly done.

This section discusses how and when stems and branches grow— information that will help you understand how to prune and when best to do it. You'll also review the four basic pruning cuts and learn when each should be used.

The graceful form of this Japanese maple *(Acer palmatum)* has been enhanced by years of careful pruning.

WHY DO WE PRUNE?

Choose the right plant for the right location and give it plenty of room to expand, and you probably won't need to prune too often. You may have to cut back a few stems or branches now and then as the plant matures, but pruning won't be a major task.

Sometimes, however, circumstances make pruning a necessity. A tree's branches might block your view as you back out of your driveway, creating a safety hazard; you may move into a home with a garden so woefully neglected it has turned into a jungle. These and several other key reasons to prune are listed below.

To maintain safety. Remove low-growing branches if they impede passing vehicles or obscure oncoming traffic from view. You may also need to take out split or broken branches before they have the chance to come crashing down on a person, car, or building. It's wise, too, to prune out low-hanging, whiplike branches (especially those with thorns) that might strike passersby.

To alter or rejuvenate growth. Neglected, overgrown shrubs can sometimes be turned into small multitrunked trees if you remove their lower limbs; this may be a better approach than digging out the shrub and planting another in its place.

Healthy, well-shaped plants set off a house beautifully.

To direct growth. Pruning influences the direction in which a plant grows: each time you make a cut, you stop growth in one direction and encourage it in another. This principle is important to keep in mind when you train young trees to develop a strong branching structure.

To remove undesirable growth. Prune out unwanted growth periodically: cut out wayward branches, thin growth that's too dense, and remove suckers (stems growing up from the roots) and water sprouts (upright shoots growing from the trunk and branches).

To promote plant health. Trees and shrubs stay healthier if you remove branches that are diseased, dead, pest ridden, or rubbing together.

To create particular shapes. You can prune a line of closely planted trees or shrubs as a unit to create a hedge. If you're a hobbyist who practices topiary, you'll prune trees and shrubs into fanciful shapes.

To produce more flowers or fruits. Flowering plants and some fruit trees are pruned to increase the yield of blossoms and fruit and to improve their quality. You'll need to remove spent flowers from roses throughout their bloom time, for example; for some fruit trees, you'll make many small, precise cuts each dormant season. Though this sort of pruning sometimes seems a tedious chore, remember that your efforts will pay off in lavish bloom and generous crops of fruit.

WHEN TO PRUNE

Learning when to prune a particular plant is every bit as important as learning how to do the actual job. The timing is easier to understand if you know a little about plant metabolism. Most plants produce new leaves and stem growth from some point in spring through midsummer. Photosynthesis proceeds most intensively during this time, producing food (in the form of sugars) for the plant. As full summer heat sets in, the sugars are gradually transferred to the plant's woody parts and its roots, where they're stored during winter's dormant period. When spring arrives, the stored sugars are used to start new growth. Pruning is timed to harmonize with this cycle; it is typically done either late in dormancy or during summer. For some plants, a combination of both late-dormancy and summer pruning often yields the best results.

Note: The following guidelines are most pertinent to climates with four distinct seasons and definite winter chill. In warmer-winter areas, timing will vary depending on the particular plant's native climate. If you have any doubts about the best time to prune a particular plant, ask knowledgeable nursery personnel or your Cooperative Extension Office for advice.

PRUNING IN LATE DORMANCY

Many plants, especially deciduous trees and shrubs, are best pruned in late winter or early spring, just before they break dormancy. Heavy frosts have abated, so the plants are less likely to suffer cold damage at the point where you make your cuts. Sugars are still stored in larger branches, trunks, and roots, so little food will be lost to pruning. Deciduous plants are still bare, so you can easily spot broken and awkwardly growing branches and decide how to direct growth. And because growth will soon start, your pruning cuts will stimulate new growth in the direction you want.

For flowering trees and shrubs, you'll need to know if the flowers are produced on old or new growth. If early spring flowers come on last year's wood—as in the case of forsythia, flowering trees such as peach and plum *(Prunus),* and flowering quince *(Chaenomeles)* —you'll lose many flowers by pruning before plants break dormancy. It's best to wait until flowering has finished, then prune. But plants that bear flowers on leafy new growth formed in spring, such as cinquefoil *(Potentilla),* can safely be pruned while dormant.

You'll find more on pruning particular plants later in this book.

FOR TREES, see page 98

FOR FRUIT TREES, see pages 184–185

FOR SHRUBS, see pages 107–108, 119

FOR ROSES, see page 117

FOR VINES, see pages 141–142

This Japanese plum tree is pruned during winter dormancy. Twiggy branches are removed, opening up the tree's center to admit more light and air.

Picking bouquets from flowering trees and shrubs such as this lilac *(Syringa)* is a pleasant form of pruning.

REMOVING DISEASED GROWTH

Sometimes the only way to stop the progress of diseases such as anthracnose, canker and rots, and fireblight is to cut away the diseased tissue. When you remove a diseased limb, make the cut far enough below the afflicted area to leave only healthy tissue at the point of the cut; a point about a foot below the diseased part is usually sufficient.

It's easy to spread disease to healthy tissue via cutting blades. You may accidentally brush your tools against stems or leaves after cutting infected wood; you may even briefly forget that you've been pruning diseased wood and make your next cut into a nearby healthy branch. To avoid transmitting infection, *it's crucial to dip your tools in disinfectant before making each new cut.* Use full-strength rubbing alcohol or a solution of 9 parts water to 1 part household bleach.

Do not compost the diseased material you remove, and dispose of it promptly. When the job is done, disinfect your tools thoroughly one last time. Rinse them to remove all traces of disinfectant (it can corrode metal), then dry them before putting them away.

PRUNING IN SUMMER

A second time to prune is in late summer, when sugars needed for the next year's growth are moving into large limbs, trunks, and roots and will not be seriously depleted by pruning. Some gardeners like to thin plants in summer, since it's easier to see how much thinning is really needed when branches are still thickly foliaged. And because growth is slower at this time of year, pruning is less likely to stimulate new growth—an advantage when you're thinning. In cold-winter regions, don't do summer pruning later than one month before the first frost; if you do, an early frost may damage the plant at the point of the cuts.

SOME NOTES ON PRUNING EVERGREENS

Though evergreen trees and shrubs do not drop their leaves, they approach a near-dormant state during the winter months. The group includes broad-leafed evergreens—such as boxwood *(Buxus)* and camellia—and conifers, among them spruce *(Picea),* pine *(Pinus),* and many others (a very few conifers are deciduous; the larch, *Larix,* is an example).

Broad-leafed evergreens are usually best pruned in late dormancy or in summer, as outlined above. For flowering broad-leafed evergreens, however, timing is a bit more precise; you'll need to prune with an eye toward preserving flower buds. Prune after bloom for evergreens flowering on last season's growth; prune before spring growth begins for those that bloom on new growth.

Most conifers are pruned only in their first 2 or 3 years, in order to direct their basic shape; from then on, they're best left alone. Some of the most badly botched pruning you'll see is on conifers that have been pruned too severely, usually to keep them confined to a too-small location—though a few conifers, including arborvitae *(Platycladus* and *Thuja),* yew *(Taxus),* and hemlock *(Tsuga),* lend themselves to shearing into hedges. When you do need to prune a conifer, the timing will depend on whether the plant is a whorl-branching or random-branching type.

The branches of dawn redwood *(Metasequoia)* grow randomly along its trunk.

Cut back new spring growth to control the size and shape of whorl-branching conifers such as this pine.

In whorl-branching conifers, the branches radiate out from the trunk in whorls. Members of this group include fir *(Abies)*, spruce *(Picea)*, and pine *(Pinus)*. These trees produce all their new growth in spring; buds appear at the tips of new shoots as well as along their length and at their bases. On pines, the new shoots are called candles, since that's what they look like until the needles open out.

Prune whorl-branched conifers in early spring. To induce branching, you can pinch or cut anywhere along the new growth, being sure to do so before the shoots harden. When the tree is still relatively small, you can nip back the pliant new growth of the leader (the central upward-growing stem) and all side branches to make a denser, bushier plant. If you cut into an older stem, however—even at a point where it bears foliage—no new growth will sprout from below the cut.

Unlike whorl-branching sorts, random-branching conifers have branches that grow randomly along the trunk. These plants don't limit their new growth to spring, but grow in spurts throughout the growing season. Trees of this type include cedar *(Cedrus)*, cypress *(Cupressus)*, dawn redwood *(Metasequoia)*, redwood *(Sequoia)*, giant sequoia *(Sequoiadendron)*, bald cypress *(Taxodium)*, and hemlock *(Tsuga)*. These can be pruned much as you would deciduous and broad-leafed evergreen trees. New growth will sprout from below your pruning cuts as long as the remaining branch bears some foliage; in general, no new growth will develop from bare branches (hemlock is an exception). It's best to prune random-branching conifers right before new growth begins in spring, though they do allow you a little more leeway in timing than whorl-branching types do.

GROWTH BUDS

Pruning cuts are made near a growth bud. The resulting growth will vary depending on the bud. If your pruning is to have the effect you want, you'll need to learn to recognize three different growth buds.

A *terminal bud* grows at the tip of a shoot and causes the shoot to grow longer. These buds produce hormones that move downward along the shoot, inhibiting the growth of other buds on that shoot.

Lateral buds grow along the sides of a shoot and give rise to the sideways growth that makes a plant bushy. These buds stay dormant until the shoot has grown long enough to diminish the influence of the hormones produced by the terminal bud, or until the terminal bud is pruned off; then they begin their growth. If you remove lateral buds, you'll redirect growth to the terminal bud; the shoot will lengthen dramatically and tend to grow upwards.

Latent buds lie dormant beneath the bark. If a branch breaks or is cut off just above a latent bud, the bud may develop a new shoot to replace the wood that has been removed. If you need to repair a damaged plant, look for a latent bud and make your pruning cut above it.

PARTS OF A BRANCH

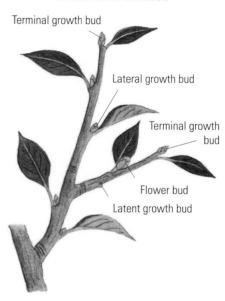

Terminal growth bud

Lateral growth bud

Terminal growth bud

Flower bud

Latent growth bud

TIP: Unless you are shearing a hedge, don't make random cuts into a stem or branch. Though results vary, the stem often dies back from the cut to the next growth bud. At the very least, you'll get erratic growth patterns; at worst, the entire plant may die. Even if you make only a few such cuts, groups of long sprouts may emerge from each one, making for an unsightly-looking branch.

CUTTING ABOVE A BUD

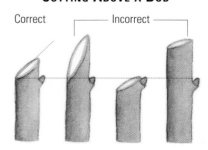

Correct | Incorrect

45° angle | Too angular | Too low | Too high

Thinning

Heading

Pinching

Shown here are three types of pruning cuts: pinching removes the terminal growth; heading removes part of the shoot; and thinning eliminates the entire shoot.

HEADING

Heading cuts produce clusters of shoots from the buds below the cuts.

PRUNING CUTS

There are four basic pruning cuts, each aimed at producing a different effect. For cuts that involve cutting above a growth bud, make your cut as shown on page 51: angle it at about 45°, with the lowest point of the cut opposite the bud and even with it, the highest point about ¼ inch above the bud.

PINCHING

One of the easiest "cuts" to make can be achieved without cutting: you simply pinch off a terminal bud with your thumb and forefinger. Pinching stops the stem from elongating and encourages bushy growth. It is typically done on annual and perennial flowers and on some vegetables; it's also effective for directing growth on small-leafed shrubs to give the plant an even shape.

HEADING

For heading, you cut farther back on the shoot than you would for pinching. In most cases, the lateral bud has already grown a leaf, and you make the cut right above the leaf. Usually done with hand-held pruners, heading stimulates the buds just below the cut, encouraging dense growth. Heading is a more aggressive approach than pinching when you're shaping certain small shrubs and flowering perennials.

TOOLS FOR PRUNING

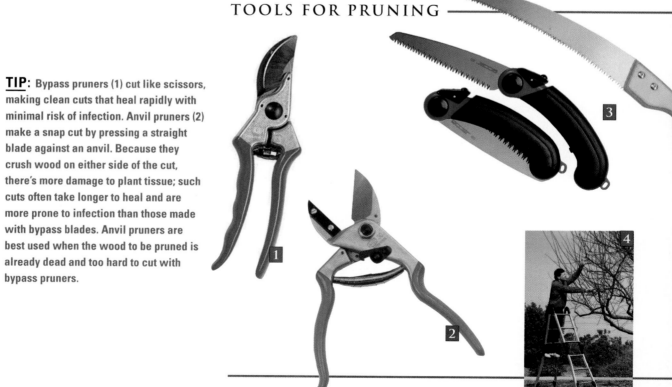

TIP: Bypass pruners (1) cut like scissors, making clean cuts that heal rapidly with minimal risk of infection. Anvil pruners (2) make a snap cut by pressing a straight blade against an anvil. Because they crush wood on either side of the cut, there's more damage to plant tissue; such cuts often take longer to heal and are more prone to infection than those made with bypass blades. Anvil pruners are best used when the wood to be pruned is already dead and too hard to cut with bypass pruners.

THINNING

Thinning reduces the bulk of a plant with minimal regrowth: each cut removes an entire stem or branch, either back to its point of origin on the main stem or to the point where it joins another branch. Because you remove a number of lateral buds along with the stem or branch, you're less likely to wind up with clusters of unwanted shoots than you are when you make heading cuts. (A common mistake of inexperienced gardeners is to make a heading cut when what's needed is a thinning cut.) Use hand-held pruners, loppers, or a pruning saw to make thinning cuts, depending on the thickness of the member being cut.

SHEARING

Shearing, customarily used to create a hedge or a bush with spherical or square form, is a form of heading that makes no attempt to cut back to a bud. However, because plants chosen for this treatment typically have many lateral buds close together, you'll usually end up cutting near a bud. Shearing stimulates many buds to produce new growth, so you'll be repeating the job regularly once you start. Since this method cuts right through leaves, it's best done on small-leafed plants, where damage is less noticeable. Use hand-held or electric hedge shears for this kind of pruning.

THINNING

Thinning cuts open up a plant and result in the least amount of regrowth.

SHEARING

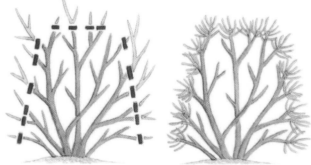

Shearing is really random heading. It produces an outer layer of dense, twiggy growth from buds below the cuts.

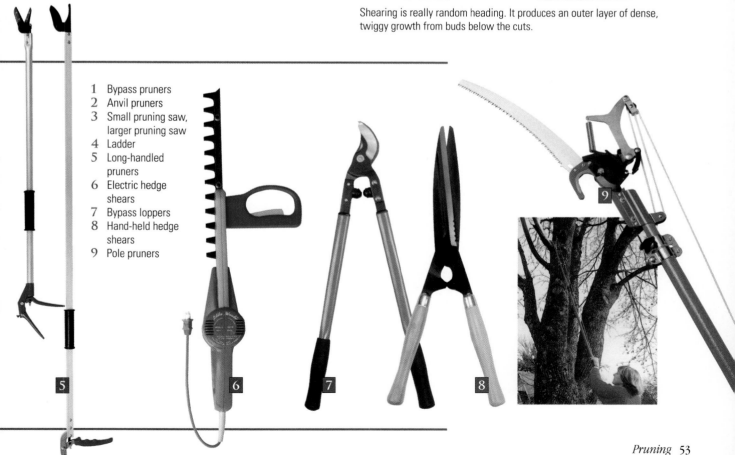

1 Bypass pruners
2 Anvil pruners
3 Small pruning saw, larger pruning saw
4 Ladder
5 Long-handled pruners
6 Electric hedge shears
7 Bypass loppers
8 Hand-held hedge shears
9 Pole pruners

PROPAGATING PLANTS

In gardening usage, "propagation" is a general term for the many ways of starting new plants. Familiar methods include sowing seeds, taking cuttings from stems, leaves, or roots, and ground and air layering. Division is another means of propagation; you'll find instructions for dividing perennials and bulbs on pages 155 and 166, respectively. Once you learn to propagate your own plants, you'll be able to try many kinds that may not be offered at your local nursery. You can grow large numbers of plants more economically, too: for the price of a six-pack of lettuce seedlings, for example, you can buy a packet of 600 seeds.

SOWING SEEDS

Many annuals, wildflowers, and vegetables can be seeded directly in the garden, either broadcast over a bed to give a planted-by-Nature look (see instructions on facing page) or sown in the traditional rows of a vegetable or cutting garden. Many other plants, however, are best raised from seed sown in containers. These include slow-growing perennials, plants with expensive or very fine seed, and warm-season vegetables and annuals that you want to start when the garden soil is still too cold and wet for in-ground planting.

PREPARING THE SOIL

Whether you're sowing a wildflower mixture or several kinds of annuals for a showy border, start by preparing the soil. Remove weeds, then loosen the soil and work in amendments with a spading fork, shovel, or rototiller. Add a complete fertilizer in the amount directed on the label. Finally, smooth the soil with a rake. If rain doesn't do the job for you, moisten the bed thoroughly a few days before you intend to plant. At sowing time, the soil should be moist but not soggy.

PLANTING IN ROWS

To grow vegetables or annuals in rows, prepare the soil as described above, but do not dig in fertilizer; it will be applied later (see below).

Next, make furrows for the seeds, following the packet instructions for depth of furrows and spacing between them. If possible, lay out the rows in a north-south direction, so that both sides will receive an equal amount of sunlight during the day. Form the furrows with a hoe, rake, or stick; for perfectly straight rows, use a board or taut string as a guide, as shown at right. Now dig two furrows alongside each seed furrow— one on either side, each 2 inches away from and 1 inch deeper than the seed furrow. Apply fertilizer in these furrows, following label recommendations for amount of fertilizer per foot of row. This technique puts the fertilizer where plant roots can best use it.

Sow seeds evenly, spacing them as the packet directs. You can tear off a small corner of the packet and tap the seeds out as you move along, or pour a small quantity of seed into your palm and scatter pinches of seed as evenly as possible. Larger seeds, such as beans, can be placed individually by hand.

Water the furrows with a fine spray; then keep the soil surface moist but not dripping wet until the seeds sprout. Thin overcrowded seedlings while they're still small; if you wait too long to thin, the plants will develop poorly, and you'll have a harder time removing an individual plant without disturbing those around it.

SOWING SEEDS IN CONTAINERS

Many plants get off to a better start when sown in containers and transplanted to garden beds later in the season. (For a few exceptions, see "Flowers and Vegetables to Direct-sow," page 56.) It's easier to provide plants in containers with the warm temperatures

KEEPING ROWS STRAIGHT

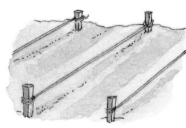

Lay a board on the soil surface (top picture); then plant or make a furrow along its edge. Or stretch string between two stakes and plant beneath it (bottom picture).

Various seed-starting trays and pots are available at nurseries and through mail-order catalogs.

and bright light they need for quick growth, and easier to protect them from insects and birds as well. The seed packet information will help you decide when to plant; most annual flowers and vegetables should be sown 4 to 8 weeks before it's time to transplant them to the garden.

CONTAINER CHOICES. Convenience, cost, and reusability will determine which containers you use. If you won't be around to water daily or don't plan to transplant seedlings into another container before planting them out, use 2- to 4-inch-diameter containers or flats with individual cells.

Plastic flats with no dividers are an old favorite. They're readily available from garden supply stores and mail-order catalogs, and free when you buy seedlings at nurseries.

Plastic cell-packs and 2- to 4-inch plastic pots, recycled from nursery purchases, are easy to obtain and use.

Peat pots are inexpensive but not reusable. But because you plant out seedlings pot and all, such pots minimize disturbance to roots. Keep them moist (so roots can penetrate them easily) as shown at left.

Plastic foam flats with tapered individual cells are sold by nurseries and through seed catalogs. They come in several cell sizes; some have capillary matting that draws water from a reservoir, making seedling care much easier.

In addition to the containers listed above, you can use household items—

TOP: To help peat pots retain moisture after seeding, set them in 1½ inches of moist soil in a flat.

BOTTOM: Plant two seeds in each cell of plastic foam flat; later thin to one seedling per cell.

BROADCASTING SEEDS IN A PREPARED BED

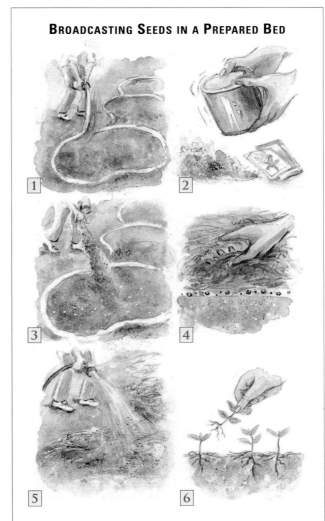

1 For a patterned planting, outline the areas for each kind of seed with gypsum, flour, or stakes and string. You may want to put a label in each area.

2 To achieve a more even distribution, shake each kind of seed (or an entire wildflower seed mixture) in a covered can with several times its bulk of white sand.

3 Scatter the seed-sand mixture as evenly as possible over the bed or individual planting areas; then rake lightly, barely covering the seeds with soil. Take care not to bury them too deeply.

4 Spread a very thin layer of mulch (such as sifted compost) over the bed to help retain moisture, keep the surface from crusting, and hide the seeds from birds.

5 Water with a fine spray. Keep the soil surface barely damp until the seeds sprout; once seedlings are up, gradually decrease watering frequency.

6 When seedlings have two sets of true leaves, thin those that are too closely spaced. Transplant the thinned seedlings to fill empty spaces in the bed.

FLOWERS AND VEGETABLES TO DIRECT-SOW

Certain easy-to-grow plants do best when sown directly in the garden, because they have delicate root systems or taproots that make successful transplantation from containers difficult. Such plants include sunflower *(Helianthus)*, sweet pea *(Lathyrus)*, love-in-a-mist *(Nigella)*, nasturtium *(Tropaeolum)*, and most wildflowers; and beans, carrots, corn, peas, and radishes.

BUYING AND STORING SEEDS

Be sure the seeds you buy are fresh; they should be dated for the current year. For many plants, seed may be sold in three different forms: loose, pelletized, and in tapes. Loose seeds, traditionally sold in packets, are familiar to all gardeners. Pelletized seeds, also sold in packets, are individually coated (like small pills) to make handling and proper spacing easier. Seed tapes are strips of biodegradable paper with seeds embedded in them, properly spaced for growing to maturity. You just unroll the tape in a prepared furrow and cover it with soil.

Store extra seeds in an airtight jar or other container in a cool, dry place. With proper storage, many kinds of seeds remain viable for a year, and some stay good for several years.

plastic cups, yogurt containers, cut-down milk cartons, foil baking pans. Be sure to punch several drainage holes in any container that lacks them, since seedlings will die if water collects around their roots.

If you're reusing old pots, scrub them out and soak them for 30 minutes in a solution of 9 parts water to 1 part household bleach to destroy any disease organisms.

GROWING MEDIUM. Use the seed-starting mixes or potting soil sold at nurseries, or make your own mix by combining 1 part each of peat moss, vermiculite, and perlite. Dampen the mix before using it by pouring it into a clean bucket, then stirring in enough water to make it moist but not soggy.

Fill each container to within ½ inch of the rim with the damp mix, firming it gently with your fingers, a block of wood, or the base of a jar. Check the seed packet for recommended planting depth. You can make furrows in the containers or scatter the seeds over the surface. If you're using containers with individual cells, plant two seeds per cell. Cover the seeds with the proper amount of prepared mix, taking care not to cover them too deeply. To prevent later confusion, label each container with the plant name and sowing date. Loosely cover the containers with wet newspaper, damp burlap, or aluminum foil; this helps keep the soil moist but still allows air to get in, preventing the growth of fungus.

If the seeds need light to germinate (this will be noted on the packet), gently press them into the potting mix, but do not cover them with more mix. Loosely cover the containers with a sheet of clear plastic.

Fluorescent lights on an adjustable stand give seedlings the light they need.

Place the containers in a warm spot. After 3 days, check daily for germination. As soon as you see green leaves arching out of the soil, uncover the containers and move them into bright light (but not direct sunlight): without adequate light, the seedlings will quickly become spindly and weak. If you aren't using a greenhouse, move the plants to a sunny south window; or give them 12 to 14 hours of fluorescent light per day, setting the lights 6 to 8 inches above the tops of the plants.

Water the containers when the surface of the potting mix feels dry. To avoid disturbing the seeds (and, after germination, the roots), spray with a fine mist. Or place the containers in a tray or sink holding a few inches of water; the mix will absorb adequate moisture within a few hours.

After the seedlings form their first set of true leaves, fertilize them weekly, using a fertilizer sold for starting seeds or a liquid type diluted to half strength.

When the seedlings have developed their second set of true leaves, it's time to transplant or thin them. If you don't need many plants, you can thin them in place: just pinch or snip off the excess seedlings, leaving the remaining ones spaced about 2 inches apart. Seedlings in individual pots or cells should be thinned to one plant per pot or cell. If you want to save most of the plants that have germinated, you'll need to transplant them to larger containers for growth to planting-out size. It's best to use individual pots or cell-packs for this purpose, so that seedlings won't suffer much root disturbance when planted out in the garden.

To transplant seedlings, fill each new container with moist planting mix. Loosen the soil around the seedlings (a kitchen fork or spoon is handy for this); then carefully lift them out, one at a time. Or lift a clump of seedlings and gently separate individual plants

THINNING SEEDLINGS　　　　**TRANSPLANTING SEEDLINGS**

LEFT: Thin seedlings to 1 to 2 inches apart by pinching them off with your fingers or snipping them off with scissors. RIGHT: Transplant seedlings to the garden or to a larger container when they have at least their second set of true leaves.

by carefully teasing apart the tangled mass of roots. Handle seedlings by their leaves to avoid damaging the tender stems. Poke a hole in the new container's planting mix, place the seedling in the hole, and firm soil around it. Water the transplant right away. Keep the containers out of direct sunlight for a few days to let the transplants recover from the move.

About 10 days before the seedlings are ready to plant outside, harden them off so they can withstand bright sun and cooler temperatures. Stop fertilizing them, and set them outdoors for several hours each day in a wind-sheltered spot that receives filtered light. A cold frame (see page 93) is useful for hardening off seedlings. Over the next week or so, gradually increase exposure until the plants are in full sun all day (shade lovers are an exception; they shouldn't be exposed to day-long sun). Then set them out in the garden as illustrated on page 34.

CUTTINGS

Propagating plants from cuttings allows you to increase your supply of a special perennial, shrub, or tree already in your garden, or to start plants from a friend's garden. Unlike most plants raised from seed, those grown from cuttings are identical to the parent plant. Cuttings taken from the stems of plants are of three types, depending on the maturity of the parent plant: softwood, semihardwood, and hardwood. Some kinds of plants can also be started from leaf or root cuttings.

SOFTWOOD AND SEMIHARDWOOD STEM CUTTINGS

Taken during the active growing season from spring until late summer, *softwood cuttings* are the easiest stem cuttings to take and the fastest to root. They come from relatively soft, flexible new growth. Many perennials, shrubs, and trees can be propagated by softwood cuttings, including coleus, forsythia, crape myrtle *(Lagerstroemia)*, geranium *(Pelargonium)*, penstemon, mock orange *(Philadelphus)*, plum, pomegranate, rose, and weigela (to name just a few). *Semihardwood cuttings* are taken somewhat later in

Continued on page 60 >

DAMPING OFF

If your seedlings suddenly collapse and die, one of the fungal diseases called "damping off" or "seed and seedling rot" may be to blame. In one type of damping off, the seedling's stem collapses at or near the soil surface; in another type, the seedling rots before it emerges from the soil, or the seed decays before it even sprouts.

To prevent these problems, use pasteurized potting mix and new or thoroughly washed and disinfected containers. Try using seeds treated with a fungicide. Take care not to overwater seedlings; be sure to provide good air circulation and ventilation, so tops of seedlings stay dry and standing moisture is kept to a minimum. Thinning seedlings to eliminate crowding is also helpful.

ROOTING SOFTWOOD AND SEMIHARDWOOD CUTTINGS

1   Prepare containers first. Use clean pots or flats with drainage holes. Fill them with a half-and-half mixture of perlite and peat moss, or with perlite or vermiculite alone. Dampen the mixture.

2   Gather cuttings early in the day, when plants are fresh and full of moisture. The parent plant should be healthy and growing vigorously. With a sharp knife or bypass pruners, cut off an 8- to 12-inch length of stem.

    Prepare the cuttings by removing and discarding any flower buds, flowers, and side shoots. Then slice the stem into 3- to 4-inch pieces, each with at least two nodes (growing points). Make each cut just below a node, since new roots will form at this point. Strip the lower leaves from each cutting.

3   Dip the cut end in rooting hormone powder, if desired. (Many kinds of plants will root without the use of hormones.) Tap off excess powder.

    Using the end of a sharp pencil, make holes in the rooting medium an inch or two apart; then insert the cuttings. Firm the medium around the cuttings and water with a fine spray. Label each container with the name of the plant and the date. Set containers in a warm spot that's shaded but not dark.

    Enclose each container in a plastic bag, fastening the bag closed to maintain humidity. Open the bag for a few minutes every day to provide ventilation.

4   Once the cuttings have taken hold and are growing roots, they will begin to send out new leaves. To test for rooting, gently pull on a cutting; if you feel resistance, roots are forming. At this point, expose the cuttings to drier air by opening the bags; if the cuttings wilt, close the bags again for a few days.

    When the plants seem acclimated to open air, transplant each to its own pot of lightweight potting soil. By the next planting season, the new plants should be ready to go out in the garden.

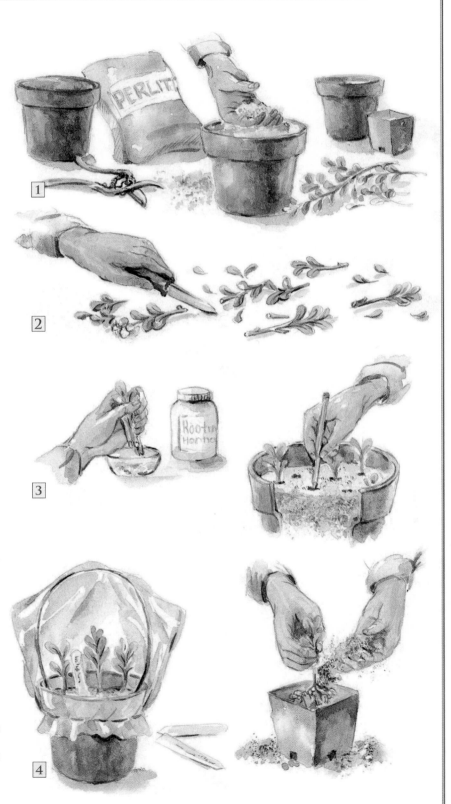

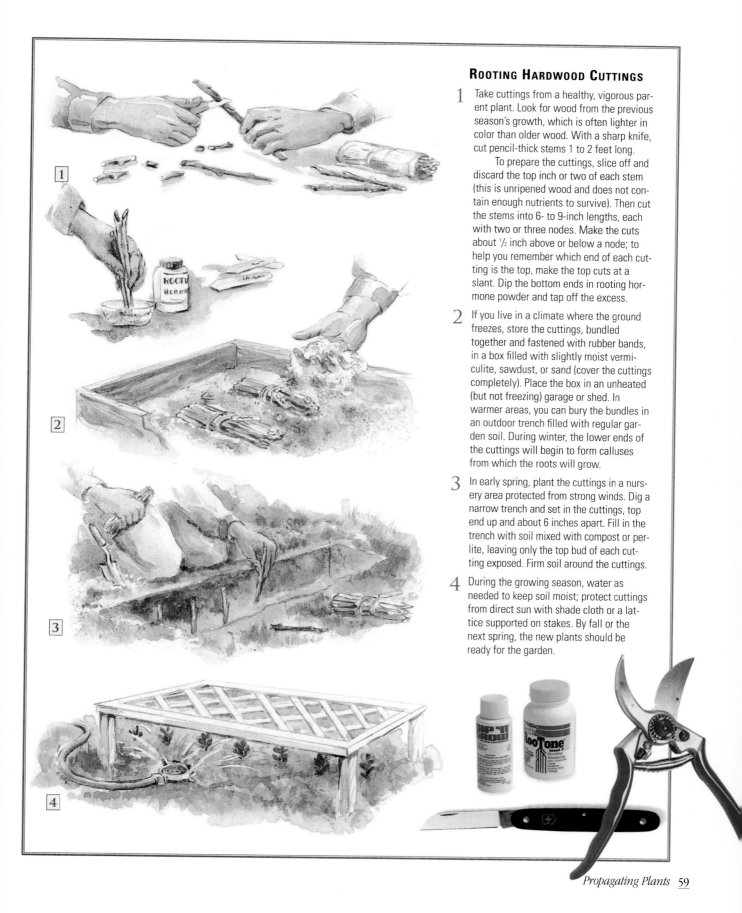

ROOTING HARDWOOD CUTTINGS

1 Take cuttings from a healthy, vigorous parent plant. Look for wood from the previous season's growth, which is often lighter in color than older wood. With a sharp knife, cut pencil-thick stems 1 to 2 feet long.

To prepare the cuttings, slice off and discard the top inch or two of each stem (this is unripened wood and does not contain enough nutrients to survive). Then cut the stems into 6- to 9-inch lengths, each with two or three nodes. Make the cuts about $\frac{1}{2}$ inch above or below a node; to help you remember which end of each cutting is the top, make the top cuts at a slant. Dip the bottom ends in rooting hormone powder and tap off the excess.

2 If you live in a climate where the ground freezes, store the cuttings, bundled together and fastened with rubber bands, in a box filled with slightly moist vermiculite, sawdust, or sand (cover the cuttings completely). Place the box in an unheated (but not freezing) garage or shed. In warmer areas, you can bury the bundles in an outdoor trench filled with regular garden soil. During winter, the lower ends of the cuttings will begin to form calluses from which the roots will grow.

3 In early spring, plant the cuttings in a nursery area protected from strong winds. Dig a narrow trench and set in the cuttings, top end up and about 6 inches apart. Fill in the trench with soil mixed with compost or perlite, leaving only the top bud of each cutting exposed. Firm soil around the cuttings.

4 During the growing season, water as needed to keep soil moist; protect cuttings from direct sun with shade cloth or a lattice supported on stakes. By fall or the next spring, the new plants should be ready for the garden.

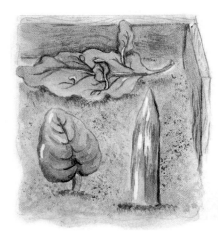

THREE TYPES OF LEAF CUTTINGS

Rex begonias are propagated by making cuts in the large veins on the underside of mature leaves. Lay the leaf flat, cut side down, on the rooting medium; then enclose the container in a plastic bag. In time, new plants will grow at the point where each vein was cut.

To root leaf cuttings of African violets, insert a young leaf with an inch or two of stem into a rooting medium made of 1 part peat moss and 1 part vermiculite, perlite, or coarse builder's sand. Enclose the container in a plastic bag to retain humidity. New plants form at the base of the stem.

To root leaf cuttings of mother-in-law's tongue, cut a leaf into 3- to 4-inch-long sections. Insert these pieces into the rooting medium, covering as much as three-fourths of their length. A new plant will eventually form at the base of each piece.

the growing season, usually in summer or early autumn. A semihardwood stem is firm enough to snap if bent sharply; if it just bends, it's too mature for satisfactory rooting. Among the plants that can be propagated from semihardwood cuttings are boxwood *(Buxus)*, camellia, citrus, escallonia, euonymus, holly *(Ilex)*, olive, and rhododendron.

The procedure for rooting these two types of stem cuttings is the same; see page 58.

HARDWOOD CUTTINGS

You make hardwood cuttings in autumn or early winter, when plants are dormant. Many deciduous shrubs and trees can be propagated by this method, including most of those mentioned above under softwood and semihardwood cuttings; other candidates include currant, fig, gooseberry, grape, privet *(Ligustrum)*, mulberry *(Morus)*, quince, and spiraea. To root hardwood cuttings, see page 59.

LEAF CUTTINGS

Some plants will root successfully from a leaf or a portion of one; examples include rex begonia, African violet *(Saintpaulia)*, and mother-in-law's tongue *(Sansevieria)*. Follow the techniques described at left.

ROOT CUTTINGS

Any plant that produces sprouts from its roots will grow from root cuttings. Some examples are bear's breech *(Acanthus)*, Japanese anemone, blackberry, trumpet vine *(Campsis)*, globe thistle *(Echinops)*, Oriental poppy *(Papaver)*, and raspberry.

Make root cuttings when the plant is dormant—in late fall or early winter, for most species. You can dig up an entire plant or just a section of its roots. With a sharp knife, remove vigorous, healthy pieces of root 2 to 4 inches long; those growing close to the crown will form new plants most quickly. (Note that rooting hormone is not needed, and in fact may actually delay rooting.) If you only have a few root cuttings, you can place them upright in a container filled with damp potting mix, with the top cut ends (the ends that were closest to the crown on the parent plant) just at soil level. For larger numbers of cuttings, fill a flat to within an inch of the top with potting mix; lay the cuttings flat on top of the mix, then cover them with ½ inch more mix.

Water the planted containers well. Then place them in a growing area such as a greenhouse or cold frame and provide protection from direct sun. Once stems and green leaves have formed, move the containers into full light and water them as needed. When the young shoots are several inches tall and new roots have formed (check by gently digging up a cutting), transplant them to individual pots and feed with liquid fertilizer.

ROOT CUTTINGS

To start a few root cuttings, insert them upright in a pot. For a larger number, lay the cuttings in a flat.

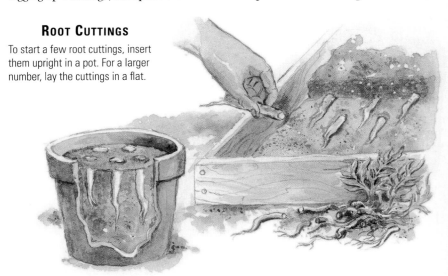

GROUND LAYERING

1   In spring, select a young, healthy, pliable shoot growing low on the plant to be layered. Loosen the soil where the shoot will be buried and work in a shovelful of compost. Dig a shallow hole in the prepared area.

   With a sharp knife, make a cut where the shoot will touch the soil; cut about halfway through the shoot, starting from the underside. Dust the cut with rooting hormone powder and insert a pebble or wooden matchstick to hold it open.

   Lay the shoot (the layer) in the hole and fasten it down with a piece of wire or a forked stick. Some gardeners tie the layer's tip to a stake to help it grow upwards.

2   Fill in the hole, firming the soil around the layer. A rock or brick can be placed on top to help hold the layer in place.

   During the growing season, keep the soil around the layer moist. Adding a few inches of mulch will help retain moisture.

   When you are sure roots have formed (this may take anywhere from a few months to more than a year; gently dig into the soil to check), cut the new plant free from the parent. Dig it up, keeping plenty of soil around the roots, and move it to its intended location.

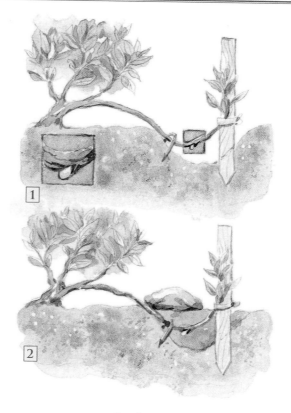

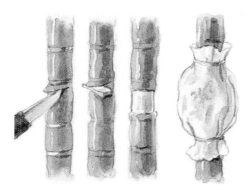

AIR LAYERING

Air layering is most successful if done while a plant is growing actively. To encourage such growth in houseplants, fertilize the plant to be layered, then place it in a sunny window. When new leaves appear, proceed with layering.

   Begin below a node. Make a slanting cut (insert a wooden matchstick to keep it open) or remove a ring of bark. Dust cut with rooting hormone, encase in damp sphagnum moss, and cover with plastic wrap to keep moss moist.

LAYERING

Layering is a propagation method that encourages new roots to form on branches still attached to the parent plant. The parent supplies the layer—the new plant—with water and nutrients during the rooting process.

GROUND LAYERING

Also called simple layering, ground layering is an easy way to produce a few new plants, though it may take as long as a year. Some plants, such as trailing blackberry, reproduce naturally by ground layering. Numerous others are well suited to this method, among them forsythia, gooseberry, grape, hazelnut, mountain laurel *(Kalmia)*, rhododendron, rose, spiraea, and lilac *(Syringa)*.

   To ground layer, follow the steps above.

AIR LAYERING

Air layering (shown above) involves the same principle as ground layering, but it's used for branches higher on a plant. It is often employed to propagate large house plants (overgrown rubber plants, for example), but it's also successful in some outdoor shrubs and trees, including citrus, witch hazel *(Hamamelis)*, magnolia, and rhododendron.

   If layering is successful, roots will appear in the sphagnum moss after several months; you can then sever the newly rooted stem from its parent and pot it or plant it out. At this point, it's usually a good idea to remove about half the new plant's leaves, to prevent excessive moisture loss through transpiration while the new plant gets established on its own.

   If no roots form, the cut you made will form a callus, and new bark will eventually grow over it.

PESTS, DISEASES, AND WEEDS

Nothing is more frustrating than finding a prized plant eaten to the ground by insects, languishing from an unknown malady, or constantly encroached upon by persistent weeds. Once you identify the problem precisely, though, you'll be on your way to solving it. In this chapter, you'll find photos and descriptions of some of the most common garden pests, diseases, and weeds, and you'll learn a common-sense approach to keeping them under control.

You won't find many problems in this Santa Fe garden. The plants are appropriate for the climate, and the gardener gives them what they need to thrive. And because they're of many kinds and many heights, they offer a habitat for beneficials and birds—your partners in pest control.

TODAY'S APPROACH TO GARDEN PROBLEMS

In years past, the preferred solution to garden problems was to eradicate the trouble with pesticides. As we've since learned, however, it is neither possible nor desirable to completely eliminate every problem that besets our plants—and by trying to do so, we may cause immediate or long-term harm to people, animals, and the environment. Today, the focus is on *prevention* and *management,* not eradication. This approach, called Integrated Pest Management (IPM), had its origins in the agricultural industry, but it is just as applicable to home gardens.

PREVENTION

Whatever your garden's size or style, good plant health is your first line of defense against potential problems of any kind. Strong, vigorous plants are better able to resist pests that fly or crawl into the garden and disease spores that drift in on the wind; a thick, healthy lawn foils weed invasion before it can begin. Make it a priority to give each plant the water, fertilizer, and light it needs to thrive.

There are other steps you can take to keep problems away. Remember that landscaping choices can contribute to a healthy garden: if you include a variety of plants of different heights, you'll provide a habitat for insect-eating birds and other creatures that help keep pest populations under control. Pay attention to maintenance: keep an eye on the accumulation of debris such as old leaves, pieces of wood, pulled annual flowers, and fallen seedpods. Although such materials—if nondiseased—can act as a good natural mulch (and a source of nutrients as they decay and work into the soil), they also provide a favorite home for ground-dwelling pests. If pests of this sort are a nuisance for you, you may want to clear away their hiding places periodically.

This kind of cleanup aids in disease prevention, as well—as do proper watering, careful transplanting, and the use of disease-resistant plants. For further disease-prevention advice, see page 76.

Numerous tactics will aid you in keeping weeds from invading your garden; ground covers and mulches offer just one effective means of thwarting these plant pests. For more suggestions, turn to page 81.

IDENTIFICATION

Keeping the garden healthy goes a long way toward preventing trouble, but every now and then a problem is bound to crop up—and before you can deal with it, you need to identify it. The following pages describe a number of common pests, diseases, and weeds. You can also turn to local nurseries and garden centers for help; knowledgeable personnel often can identify your problem if you bring in a few diseased leaves or a captured insect for inspection. Your Cooperative Extension Office is another excellent resource. To contact the nearest one, check the telephone listings for your county (the number is sometimes listed under "Agricultural Extension") or closest state university. Funded through local colleges and universities, these offices are chartered to establish horticultural programs for local residents and to answer gardening questions.

Cooperative Extension Offices publish a wide variety of pamphlets on topics of interest and importance to local gardeners.

MANAGEMENT WITHOUT PESTICIDES

Once you have identified a problem, you'll need to decide on a course of action. First, remember that some problems are minor or fleeting enough to be ignored: you probably can live with a chewed leaf or two, and some insect infestations may persist for only a week or so, then resolve by themselves as the pests mature or move on. Other problems, however, will be serious enough to require controls. When this happens, don't immediately turn to pesticides. Other, less toxic options may work perfectly well.

Note: If a particular plant looks sickly no matter what you do, the best course may be to abandon rescue attempts. Dig it up and replace it with something else.

PHYSICAL CONTROLS

These are all simple, time-honored tactics; you remove pests by mechanical means. Check the discussions of individual pests, diseases, and weeds for more ideas.

Hard blasts of water from the hose knock many pests (aphids and spider mites, for example) from their perches.

Handpicking is a straightforward way to get rid of pests such as hornworms and snails.

Sticky traps—paper or cardboard covered with a sticky material like castor oil, natural gum resin, or vegetable wax—are useful. Place 6- by 6-inch sheets on sticks in a vegetable bed to attract flying insects. You can also wrap a stiff paper band (at least 3 inches wide) covered with sticky material around a tree trunk and leave it in place for a few weeks; it will keep insects from crawling up into the branches.

Barriers work well against many pests. Thwart crawling marauders such as snails and slugs by encircling planting beds with a 4- to 5-inch-wide ring of sawdust or a 4-inch-high "fence" of copper strips. A below-ground chicken-wire lining in a vegetable or other garden bed will discourage gophers; wire frames on top of planting beds keep pests such as rabbits, opossums, raccoons, and skunks out. Floating row covers (see page 173) keep insects and birds off some ground crops; netting prevents birds from snacking on ripening fruits and vegetables.

TOP: Handpick tomato hornworms using kitchen tongs.

BOTTOM: Sticky traps attract a wide variety of flying insects.

HELP FROM INSECTS AND OTHER CREATURES

A number of beneficial creatures can aid you in pest control; you'll find photos of some of these on pages 67 and 68. Among the group are many near-invisible flies and wasps, such as syrphid and tachinid flies, trichogramma and encarsia wasps, and predatory midges. These creatures kill whiteflies, aphids, and other pests by laying eggs inside pest larvae; when the eggs hatch, the host serves as food. Local agencies sometimes introduce certain of these beneficials to entire neighborhoods or cities to combat a severe pest problem; you'll also find a few types available for sale from specialty garden supply companies. The best way to recruit these tiny allies, however, is to grow flowers that provide them with nectar; they'll come to your garden to feed, then remain to lay their eggs. They can most easily extract nectar from plants with very small flowers, such as sweet alyssum *(Lobularia maritima)*. They're also attracted to daisy-family plants; the flat flower heads both provide nectar and make ideal landing strips.

Ladybugs are familiar garden helpers. You may be tempted to buy them from a garden supply firm, intending to blanket your garden—but if they are to stay, they must be introduced just as they are ready to lay eggs, and this timing is difficult to achieve. What's more likely is that most of them will fly out of the garden in a matter of hours. Focus on maintaining a healthy garden filled with plants that vary in type and size, and the ladybugs will arrive on their own.

Parasitic nematodes (a different sort from the nematodes that attack plant roots) feed on many kinds of soil-dwelling pests and borers. They're sold in dormant form at many garden centers.

Attract beneficials with flowering plants such as sweet alyssum *(Lobularia maritima),* shown in top photo, and Shasta daisy *(Chrysanthemum × superbum),* bottom photo.

To use them, you simply mix the packaged nematodes with water and apply the solution to the soil with a watering can.

Though some birds do like to nibble on fruit and vegetable crops, they're also quite willing to eat insect pests. Attract them to your garden by providing food, shelter, and water, and they will repay your attention. Chickadees, for example, will visit your rose bushes each day and eat all the aphids they find.

MANAGEMENT WITH PESTICIDES

If nontoxic controls won't do the job, you may have no choice but to use a pesticide. "Pesticide" is a general term for any product that destroys or repels pests, or that prevents or mitigates their attack. The group includes insecticides, used against insects and related creatures of various types; fungicides, which control many plant diseases; and herbicides, which kill weeds.

The U.S. Environmental Protection Agency (E.P.A.) has strict rules for pesticide classification and labeling. Because all pesticides can be dangerous if used incorrectly, the regulations apply both to products we think of as quite benign (such as soap sprays) and to those so toxic they can be applied only in tightly controlled situations by persons certified to use them.

READING A PESTICIDE LABEL

When you read a pesticide label, start by looking at the list of active ingredients. Here you'll find the common name of each ingredient—information that's useful when you're comparing brands or following recommendations that refer to products by the common rather than trade name (as in this book, for example).

Also look for the signal word—"caution," "warning," "danger," or "poison." This word alerts you to the product's immediate toxicity; "caution" indicates the lowest toxicity, "poison" the highest. As a general rule, it's a smart idea to start your control attempts with the least toxic choice possible.

Labels specify which pests the product controls; give a list of plants on which it can be used, also noting whether it is safe for food crops; provide storage and disposal information; state any special precautions; and give first-aid instructions in the event of unsafe exposure.

Once you have purchased a pesticide, mix it exactly as the instructions direct. A solution that is too weak may be ineffective; one that's too strong may kill the plant you're treating and be harmful to you and the environment. Then apply the product precisely as directed. If the instructions tell you to wear goggles or a breathing mask, it is essential that you do so.

BRAND
Pesticide

ACTIVE INGREDIENTS

SIGNAL WORD
Product code identification

Signal word

Active ingredients

When you buy any pesticide, read the label carefully. Check the product's common name (the name listed on the label under "active ingredients"), which often differs from the trade name; the insecticide carbaryl is marketed under the trade name Sevin, for example. In this book, we refer to pesticides by common name. Also look for the signal word on the label; it will give you an idea of a product's immediate toxicity. The four signal words are "caution," "warning," "danger," and "poison"; "caution" indicates the lowest toxicity, "poison" the highest.

As a general rule, start your control attempts with the less toxic products. Soaps, oils, sulfur, pyrethrin, and *Bt* all fall into this class of "milder" pesticides; when used carefully, according to label directions, they pose minimal danger to you and the environment.

TIP: A U.S.D.A. formula combining oil and soap is effective in killing soft-bodied insects. Mix 1 cup peanut, safflower, corn, soybean, or sunflower oil with 1 tablespoon liquid dishwashing detergent. To make the spray, use 1½ teaspoons of the oil-detergent mixture for each cup of water.

SOAPS, OILS, AND SULFUR

These products are effective against many problems and have relatively few drawbacks. They must, of course, be used with care: some individuals may be allergic to them, and they can cause eye or skin irritation. Soaps and oils are extremely dangerous to fish.

SOAPS are especially effective in killing soft-bodied insects: when the spray hits them, it penetrates their bodies and causes cell membranes to burst. Unfortunately, soaps kill not only pests but beneficial insects as well—including bees, which are in decline throughout North America. You can, however, time the application of soap spray to minimize hazard to bees. Since bees typically return to the hive in late afternoon, spray in early evening; by morning, the soap will have dissipated. You'll also save beneficials by resisting the urge to spray a wide area "just for good measure." Spray only those plants exhibiting symptoms.

Some soaps are effective in killing weeds. Those marketed as weed killers have a higher proportion of soap to water than those sold to kill insects.

When you prepare soap sprays, keep in mind that they will be more effective when mixed with soft water than with hard water: soft water produces a sudsier spray that is better able to reach all surfaces of a plant.

OILS serve several purposes and come in two weights. The heavier sort, called *horticultural oil* or *dormant oil*, is applied in late winter (before foliage appears) to kill certain disease spores as well as eggs and

Bees are crucial pollinators for many plants, from flowering ornamentals to fruit trees. When you use pesticides, do so carefully to minimize harm to these beneficial insects.

dormant stages of some pests. It cannot be used after leaves emerge, since it will scald foliage. Some manufacturers combine horticultural oil with lime sulfur (see "Sulfur," below) and market it as "dormant spray"; read labels carefully if you want oil alone.

Summer oil is the lighter oil; it can be used on plants in leaf. Unlike horticultural oil, it generally doesn't scald foliage. It can sometimes interfere with transpiration, however, so spray just one branch and watch it for signs of wilting before you treat the entire plant. Summer oil smothers both soft-bodied and hard-bodied insects when applied directly to them; it can also prevent rust and mildew spores from taking hold.

SULFUR—the finely ground mineral—is effective on a variety of flowers, fruits, and vegetables in preventing powdery mildew, rust, and black spot. It can also control mites and several insect pests. It is toxic to a few plants, including cucumber, raspberry, and apricot, so check the label carefully to make sure it is safe for your intended target. Unlike lime sulfur (see below), *elemental sulfur cannot be used in conjunction with oils:* the combination will kill plants. Wait 1 month before applying sulfur to any plant that has been treated with an oil spray.

Buy sulfur as a wettable powder, then mix it with water and spray the solution to coat plant surfaces evenly. Keep in mind that sulfur is sometimes combined with other pesticides, many of which have higher toxicity levels. Read labels closely to see if you're buying sulfur on its own or mixed with something else. The signal word will give you a clue; sulfur rates "caution," but combination products of higher toxicity will be labeled "warning."

Lime sulfur (calcium polysulfide) is effective against the diseases and pests noted above for elemental sulfur. It can be purchased separately or in combination with horticultural oil (as dormant spray). Because it is caustic, you are required by law (as stated on the product label) to wear protective clothing, goggles, and a breathing mask when you're applying it.

PYRETHRIN

In jungles, rain forests, and other wilderness areas around the world, researchers have found plants whose natural toxins will kill pests. One of the most effective of these is pyrethrin, derived from a daisy-flowered plant, *Tanacetum cinerariifolium* (formerly *Chrysanthemum cinerariifolium*). Pyrethrin kills many soft-bodied and some hard-bodied insects, has a low level of toxicity,

USING PESTICIDES SAFELY

When using any pesticide, read the label instructions carefully and follow them exactly. Also keep the following tips in mind.

❧ When you dilute concentrated liquids for application, work on a sturdy outdoor surface and wear waterproof gloves and a long-sleeved shirt. Measure the concentrate exactly, using standard measuring cups and spoons. Clean up any spills at once, following the package directions.

❧ Keep pressure-pump applicators of different sizes on hand so you can easily prepare only the amount you need.

❧ If the directions for a particular pesticide tell you to wear goggles and a breathing mask during the application process, do so.

❧ When you're applying pesticides, protect your skin by wearing waterproof gloves and shoes, a long-sleeved shirt, and long pants. Tuck your hair under a hat.

❧ Keep pesticides well away from children and pets. If necessary, store them in a locked cabinet in a garage or storage area.

❧ Don't put unused pesticides in the trash. For instructions on proper disposal, contact your local sanitation service or the state pesticide agency.

and dissipates rapidly. It is not, however, harmless; mix, apply, and dispose of it as carefully as you would any other pesticide. It kills beneficial insects as well as pests, so use it judiciously. Some pyrethrin-based products are combined with other, more toxic pesticides; read labels closely to see what you're getting.

BACTERIAL PESTICIDES

Bt (Bacillus thuringiensis) is a bacterial pathogen that paralyzes and destroys the stomach cells of insects that consume it: once they eat a *Bt*-coated leaf, they stop feeding, then die within several days. Because *Bt* must be ingested to be effective, it is more selective than sprays that simply kill on contact—and that means it's less likely to upset the insect balance in your garden.

The type of *Bt* most commonly sold kills many leaf-eating caterpillars—including, unfortunately, those that will eventually become butterflies. If you want butterflies in your garden, try to use *Bt* only on those plants hosting pest caterpillars. You'll also find special strains of *Bt* aimed at specific pests; *Bt tenebrionis,* for example, is effective against Colorado potato beetle larvae.

SYNTHETIC PESTICIDES

Synthetic (laboratory-produced) pesticides are the solution of last resort, to be used only after you have exhausted all other, less toxic approaches to coping with a particular pest, disease, or weed. Despite their higher toxicity, such products sometimes offer the best—or only—way to save a precious plant from insect attack or halt a rampant disease or weed infestation.

Appropriate pesticides for specific problems are identified by name in the following sections on pests (pages 67–75), diseases (pages 76–80) and weeds (pages 81–88). Keep in mind, however, that pesticide regulations change rapidly. Some of the products mentioned in this book may later be removed from the list of pesticides approved in your state, or their application directions may change; and, of course, new products may be added. If you have questions concerning current regulations, consult a local nursery or your Cooperative Extension Office.

TOOLS FOR APPLYING PESTICIDES

1 Backpack pressure-
   pump applicator
2 Pressure-pump
   applicators
3 Breathing mask
4 Gloves
5 Goggles
6 Protective clothing

There's little good to be said about tent caterpillars; infestations can defoliate entire trees. Here, the pests ravage a walnut tree.

PESTS

Some garden residents have few redeeming features: Japanese beetles, for example, seem to do nothing but cause trouble, devouring flowers, vegetables, and lawns. Other creatures, though, are pests only some of the time. Birds are allies when they help reduce the insect population, enemies when they eat ripening cherries; white cabbage butterflies look pretty as they flit among the flowers, but as vegetable-eating caterpillars they're a nuisance. Learning just which creatures are pests—and when—is an integral part of successful pest management.

RECOGNIZING INSECTS AND RELATED CREATURES

It's easy to recognize larger pests, such as deer and rabbits—but it's not so simple with the smaller ones. They're often too tiny or too fast-moving to be easily seen, and they tend to conceal themselves well. Sometimes they look like their beneficial relatives: most of us can't tell the difference between a spined soldier bug (helpful) and a squash bug (hateful). Sometimes they manage to let other creatures take the rap. Pillbugs, for example, are often wrongly convicted through circumstantial evidence: we find them at the scene of the crime and assume they did the damage. And some pests confuse us because they change their appearance as they mature: one day they're grubs living in the ground, the next they're shiny beetles scampering among the plants.

In the following pages, we discuss the creatures, both harmful and helpful, you're likely to find in your garden. For more detailed descriptions of some common pests and the damage they typically cause, turn to page 68. For information on animal pests such as deer and squirrels, see page 74.

Note: For convenience, gardeners typically refer to most pests simply as "insects." But while many garden pests are in fact true insects—aphids, grasshoppers, and squash bugs, for example—others are only insect*like.* As far as the gardener is concerned, they're related to true insects in the harm they do; but they belong to different scientific classes. Examples of such creatures include spider mites (arachnids), nematodes (roundworms), and slugs and snails (mollusks).

LOOKING OUT FOR GARDEN HELPERS

Some insects and related creatures routinely consume many pests and rarely cause problems. As a group, they're called beneficials. Perhaps the best-known example is the ladybug, which eats many sorts of pest larvae; you'll find photos of four more beneficials on page 68.

Note that some of the spiders, bees, and wasps you'll see as you tour your yard also help keep the garden healthy. Many spiders, for example, eat numerous sorts of pests. Be on the alert, however, for two poisonous spiders to avoid: the black widow, which has a shiny black body with a red hourglass-shaped mark on the abdomen, and the brown recluse, which is matte brown with a darker brown, violin-shaped mark on its head. Though most spiders will flee rather than bite, a bite from either of these two requires immediate medical attention.

Without the help of bees as pollinators, we'd lose many of our favorite fruit crops. Besides the familiar honeybee, your garden may also host bumblebees and various other solitary bees

We all like ladybugs; they're a favorite motif for everything from greeting cards to fabrics. They've earned their good reputation by consuming all kinds of garden pests.

Assassin bugs eat aphids, mites, and certain harmless insects.

Damsel bugs and their nymphs feed on aphids, leafhoppers, and small caterpillars.

Ground beetles hunt and eat other insects, caterpillars, and soil-dwelling maggots and grubs; larger species eat snail and slug eggs.

Though adult lacewings feed only on nectar and honeydew, their larvae devour aphids, leafhoppers, mealybugs, mites, thrips, whiteflies, and other small pests.

and wasps (as well as minuscule parasitic wasps that you won't even see). The solitary types are relatively slow moving and rarely aggressive. In contrast, the wasps and bees that bother people (yellow jackets and Africanized bees, for example) typically live in group nests or hives and are normally quite aggressive.

Because many helpful (and simply inoffensive) insects and related creatures are killed by any pesticide, even something as seemingly innocuous as a soap spray, it's important to limit treatment to just those areas suffering from problems. Don't spray the garden wholesale. If you need to get rid of aggressive wasps and bees, hire a professional for the job.

For more on beneficials, see page 63.

SOME COMMON PESTS

Profiled on the next pages are some of the most troublesome garden pests, including insects and related creatures as well as animals. For each, we briefly describe its appearance and the damage it causes, then offer suggestions for both nonchemical and synthetic chemical controls. For further information on the suggested chemical controls, see page 75.

INSECTS AND RELATED CREATURES

The following pests are familiar garden troublemakers throughout much of North America.

ANTS

Ants rarely cause problems directly. Instead, they make trouble by driving away creatures that might eat or parasitize aphids and whiteflies—two pests that do considerable damage. These pests excrete honeydew, a sugary sap ants like to eat. Some ants invade houses during rainy weather. Outdoors, their nests often grow larger when temperatures are mild—a nuisance for the gardener. Fire ants, found in the Southwest, inflict a painful sting and often build their mounds in lawns or compost heaps.

To reduce food sources for ants, keep aphid and whitefly populations under control, as noted below and on page 73. These pests sometimes live in tree canopies high above the ground; the only sign of their presence is a trail of ants marching up and down the tree trunk. To keep ants from reaching their goal, encircle tree trunks with sticky bands for several weeks. Pyrethrin kills ants on contact. Fire ants may relocate if their nests are repeatedly drenched with boiling or soapy water.

For chemical control, place baited ant traps sold for indoor use in the garden. Spray with carbaryl or diazinon to kill large infestations around patios. Drench or dust fire ant mounds with chlorpyrifos or diazinon.

APHIDS

Aphids are soft-bodied, slow-moving insects, often with a fat abdomen; they cluster on the new growth of many plants, sucking fluids from tender shoots and causing wilting or distortion. They come in various colors, including green, pink, red, and black; some are winged. Some kinds appear only at particular times of year; others seem to have a preference for a specific plant or plants. The honeydew they excrete attracts ants and can encourage sooty mold (page 79). Where there's a severe infestation of both aphids and ants, you must control both insects.

Aphid infestations often seem to develop overnight, but they rarely last longer than a few weeks. Knock the pests off plants with sharp blasts of water; you'll also get help from many natural predators, including lacewings, damsel bugs, ladybugs, syrphid flies, predatory midges, parasitic wasps, lizards, and small birds. Hot weather will kill aphids.

Ants

If you want help from beneficials, avoid chemical controls. Later in the season, when aphids have naturally died out and beneficials have departed, wash off honeydew residue or sooty mold with soap spray or plain water.

BAGWORMS

Most commonly found east of the Rockies, these pests are not worms at all; they are the larvae of certain moths. They strip foliage from trees and shrubs, starting at the top of the plant and eating it bare. They weave dangling silken bags as they feed. Later, they retreat to the bags, pupate, and emerge as moths. Females remain within the bags to lay eggs; caterpillars hatch in spring, often blowing from one tree to the next on thin threads.

Bt is the preferred control. Spray when caterpillars are just emerging, since they feed heavily at this stage. If the infestation is light, cut off and burn infected stems and branches.

Chemical controls include acephate, carbaryl, diazinon, and malathion; apply them when you see worm-infested trees.

BORERS

In their larval stage, many beetles bore into trees or tunnel just beneath the bark. As they feed, they encircle entire branches and even the trunk, cutting off the tree's supply of water and nutrients. Early symptoms include wilting and yellowing foliage on a single branch; you may also see small holes bordered by sawdust, excrement, or sap. Some borers enter below the soil line; if these are attacking, you'll see evidence only at the plant base. Fruit and nut trees, ash, dogwood, lilac, and cane berries are especially vulnerable, particularly if they are stressed or in poor health.

Prevention is the best solution. Keep trees healthy with proper fertilizing and watering; be especially attentive to water during drought years. Avoid damaging bark. If you need to prune, do so in midsummer, so that wounds are healed by spring when larvae are present. Cut off and burn infected branches.

Chemical controls may help if you spray when adult beetles are laying eggs in summer. Use chlorpyrifos.

CATERPILLARS

Caterpillars, the larval stage of moths and butterflies, include bagworms, gypsy moths, leafrollers, and tent caterpillars (all four are covered in this section). Other caterpillars that cause trouble in fruit and vegetable gardens are cabbage worms,

Aphids

Bagworms

Borer

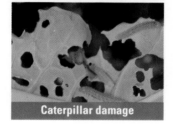

Caterpillar damage

codling moths, and hornworms. Adult *cabbage worm* butterflies lay eggs on foliage of crops such as broccoli, Brussels sprouts, cabbage, and cauliflower; the eggs hatch in a few days, and the pale green caterpillars then consume the leaves. *Codling moths* afflict apples and other fruits. They lay eggs on mature blossoms, just as fruit begins to set; when the caterpillars (white with brown heads) hatch, they feed inside the fruit as it grows. *Hornworm* moths lay pale green eggs on leaf undersides of plants such as eggplant, pepper, potato, and tomato; the bright green caterpillars (large enough— up to 5 inches long!—to give many a gardener a start at first sight) then devour foliage and strip stems bare.

Cabbage worms pupate on stems of the plants they eat, making it difficult to eliminate them in the pupal stage. Instead, cover vegetable plants with floating row covers (see page 173) to prevent adults from laying eggs on them. To reduce codling moth populations, clear ground of all debris each fall; pupae overwinter in debris at ground level. Hornworms pupate underground. Till soil each spring to expose and dry out pupae; rotate susceptible plants to new locations each year. Handpick any hornworms you see. All three of these caterpillars are susceptible to *Bt,* but it must be sprayed when they are just emerging and feeding heavily.

Chemical controls against caterpillars include carbaryl and malathion. In the case of codling moths, you must spray before the just-hatched caterpillar burrows into the fruit. If codling moth is a known problem in your area, routinely spray susceptible trees just as fruit begins to set.

COLORADO POTATO BEETLES

Both adult beetles and larvae feed voraciously on foliage of vegetables and flowers such as potatoes, peppers, tomatoes, eggplant, and nicotiana. They hatch from clusters of bright yellow eggs laid on leaf undersides. As adults they're quite noticeable, due to their showy polka-dot vests and striped pants.

When the growing season ends, remove all spent plants immediately. In spring, till soil to expose overwintering pupae. A thick mulch may keep adults from reaching their target plants from the soil. Many beneficials help manage this pest, including ladybugs, lacewings, and spined soldier bugs. *Bt tenebrionis* is an effective control if applied when larvae are young and feeding heavily. Pyrethrin also works well; it is safe around food crops if used correctly.

Several chemical controls are listed by the manufacturers as effective against Colorado potato beetles, but in fact the pest is becoming resistant to many of these.

🐛 CUCUMBER BEETLES

These tiny beetles (just ¼ inch long) are yellowish green, with black spots or stripes. The larvae eat roots of crops such as corn; adults feed on foliage of cucumber, muskmelon, pumpkin, and squash, as well as on flowers such as aster, dahlia, and rose. While adults do cause some damage by eating leaves and blossoms, they do more harm by spreading bacterial wilt (page 77) among certain vegetables as they feed.

To control cucumber beetles, clean up and discard all plant debris in fall; it can serve as an overwintering site. Use floating row covers (see page 173) to prevent adults from reaching plants. Pyrethrin may control adults; parasitic nematodes will reduce the larval population. To save vegetable plants in the face of an infestation, look for varieties resistant to bacterial wilt.

Carbaryl is an effective chemical control against adults.

🐛 EARWIGS

In limited numbers, earwigs perform a beneficial function by eating soft-bodied insects like aphids. However, they also eat soft plant parts— and if they're present in quantity, they can cause considerable damage to flower petals and corn silk. They feed at night and hide during the day under pieces of wood, flower pots, and the like. To trap them, put out loosely rolled newspaper under shrubs or among flowering plants in the evening; in the morning, dispose of paper and earwigs. Or sink low containers (such as tuna cans) into the ground at several places around the garden; add ½ inch of vegetable oil to each. The pests will fall in; collect and dispose of them each morning.

Chemical controls include earwig bait, which usually contains carbaryl or propoxur. Some products include fish oil as an attractant; don't use this type if there is any possibility of cats or other pets being attracted to it.

🐛 FLEA BEETLES

Their tiny size and jumping movements give these beetles their name. As adults, they riddle plant leaves with small holes, leaving the foliage dry and desiccated. They are especially fond of seedlings and can consume entire plants before you're aware of their presence. To determine if

Colorado potato beetle

Cucumber beetle

Earwig

ABOVE: **Flea beetles**
BELOW: **Grasshopper**

flea beetles are present, place a white card on the ground among the plants or on a lawn; the pests are attracted to white, and if they're near you'll soon see them jumping on the card's surface. The white larvae feed on roots, including root crops such as potatoes. They're small, but you can find them by probing the soil.

To control flea beetles, keep the garden clear of plant debris that could serve as overwintering sites for adult beetles. Till the soil in fall to expose grubs. Parasitic nematodes will control grubs underground. Pyrethrin may help control adults.

Chemical controls effective against adult beetles include chlorpyrifos and diazinon.

🐛 GRASSHOPPERS

While grasshoppers may be present in limited numbers in many areas, it's the periodic population explosions that cause devastating damage, especially in hot-summer parts of the country. Plants can be eaten right down to the ground.

Each adult female grasshopper lays up to 75 white or cream-colored, rice-shaped eggs directly in the soil; when you cultivate soil between fall and spring, be on the lookout for egg clusters and destroy any you find. Floating row covers (see page 173) or netting are often your best defense against attack. If only a small number of grasshoppers are present, you may be able to control them by handpicking adults in the cool of the morning, when they won't jump or fly away.

Young, wingless grasshopper nymphs appear in spring and can be controlled with chemicals. Use bran and carbaryl bait or products containing acephate, carbaryl, chlorpyrifos, diazinon, or malathion. Observe the pests' evening behavior to locate roosting sites, then spray after dark.

🐛 GYPSY MOTHS

Newly hatched gypsy moth caterpillars float through the air on silken strands and travel in hordes from plant to plant, often defoliating entire trees. While some trees can recover from such infestations, many—including most conifers—cannot. The pests pupate during the summer in the same trees they infested as caterpillars. They mate as flying adult moths; the pregnant females then become so heavy that they must crawl rather than fly into nearby trees to lay their eggs.

Control gypsy moths by handpicking the chamoislike egg masses and caterpillars. Wrap tree trunks with sticky barriers to keep female moths from climbing up to lay eggs. Assassin bugs, spined soldier bugs, parasitic wasps, and tachinid flies will parasitize caterpillars and kill them. A special *Bt* strain, *Bt kurstaki,* will kill caterpillars while they are still small.

Chemical controls such as acephate or carbaryl will control larger, more mature caterpillars, but be aware that these will also kill the pests' natural enemies.

JAPANESE BEETLES

The metallic green head and copper-colored wing covers make this beetle easy to recognize. It devours many members of the rose family, marigold, zinnia, and most vegetables. The small, grayish white grubs feed on roots and are especially troublesome in lawns. Japanese beetles are most common east of the Mississippi, but they have been found in Southern California.

Employ a variety of management techniques. Till the soil in the fall to expose grubs to birds. Keep floating row covers (see page 173) on vegetable crops. Handpick any adults you see. Drench lawns with parasitic nematodes or milky spore disease (a disease caused by *Bacillus popilliae* and *B. lentimorbus*); you may need to treat extensive areas, including neighboring lawns, for this to be effective. Pyrethrin may control adults.

Chemical controls include acephate and carbaryl (for adults) and diazinon (for grubs in lawns).

LEAF MINERS

"Leaf miner" is a catchall name for certain moth, beetle, and fly larvae that tunnel within plant leaves, leaving twisting trails on the surface. As larvae mature, they drop to the soil to pupate. The tiny adults are rarely seen; they lay eggs on leaf undersides. Leaf miners cause primarily cosmetic damage (a particular problem on hollies in the landscape), but they may also ruin leafy vegetables such as chard, lettuce, and spinach.

Cover soil with black plastic mulch so that larvae can't burrow underground; this is an effective control under ornamental plants. In vegetable gardens, till soil between rows to expose pupae; use floating row covers (see page 173) over new garden areas to prevent infestation by adults flying in from nearby locations.

Because larvae are protected by leaf membranes, chemical controls are not effective.

Gypsy moths

Japanese beetle

Leaf miners

Leafroller

Mealybugs

LEAFROLLERS

The name "leafroller" is given to several kinds of caterpillars that chew foliage and roll it around themselves, thus protecting themselves from predators such as birds. On many plants, they cause only minimal damage. However, leafrollers that feed on trees such as aspen, horsechestnut, maple, oak, poplar, and willow may do serious damage as they devour new growth; some trees may be completely defoliated.

Leafrollers have many natural enemies, including birds and trichogramma wasps. *Bt* may control young caterpillars when they are feeding heavily. Eggs are laid directly on trees; you may be able to smother them by spraying deciduous trees with horticultural oil during dormancy.

For chemical control, use acephate, carbaryl, or diazinon when caterpillars are feeding.

MEALYBUGS

Common on houseplants, mealybugs can also be a problem outdoors in mild-winter areas. They're similar to scale insects and aphids. The name refers to the female's powdery wax coating, a shield that prevents insecticides from penetrating. In large colonies, mealybugs cause extensive damage to soft tissues of plants: leaves are distorted and yellowed, growth is stunted. They excrete honeydew, which attracts ants and can encourage sooty mold (page 79).

Daub mealybugs on houseplants with a swab dipped in rubbing alcohol. In the garden, dislodge them with jets of water or treat with soap spray or horticultural oil. Some natural predators such as ladybugs and lacewings consume mealybugs.

Chemical controls include acephate, diazinon, and malathion, but hold off on these if you want help from beneficials.

NEMATODES

Nematodes are not insects, but minuscule worms less than $\frac{1}{16}$ inch long. Some are beneficial, parasitizing plant pests—but others are pests that eat roots and, occasionally, foliage. They infest a wide variety of plants, including woody types as well as flowers and vegetables. Symptoms are similar to those of overwatering: plants become stunted and yellow, deteriorate slowly, and usually die. Diagnosis is not simple; a professional soil test is usually needed.

Nematodes are most common in sandy, moist soils in warm-weather climates such as the Southeast. Control is difficult;

soil solarization (see page 83) may help. Contact your local Cooperative Extension Office for advice.

Complete soil fumigation will control nematodes, but the job can be done only by a professional certified to work with the required pesticides.

ROOT WEEVILS

These small, flightless, black or gray pests feed throughout the growing season, chewing notches in leaf edges of many plants, especially azaleas, rhododendrons, roses, and viburnum. In late summer, they lay eggs on the soil or in the folds of leaves. After the eggs hatch, the legless larvae burrow into the soil and eat roots.

Control is not easy. Floating row covers (see page 173) may keep adults from landing on plants. Parasitic nematodes are effective in controlling larvae.

For chemical control of adults, use acephate.

ROSE CHAFERS

These beetles are especially bothersome on roses and peonies. The adults feed in swarms, attacking flowering plants first, then going on to others. They eat holes in blossoms and chew leaves to lace. In their grub form, they infest lawns and damage grass roots much as Japanese beetles do; you'll find patches of lawn that are severed at the roots and can be rolled up like carpet. Rose chafers are particularly troublesome in sandy soils.

You may find both rose chafers and Japanese beetles on your roses at the same time, and controls for the two are similar. Handpick any adults you see; pyrethrin may also be used against them. To kill larvae, drench lawns with parasitic nematodes.

Chemical controls effective against adults include acephate and carbaryl. Diazinon can be used to kill larvae in lawns.

SCALE INSECTS

Found in practically every part of the country, scales are sucking insects closely related to mealybugs and aphids. Like mealybugs, they have a protective waxy, shell-like coating—but while mealybugs are mobile (albeit slow moving), scales are stationary for almost their entire lives (juvenile scales do move about, but they soon settle down in one spot). They look like small brown or black bumps on branches and leaves; some excrete honeydew, which attracts ants and fosters sooty mold (page 79).

Nematodes

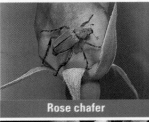
Root weevil

Rose chafer

ABOVE: Scale insects
BELOW: Slug

Afflicted plants lose vigor and wilt; new growth is distorted. Branches and even whole plants may die. If infestation is light, you may be able to control it by picking scales off the plant or scraping them off with a plastic scouring pad. If the plant is deciduous, spray it with horticultural oil in winter to suffocate the pests.

Juvenile scales crawl slowly and are best controlled by natural predators; they can also be blasted off plants with strong jets of water.

Do not use chemical controls unless the plant is very valuable and all else has failed; chemicals kill the pests' natural enemies and may exacerbate scale elsewhere in the garden. Chemical controls for juvenile scales include acephate, carbaryl, diazinon, and malathion.

SLUGS AND SNAILS

In many parts of the country, slugs and snails are one of the most vexing garden pests. They are similar creatures (slugs are merely snails without shells) and feed on many ornamental plants, vegetables, and flowers by chewing tissue with their rasping mouth parts; they leave telltale silvery slime trails as they glide along. They are a major problem for citrus trees.

Shiny black ground beetles eat some snail and slug eggs. Handpicking is an effective way to reduce adult populations. To speed up the process, attract the pests to a certain spot in the garden by placing a slightly elevated board there; they'll congregate in the cool shade on the bottom of the board, ready for fast and easy disposal. Some gardeners set traps containing stale beer slightly below ground level; the pests are drawn to the beer, crawl into the traps, and drown.

To protect citrus and other trees, encircle the trunks with a 4-inch-wide band of copper stripping; slugs and snails won't crawl over it. You can also set copper strips in the ground vertically to form a sort of fence around valuable plants or an entire bed, or surround plants or beds with 4- to 5-inch-wide sawdust "moats" (such sawdust rings are less effective in wet weather and rainy climates).

Chemical controls include bait or meal containing metaldehyde or methiocarb. Be careful with such controls if children or pets use the garden, since bait is attractive to them.

SPIDER MITES

To the naked eye, these tiny spider relatives look like red, green, or yellow flecks on

Spider mites

Squash bug

Tarnished plant bug

Tent caterpillars

Thrips

Whiteflies

foliage. They are especially prevalent in inland areas with warm summers, where they attack a wide variety of trees, shrubs, and vines. Leaves of infested plants turn yellow and may be covered with fine webbing. To confirm a diagnosis, hold a piece of white paper below leaves and tap them. If mites are present, they'll drop onto the paper and look like so many rapidly moving specks.

Wash mites off plants with strong blasts of water, then follow up with soap spray. Any dust that settles on plants in late summer encourages mites, and they also prefer dry air, so regular rinsing of leaves with water is an excellent control. Summer oil and sulfur will also control spider mites, but do not use them together; they are toxic to plants in combination. If you first use one, don't use the other for 1 month.

Chemical controls are not recommended.

SQUASH BUGS

As the name implies, squash bugs attack squash-family plants, especially winter squash and pumpkins. The adults are dark brown or black, almond shaped, and about ½ inch long. They suck plant juices, causing leaves to wilt; they also feed on fruit.

In spring, adults lay masses of hard brown eggs crowded together on the undersides of leaves; look for these and destroy any you find. Adults spend nights under flat objects, so lay out boards in the evening, then turn them over early in the morning and kill any bugs you find (they emit an unpleasant odor when crushed).

For chemical control of adult bugs, use carbaryl.

TARNISHED PLANT BUGS

These fast-moving, shield-shaped insects are named for their mottled brown coloration. They suck plant juices from the buds, fruit, and stems of many flowers, fruits, and vegetables, causing shoots to blacken and drop or become deformed. When they feed on fruits, they leave sunken, catfaced scars.

Adults overwinter in plant debris, so do a garden cleanup each fall. Plant under floating row covers (see page 173). Sticky traps may attract the pests; soap sprays will kill those you hit directly. Spined soldier bugs are natural predators.

Chemical controls effective against adults include carbaryl and malathion.

TENT CATERPILLARS

Tent caterpillars form huge, weblike nests in many trees and shrubs. They venture out during the day to feed, then return to their nests each night. Bad infestations can defoliate entire trees.

The most effective control is to cut off the limb containing the nest; do so at dusk, when more caterpillars are home for the evening. If removing an infested limb would seriously deform the plant, break up the nest with a stick and spray the inside with *Bt*. Handpick sticky egg masses from plants in late winter and early spring. Wrap plant trunks with sticky barriers to keep pregnant females from climbing up to lay eggs.

Carbaryl, diazinon, and malathion are effective chemical controls against caterpillars.

THRIPS

Almost microscopic in size, thrips feed by rasping soft flower and leaf tissue, then drinking the plant juices. Leaf surfaces often take on a shiny silvery or tan cast; on their undersides, you'll find black, varnishlike fecal matter. Thrips infest a wide variety of plants. In severe cases, blossoms and leaves are often twisted or stuck together.

Plants under stress, especially those that are underwatered, are most susceptible to thrips. During dry, hot periods, hose down the leaves of plants that prefer moist environments (such as rhododendrons). Thrips are effectively managed by natural enemies, including ladybugs, lacewings, and predatory mites. Soap sprays can also be effective.

Chemical controls include acephate, diazinon, chlorpyrifos, and malathion.

WHITEFLIES

You know whiteflies are present when you touch a plant and a mass of tiny, white, winged insects fly out of it. Turn over a leaf and you'll see other adults as well as stationary pupae and nymphs. Both adults and nymphs suck a plant's juices, debilitating it moderately or severely depending on the size of the pest population. Symptoms range from yellow stippling on leaves to browned, curled foliage. The pests also excrete honeydew, which attracts ants and fosters sooty mold (page 79).

Natural enemies such as parasitic wasps normally help keep whiteflies under control. For severe infestations, you can purchase wasps and introduce them into the garden; the most common is *Encarsia formosa.* Or check with your local Cooperative Extension Office to find out if a different wasp might better manage the problem. You can also hose off plants with strong jets of water.

Chemical control is not recommended. Insecticides don't easily penetrate the pupae and nymphs, and more adults fly away than are caught by the spray. You'll kill more helpful wasps than you will whiteflies, and the pest population will simply increase.

ANIMALS

Those who garden near open space or forest are likely to share their gardens—willingly or not—with a multitude of animals. But urban areas, too, can be frequented by animals such as squirrels, and deer are found on the outskirts of many communities.

BIRDS

In most situations, birds are welcome in the garden. They eat many insect pests, and if you provide them with shelter, water, and food, they'll stay nearby and help you in your pest-control efforts.

Sometimes, however, birds are a bother; they eat seedlings and peck at ripening fruits and vegetables. To keep them away from newly sprouting seedlings, cover the plants with floating row covers (see page 173). In small beds, poke brushy twigs into the ground where seeds are planted; this maze of brush acts as a barrier. Netting can be draped over trees or vegetable plants as the crop ripens. Shiny strips of reflective material twist in the wind and may scare birds away.

DEER

Deer are attractive to look at, but they're the bane of many a gardener's existence: they like to nibble on the tender shoots or flowers of a great many plants, and they can decimate a garden overnight. They've learned that gardens on the edges of populated areas provide a reliable food supply.

Though deer aren't picky eaters, strong-smelling and unpleasant-tasting plants are the last to go. The animals' tastes seem to vary from area to area, so check with your

Common starling

Deer

Mole

Pocket gopher

Cooperative Extension Office for a list of plants least likely to appeal to the local deer population.

Fencing is the most certain protection. Fences should be 7 to 8 feet high on level ground, up to 10 feet high if the garden is on a slope. Chicken-wire cylinders will protect individual young plants. Motion sensors that activate water-spraying hoses when deer arrive at night are sometimes effective.

MOLES

Moles are notorious pests in certain parts of the country. They rarely eat plants—but as they tunnel along, they heave plants from the ground, sever tender roots, and disfigure lawns.

If only a few moles are present, you may opt to co-exist with them, since they eat many beetle larvae that prey on lawns, ornamental shrubs and trees, and vegetables. When a mole problem is out of hand, however, a spear- or harpoon-type trap is effective in reducing the animals' numbers. The traps come with instructions showing correctplacement.

Moles are difficult to kill with poison bait, since they feed primarily on living creatures.

POCKET GOPHERS

Pocket gophers are a serious problem in many parts of North America. The first sign of trouble is often a mound of fresh, finely pulverized earth in a lawn or garden bed. This alerts you to the tunneling going on below the surface. Plants suddenly die because their roots have been eaten away; tender young plants are dragged into the burrows to be eaten.

In lawns and other large areas, trapping is the most efficient control. Dig down until you find a main horizontal runway connecting to a surface hole; then place traps on either side of the runway. If the infestation is severe, pairs of traps may be required in several runways. The traps come with instructions showing correct placement. If gophers have become trap-wary, poisons inserted deep into their burrows may be effective, but be cautious with this method if dogs are present; they may ingest the poison in their attempts to dig up gophers.

To keep gophers out of vegetable and other garden beds, excavate all soil to a depth of 1 to 1½ feet before planting. Line the area completely with chicken wire, using 2 by 2s to stabilize the corners; then refill with soil.

🐾 RABBITS

Rabbits can be especially troublesome to gardeners in rural areas. When their natural food supply dwindles due to seasonal changes, they'll seek food in nearby vegetable gardens.

To protect vegetable beds, you can set up boxlike frames covered on all sides with chicken wire; the wire extends deep enough into the soil to keep rabbits from burrowing beneath it, and the box top opens to allow you access to crops.

If rabbits do manage to burrow under the barrier, consider gardening in solid-bottomed raised beds; the wire-covered frames can be anchored to the bed's wooden frame with hinges.

Rabbits

Squirrel

🐾 SQUIRRELS

Both ground squirrels and tree squirrels can be a bother (some frustrated gardeners call the latter "rats with furry tails"!). Ground squirrels live in burrows but feed above ground during the day, nibbling through the garden and climbing trees to get at nuts and fruits. Tree squirrels spend most of their lives above ground, searching for nuts and acorns and burying many for winter feeding. They are attracted to bird feeders, which they like to raid; they may then nest in nearby trees and establish local colonies.

Though squirrels can drive gardeners to distraction, in many area these animals are protected from trapping or poisoning by local regulations. Check with the relevant authorities before attempting any controls. To keep tree squirrels from hiding nuts in container plantings (and digging up plants in the process), mulch the soil with decorative small rocks.

SYNTHETIC INSECTICIDES

The insecticides below are listed alphabetically by common name (the name given on the label under "active ingredients"). If the trade name differs from the common name, it is given in parentheses.

Most of these products kill pests on contact or through direct ingestion. Acephate, however, is a systemic pesticide: applied to a plant, it is absorbed by the foliage or roots, and any pests that then ingest the plant's juices or chew its leaves are killed. Systemic insecticides must never be applied to any edible crop. For products that can be used on food crops, check the label to see how many days before harvest the insecticide may be applied.

When using any insecticide, read the label instructions carefully; then follow them exactly. Also review the safety tips on page 66.

ACEPHATE (Orthene). Systemic. Use only on ornamentals—but since it is toxic to bees and other nectar-drinking beneficial insects, do not use on blooming plants.

CARBARYL (Sevin). Commonly used in vegetable gardens; usually effective against chewing insects (caterpillars, for example) but generally not effective against sucking types like aphids. It can even make infestations by sucking insects worse by destroying their natural enemies. Highly toxic to bees and earthworms.

CHLORPYRIFOS (Dursban). A control for lawn pests, many pests of ornamentals, and certain borers that attack shade trees. Do not use on food crops.

DIAZINON. A broad-spectrum insecticide also widely used to control various lawn pests, diazinon is the only chemical control that can safely be used to control soil-dwelling pests in vegetable gardens. It is toxic to bees and birds.

MALATHION. A broad-spectrum insecticide for use on both edible and ornamental crops. Toxic to bees.

METALDEHYDE. The most common slug and snail control, metaldehyde is usually the active ingredient in various baits and some liquids. It may be used around vegetable and fruit crops, but it is toxic to pets.

METHIOCARB (Mesurol). An effective control for slugs and snails; will also kill earthworms. Do not use on food crops.

PROPOXUR (Baygon). Common in earwig baits and wasp and hornet sprays. Do not use on food crops.

Raking is a fall ritual. It keeps the garden looking neat; it also removes any fallen diseased leaves, so they won't infect new growth come spring.

DISEASES

A healthy plant, like a healthy human being, is better able to resist the microorganisms that cause disease. Focus on keeping your garden strong and vigorous, and you've already taken an important step toward preventing plant problems. Sometimes, though, diseases will appear despite your best efforts—but if you're familiar with their symptoms and the controls that can be used against them, you'll have a better chance of stopping them before they can get established.

PLANT PATHOGENS

Fungi, bacteria, and viruses are the pathogens most often responsible for plant diseases. Unlike green plants, these organisms are incapable of manufacturing their own food and must instead take it from a host plant. Fungi can live in the soil, but the bacteria and viruses that cause plant problems cannot survive outside their host.

Fungi multiply by tiny reproductive bodies called spores (their equivalent of seeds), which they produce in great quantity. Spores of some fungi enter plants through the roots; others land on leaves, where they attach and complete their life cycle. A single fungus-infected leaf may release 100 million spores, which drift through the garden and onto new hosts with even the slightest breath of air.

Bacteria need water and warmth to multiply, so the diseases they cause tend to be more prevalent in warm, wet climates.

These single-celled organisms are easily transmitted by rain, splashing irrigation water, and gardeners working among plants. They enter plants through a wound or natural opening.

Viruses are even smaller than bacteria; they can reproduce only within the actual cells of the host organism. Some viruses are transmitted by insects such as aphids, leafhoppers, and thrips; others are carried by infected seeds and pollen. Viruses also enter plants through wounds and cuts.

DISEASE PREVENTION

You can't always prevent a disease from attacking a prized plant. The bacterial infection fireblight, for example, can enter blossoms readily if there is rain just at the time of bloom; you'd have to control the weather to stop it. A mosaic virus–infected bare-root rose won't exhibit symptoms until it leafs out.

Luckily, good gardening practices will fend off many diseases. To keep plant problems under control, take the following steps.

Powdery mildew covers leaves and stems of this rose.

Keep plants healthy by giving them the water, light, and fertilizer they need to flourish.

Buy disease-resistant plants. You'll find tomatoes resistant to verticillium wilt and flowering pear trees less likely to succumb to fireblight, for example. Vegetable seed packets are labeled to indicate the particular plant's disease resistance; plant tags on fruit trees or ornamental trees and shrubs sometimes also include this information. Your Cooperative Extension Office can often provide information on plants resistant to diseases that may cause problems in your area.

Transplant carefully to minimize root damage. When broken, roots are susceptible to certain soilborne diseases.

Take care not to injure plants when you work in the garden. An open wound on a plant stem or tree trunk readily admits bacteria and fungi.

Avoid wet-weather garden work. You may unwittingly spread waterborne pathogens as you move about from one spot to the next.

Install a drip irrigation system (see pages 44–45) or use soaker hoses to minimize the splashing water that can spread waterborne diseases.

Remove diseased plants. If certain plants are constantly afflicted by disease, eliminate them from the garden and replace them with less trouble-prone choices. This solution is simpler than attempting to control the disease, and it removes sources of further infection.

Dispose of infected plants and plant parts right away. Throw them out with the trash; don't compost them. Some pathogens may be killed by the heat generated during decomposition, but it's better not to take the chance.

Keep the garden clean. Do a thorough fall cleanup each year. Remove weeds, since pathogens may overwinter on them. In mild-winter areas, strip off any diseased leaves remaining on plants; rake up and discard all diseased leaves on the ground. You may also want to rake up other garden debris; though it can serve as a good mulch (if undiseased), it also shelters ground-dwelling pests.

SOME COMMON DISEASES

The following pages profile some of the plant diseases you're mostly likely to encounter (see page 129 for common lawn diseases). For each, we note the plants it is likely to afflict and the symptoms it produces, then offer suggestions for both nonchemical and chemical controls. Note that fungicides should be used only as a last resort, when all other control tactics have been exhausted and you have no other recourse for dealing with a severe problem. Many of these products are highly toxic, rating a signal word (see page 64) of "warning" or "danger." For further information on the suggested chemical controls, see page 80.

🍂 ANTHRACNOSE

Anthracnose is a fungal disease that afflicts leaves and tender shoots as they emerge in spring. The fungus also infects older leaves, producing large, irregular brown blotches. On tomatoes and peppers, small, circular, water-soaked spots appear on the fruit and grow in size, eventually penetrating and spoiling the fruit. Small branches may show twig dieback and cankers. Because symptoms vary depending on the plant, take a sample of the infected plant part to your Cooperative Extension Office or a full-service nursery for help in diagnosis.

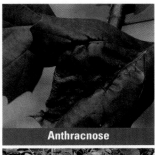
Anthracnose

Wet conditions encourage anthracnose fungi. If your area receives plentiful rainfall during the growing season, look for resistant plants. Grow vining plants on freestanding trellises or poles (well away from walls or fences) to keep them dry. Change from overhead to ground watering. Eliminate sources of future infection by pruning out all infected twigs and branches and raking up fallen infected leaves. Lime sulfur may prevent spores from attaching to plant parts.

Bacterial wilt

For chemical control, you can use chlorothalonil in spring. Spray when leaves unfold, then two or three more times at 2-week intervals.

Black spot

🍂 BACTERIAL WILT

A common disease of cucumbers, bacterial wilt also afflicts muskmelons, squash, and pumpkins. Most troublesome east of the Rockies, it is prevalent during moist weather. It is usually spread by cucumber beetles (page 70) feeding on foliage. Symptoms include rapid wilting of plants and death of young seedlings. Check for the disease by cutting a stem near the base and squeezing it; if present, bacteria will ooze out in a sticky mass.

To avoid infection of certain vegetables, look for resistant plants. Infected plants will not recover. To minimize risk of infection among susceptible plants, use floating row covers (see page 173) to keep beetles off plants; or spray with pyrethrin.

There is no chemical control.

🍂 BLACK SPOT

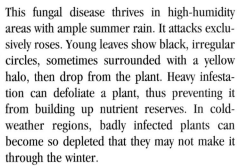

This fungal disease thrives in high-humidity areas with ample summer rain. It attacks exclusively roses. Young leaves show black, irregular circles, sometimes surrounded with a yellow halo, then drop from the plant. Heavy infestation can defoliate a plant, thus preventing it from building up nutrient reserves. In cold-weather regions, badly infected plants can become so depleted that they may not make it through the winter.

Prevent the disease by planting resistant rose varieties. Remove and destroy all diseased foliage in fall. Some gardeners have had good luck controlling black spot with weekly applications of a baking soda and summer oil spray; to make the solution, mix 2 teaspoons baking soda and 2 teaspoons summer oil with a gallon of water. Others report success with soap sprays or sulfur.

Chemical controls include chlorothalonil, triforine, and thiophanate-methyl. Repeat applications of spray will be needed as long as the weather conditions favor the development of the fungus.

CROWN GALL

The bacteria responsible for this disease infect plants near the soil line or on stems and roots, producing lumpy growths ranging from pea-size to baseball-size. Various plants are susceptible; check with your Cooperative Extension Office for a list. Besides deforming plants, the galls may cause serious damage by interrupting the flow of water and nutrients. The problem often arrives in the garden via infected nursery stock; it can be transmitted when gardeners prune infected plants, then go on to prune others without disinfecting tools first. The bacteria may also enter a plant through wounds.

To control crown gall, look for resistant varieties and check plants for symptoms before buying them. If you have had crown gall in one garden location, don't plant susceptible new plants in the same area. Remove and destroy infected plants; be sure to disinfect tools when pruning (see "Removing Diseased Growth," page 50).

There is no chemical control.

FIREBLIGHT

This bacterial disease affects only rose-family plants, among them apple, pear (including ornamental flowering pear), hawthorn, and pyracantha. The infection enters through blossoms, then spreads with the help of pollenizing insects and splashing water from rain or sprinklers. Temperatures above 60°F/16°C and high humidity favor fireblight. When a shoot suddenly dies or blackens as if scorched by fire, fireblight is the likely cause.

To prevent fireblight, avoid growing susceptible plants; or plant resistant varieties. If you see infected limbs or branches, immediately cut them out; make cuts at least 1 foot below the diseased area and disinfect tools between cuts (see "Removing Diseased Growth," page 50).

There is no chemical control.

GUMMOSIS AND CANKERS

"Gummosis" and "canker" are both terms used to describe various bacterial or fungal diseases that cause oozing, sunken lesions on trunks or limbs of afflicted trees and shrubs. The problem is most commonly seen on fruit trees, and often gets its start when the disease organism enters through a wound or borer entry hole (see page 69). Wounds are often caused by weed whips or lawn mowers; trunk sunburn may also damage

Crown gall

Fireblight

Canker

Oak root fungus

Peach leaf curl

the bark and allow entry. Keeping the plant too wet makes it easier for bacteria or fungi to establish themselves.

To prevent the problem, avoid overwatering and take care not to injure plants. Protect young trees from sun scald by wrapping the trunks loosely in burlap. If the plant is generally healthy, it will usually seal off the cankers. If the canker appears on a small limb, prune it out well below the canker; disinfect tools between cuts (see "Removing Diseased Growth," page 50).

There is no chemical control.

OAK ROOT FUNGUS

Oak root fungus (*Armillaria mellea*) is named for a favorite host, but it attacks a variety of woody plants. It is prevalent in the Southeast and in low-elevation, nondesert regions of California. The first symptoms may be dull, yellowed, or wilted leaves and/or sparse foliage; later, entire branches die. The aboveground symptoms result from root death, which cuts off the plant's water and nutrient supply. To verify the presence of oak root fungus, check under the bark of large roots or the trunk (near ground level) for a mat of whitish fungal tissue. In late autumn or early winter, clumps of tan mushrooms may appear around the bases of infected plants.

You may be able to save lightly infected plants—or at least prolong their lives—by removing soil from their bases to expose the juncture of roots and trunk to air, and by cutting out and destroying all dead and infected tissue.

To avoid the problem, choose resistant plants. Avoid placing susceptible plants in locations where oak root fungus is known to have occurred or where *Armillaria* fungi are likely to be present (on the site of an old orchard, for example). If you want to plant where a tree or shrub has been killed by *Armillaria*, remove and destroy all roots in the planting area.

There is no chemical control.

PEACH LEAF CURL

One of the worst diseases of peaches and nectarines, peach leaf curl is most active during rainy, cool springs. The spores of the fungus *Taphrina deformans* overwinter on a tree's bark, having been carried there by wind or rain; in spring, rain carries the spores to developing leaf buds. New leaves are puckered, curled, abnormally thick, and dotted with reddish blisters; entire leaves may turn red or yellow. Later in the season, powdery grayish white spores form on leaves, then blow onto bark and growth buds, setting the stage for the next cycle. Fruit may be entirely absent; if present, it is misshapen and may drop before it ripens.

To prevent peach leaf curl, plant resistant trees. Do a thorough fall cleanup and remove all debris from the ground below trees. Spray with sulfur or lime sulfur during the dormant season; timing is critical, so check with your Cooperative Extension Office for the best spraying dates. If you grow dwarf varieties, you can control the infection by covering trees with plastic sheeting during rainy weather in spring.

There is no chemical control.

POWDERY MILDEW

This fungal disease attacks a wide variety of plants, including all sorts of beans, clematis, dahlia, grape, hydrangea, rose, strawberry, tomato, and zinnia, and trees such as apple, maple, oak, peach, and sycamore. It is favored by moist air, shade, and poor air circulation, but needs dry leaves to become established. The first symptoms are small gray or white circles on leaves, stems, and flowers; then entire leaves and blooms become powdery white and distorted. Some plants remain vigorous despite the infection, but others decline or fail to set fruit. Some flowering plants can become so disfigured that they must be removed from the garden.

Powdery mildew

To prevent powdery mildew, plant resistant varieties and routinely spray plants with jets of water to wash off fungus spores. Increase sunlight to plants by avoiding overcrowding. In the fall, discard infected flowers, fruits, and plants. Sulfur may help; on roses and other flowering plants, try a baking soda and summer oil spray (see "Black spot," page 77). Some gardeners report success with the antitranspirant sprays sold to protect tender plants from cold. Such sprays keep the surface temperature of treated leaves somewhat higher than that of the surrounding air; apparently they also prevent mildew spores from attaching to foliage.

Chemical controls include triforine and thiophanate-methyl.

ROSE MOSAIC VIRUS

There are many mosaic viruses, each afflicting a different plant. Rose mosaic virus is the most common viral disease of roses. New leaves that unfurl in spring show yellow zigzag patterns, spots, and mottling; they may also be distorted. Leaves produced during summer, however, may

Rose mosaic virus

not show these symptoms. The virus's effect varies; some infected plants grow and bloom with no apparent problems, while others grow slowly, bloom less profusely, or show greater sensitivity to winter cold.

Rose mosaic virus is transmitted through infected rootstock or budwood during the commercial propagation process. If you buy an infected rose as a bare-root plant, you won't know it has the virus until it leafs out. If you discover a virus-infected plant, it's best to remove it and replace it with virus-free stock (more and more growers are trying to eliminate the virus from their stock plants).

There is no control for this virus.

RUST

A great number of rust fungi exist, each specific to a certain plant: hollyhock rust, for example, won't bother roses, and rose rust won't infect hollyhocks. Other susceptible plants include pine, fir, hawthorn, fuchsia, geranium, snapdragon, asparagus, some beans, onion, blackberry, fig, pear, and lawn grasses.

It's easy to identify rust; just turn a leaf over and look for powdery orange or brown pustules (the pustules are also sometimes purple, red, white, or black). If the problem is left untreated, pustules cover leaf undersides and show on the upper surfaces as yellow mottling. Entire leaves may turn yellow and drop.

To combat rust, buy resistant varieties. Because rust spreads fastest in wet conditions (leaves must be wet for at least 4 to 5 hours for spores to germinate), you can minimize spread by curtailing overhead watering. Remove and discard the rustiest-looking leaves; dispose of infected leaves that drop to the ground, and clean up all debris in fall. Sulfur and summer oil may help (do not apply them simultaneously; the combination is toxic to plants).

Rust

Chemical controls include chlorothalonil, triadimefon, and triforine (especially on roses).

SOOTY MOLD

Caused by a number of different fungi, this disease can afflict any plant. It shows up as a powdery, dark brown or black coating on leaves—hence the name "sooty mold." The responsible fungi live on a plant's natural secretions and on the honeydew excreted by aphids, mealybugs, and scale. While fairly harmless on its own, sooty mold may weaken a plant if combined with extensive insect damage.

Sooty mold

To control the problem, reduce the population of honeydew-excreting insects. Rinse small, ornamental plants by hand; hose down larger infected areas (such as trees or expanses of ground covers).

There is no chemical control.

🌿 SOUTHERN BLIGHT (SCLEROTIUM ROOT ROT)

This soil-borne fungal disease thrives in the warm soils and wet weather of the Southeast; it is sometimes called mustard seed fungus, a reference to the organism's small yellow resting bodies. It infects many commonly planted vegetables and flowers, some shrubs, and occasionally lawns. White, cottony growth appears on plant stems near soil level and often spreads to the surrounding soil. As the fungus gradually cuts off the flow of water through the stems, the plant rots at the base, turns yellow, and dies.

Control is difficult, because the fungus can survive in the soil for years without a host. Soil solarization (see page 83) will help; long (4-year) crop rotation is important. To minimize spread of the fungus, don't cultivate soil between plants after planting. In fall, clean up all debris and destroy infected plants, including their root balls. Till soil in winter to bury overwintering resting bodies.

Southern blight

Verticillium wilt

For chemical control of Southern blight on ornamentals, consult your Cooperative Extension Office. There is no chemical control for edible plants.

🌿 VERTICILLIUM WILT

A widespread and destructive disease, verticillium wilt is caused by a fungus that invades and plugs water-conducting tissues in roots and stems. A common symptom is wilting on one side of the plant. Leaves turn yellow, then brown; then they die. Many plants are afflicted. Highly susceptible crops, such as tomatoes, potatoes, cotton, strawberries, and various melons, frequently leave the soil infested—and the fungus can survive in the soil for years in the absence of susceptible targets. Even crop rotation will not eliminate it.

Resistant plants are the best defense against verticillium wilt. A number of resistant trees, shrubs, flowers, bulbs, and vegetables are available; contact your Cooperative Extension Office for a list of those sold in your area. Plants resistant to verticillium wilt are often also resistant to the disease fusarium wilt (see page 172).

If the problem is so severe that you must resort to chemical control, call in a professional to fumigate the soil.

SYNTHETIC FUNGICIDES

The fungicides at right are listed alphabetically by common name (the name given on the label under "active ingredients"). If the trade name differs from the common name, it is given in parentheses.

Chlorothalonil dissipates over time. The remaining products listed are systemic: applied to a plant, they are absorbed by the foliage or roots to prevent or cure infection from within. Systemic fungicides must never be used on food crops.

When using any fungicide, read the instructions carefully and follow them exactly. Also review the safety tips on page 66. The products listed here require that you wear protective clothing, goggles, and a breathing mask for application.

CHLOROTHALONIL (Daconil). Multipurpose fungicide for prevention of diseases of lawns, fruits, vegetables, and ornamentals.

THIOPHANATE-METHYL. Systemic. Effective against many plant diseases, including powdery mildew and black spot.

TRIADIMEFON (Bayleton). Systemic. Used for prevention or eradication of powdery mildew, rust, and some lawn diseases.

TRIFORINE (Funginex). Systemic. Used for prevention and eradication of powdery mildew, rust, black spot, and a variety of other diseases.

WEEDS

Weeds are plants growing where gardeners don't want them to grow. They rob desirable plants of water, nutrients, and sunlight, they may harbor insects and diseases—and beyond that, they are quite often unattractive to look at. Managing weeds, whether by removing them or preventing their growth in the first place, is an ongoing part of successful gardening. For descriptions and photos of some of the worst offenders, see pages 84–88.

MANAGING WEEDS

In most situations, you can eventually eliminate weeds through physical management; methods range from the familiar hand pulling through mowing, mulching, and smothering. To deal with the toughest cases, though, you may need to consider using chemical controls.

PHYSICAL MANAGEMENT

Hand pulling or hoeing is your first line of defense against weeds, especially annual and biennial kinds. If you're diligent for several years about removing these before they set seed, their numbers will decline significantly.

Perennial weeds are harder to manage. Once they've passed the seedling stage, they develop rhizomes, bulbs, tubers, or extensive root systems that aid in reproduction. Pulling usually doesn't remove these underground structures completely, and the weeds can resprout from fragments left behind. It's best to dig these weeds, removing as much of the root system as you can—a process you may need to repeat several times.

Don't leave pulled or hoed-out weeds lying on bare ground, since they may take root again. Leafy annual or biennial types that do not yet have flowers or seeds can safely be relegated to the compost pile, as can the top growth of perennial weeds (before seeding). But roots of perennials (dandelions and quack grass, for example) should be tossed in the trash rather than composted—as should any weeds that have set seed.

HAND WEEDING. Pulling weeds by hand is time consuming, but it's also the safest way to eliminate weeds growing close to desirable plants without risking injury to the "good" plants' roots. Fortunately, various tools are available to make the job easier. A trowel or small cultivator helps loosen the soil around

TOOLS FOR WEEDING

1 Swan-necked hoe
2 Cape Cod weeder
3 Dandelion weeder
4 Trowel
5 Three-pronged cultivator
6 Dutch hoe
7 Oscillating hoe

ORGANIC MULCHES

CHOPPED LEAVES. Whole leaves tend to mat, so chop them with a shredder or lawn mower. Compost them in piles over winter, then apply in a 3- to 4-inch-thick layer in spring.

COMPOST. An ideal mulch, assuming your compost pile heats up enough to kill any weed seeds it may contain. Apply in a 2- to 3-inch-thick layer. For more on composting, see pages 21–22.

GRASS CLIPPINGS. Apply in thin layers, building up to a layer 2 to 3 inches thick; let each layer of clippings dry before adding another, since a thick layer of fresh clippings will mat down and turn slimy. Or spread the clippings on the driveway to dry before applying.

PINE NEEDLES. Pine needles acidify the soil and are best used around acid-loving plants such as rhododendrons and azaleas. Apply in a 2- to 4-inch-thick layer.

SHREDDED BARK, GROUND BARK, BARK CHIPS, WOOD CHIPS. Apply in a 2- to 4-inch-thick layer. Thicker layers provide longer-lasting weed control.

weeds; a dandelion weeder helps pop taprooted weeds from the ground. To get weeds out of cracks in pavement, use a screwdriver, weeding knife, or putty knife.

HOEING. A time-honored method of weeding both vegetable and ornamental gardens, hoeing also loosens the top layer of soil, improving water and air penetration. Garden centers and mail-order companies offer many sorts of hoes. Narrow, pointed ones are good for weeding around vegetables. A garden hoe with a sharp edge cuts off weeds at ground level; it's the best choice for open areas, such as the spaces between rows of vegetables. Various scuffle or oscillating hoes are especially useful for weeding under spreading plants.

CULTIVATING. For larger areas, such as orchards, vacant lots, roadsides, or plots intended for future garden use, rototilling or discing will do the job. These methods not only knock down the weeds but also incorporate them into the soil, where they decay to form humus. Some weeds may sprout again from the roots or crowns, so you may need to till several times.

MOWING. Rotary mowers and weed eaters are other good choices for weed control in larger areas. Both tools cut the weeds; weed eaters leave the severed tops behind, while mowers grind them up as they cut them. Of course, these methods do leave the weeds' roots and crowns behind to grow again.

FLAMERS. Powered by propane or a mixture of propane and butane, these devices are not meant to burn weeds. Instead, they heat them to the point that their cell walls burst. Though this damage is enough to kill many weeds, types with deep perennial roots usually regrow; eradicating these requires several treatments. Take care when using flamers around mulches, and never use them in dry, fire-prone areas.

GROUND COVERS, sometimes called living mulches, are effective in preventing weed growth: like organic and inorganic mulches, they keep sunlight from reaching weeds and their seeds. For the first few seasons after you plant a ground cover, you'll usually have to do some hand weeding or apply a mulch, but as the cover grows and spreads to form a tight carpet, weed growth is much reduced. For more on ground covers, see pages 132–139.

A flamer uses heat to kill weeds by rupturing the plants' cell walls.

SMOTHERING effectively kills weeds in areas earmarked for future planting. After mowing or cutting off the top growth, lay down a mulch of heavy cardboard, newspaper (in a layer at least three dozen sheets thick), or black plastic. Overlap these materials so weeds can't grow through the cracks. Anchor the covering in place with a layer of bark chips or other organic mulch. Leave this smothering mulch in place for at least a full growing season; allow a year or more for tough weeds.

MULCHES. Like any other seeds, weed seeds require sunlight, warmth, and moisture to germinate and grow. Mulches block light from the soil below, thus preventing the seedlings from becoming established. They also help keep soil moist and modulate its temperature. You can choose from organic or inorganic mulches.

Organic mulches (see suggestions at left) gradually decompose, adding humus to the soil and giving it a loose, crumbly texture (thus making it easier to pull any weeds that do appear). Before laying down any organic mulch, clear existing weeds from the soil, since those that are already established can grow right through the mulch. Use a 2- to 4-inch-thick layer on paths and around plants, but take care not to cover the plants' bases (or crowns): too much moisture near the crown will rot many plants.

SOIL SOLARIZATION

Soil solarization takes advantage of the sun's heat, trapped under clear plastic sheeting, to control many kinds of weed seeds as well as harmful fungi, bacteria, and some nematodes. The process is carried out in summer and works best in regions that have hot, sunny weather for 4 to 8 weeks straight; daytime temperatures above 80°F/27°C are ideal. Solarization isn't very effective in coastal climates with summer fog, nor does it work well in very windy areas.

Plan to solarize areas you intend to use for fall vegetables, ornamental beds, or lawn. Follow these steps:

1 Cultivate soil, clearing it of weeds, debris, and large clods of earth. It is important to get rid of growing weeds, because clear plastic—unlike black plastic—doesn't halt growth of plants in the soil beneath it.

2 Make a bed at least 2$\frac{1}{2}$ feet wide (narrower beds make it difficult to build up enough heat to have much effect). Carve a small ditch around perimeter and rake to level surface.

Soak soil to a depth of 1 foot: moist soil conducts heat better than dry soil and initiates germination of weed seeds, which will then be killed by heat.

3 Cover soil with 1- to 4-mil clear plastic; use UV-resistant plastic if it's available, since it won't break down during solarization. Stretch plastic tightly so that it is in contact with the soil. Bury the edges in the perimeter ditch. An optional second layer of plastic increases heat and makes solarization more effective; use soda cans as spacers between the two sheets (see inset at right).

Leave plastic in place for 4 to 6 weeks (8 weeks for really persistent weeds); then remove it. (Don't leave it down longer than 8 weeks, or soil structure may suffer.) You can now plant. After planting, avoid cultivating more than the upper 2 inches of soil, since weed seeds at deeper levels may still be viable.

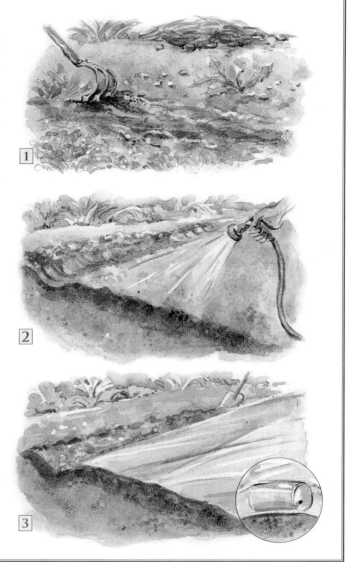

Inorganic mulches include gravel and stones, black plastic, and landscape fabrics.

Gravel, river rock, and other kinds of stones make permanent mulches that can suppress weeds effectively—as long as you install them over weed-free soil to begin with. Many gardeners place landscape fabric under gravel.

Black plastic, available in rolls, is especially helpful in the vegetable garden. Besides effectively preventing weed growth, it warms the soil early in the season, speeding the growth of heat-loving plants like melons. Place the plastic over the soil, then cut slits in it where you want to plant seeds or transplants. Remove the plastic at the end of the growing season, since by this time it will usually have degraded too much to use again.

Landscape fabrics, sold in nurseries and garden supply centers, are made of woven polypropylene, spun-bonded polyethylene, or a combination of other synthetic materials. Unlike plastic sheeting, they are porous, allowing air, water, and dissolved nutrients to reach the soil. Density and porosity vary with the manufacturer; the denser fabrics are better for suppressing weeds.

Continued >

Unroll fabric, then use scissors or a knife to cut X-shaped slits for plants. Tuck the flaps back in around the plants' bases.

Landscape fabrics are available in various widths and lengths. They're best used in permanent plantings around trees and shrubs; they aren't really suited for beds of vegetables or annuals, where you change plants often. You can install them around existing plants or cut slits in them to accommodate new ones.

Before you install the fabric, eliminate weeds. Unroll the fabric and estimate where to cut it. Use sharp scissors to cut slits (X-shaped slits work best), then carefully fit the fabric over or around the plants. Overlap seams by at least 3 inches to avoid gaps through which weeds can grow. To anchor the outer edges of the fabric to the soil, use plastic pegs, nails, or heavy wire staples.

After installation, cover the fabric with 2 to 3 inches of a weed-free organic mulch such as bark chips or with a thinner layer of pea gravel or smooth river rocks. The mulch protects the fabric from ultraviolet degradation and improves its appearance.

CHEMICAL MANAGEMENT

Synthetic herbicides are not recommended for food gardens. In home ornamental gardens, they should be your last resort, called into play only when other methods have failed. Beyond the risks they may pose to health and the environment, many of these chemicals can damage desirable plants if they drift through the air or run off in irrigation or rainwater. Some persist in the soil for long periods, injuring later plantings. And often, the entire process of herbicide use—selecting an appropriate product, reading the label, mixing and applying the spray, cleaning up—takes more effort than simply pulling or digging the weeds.

If you use herbicides, always make sure the product is safe for the desirable plants growing in and near the areas to be treated, and keep in mind that you can be held responsible for any damage to neighboring properties resulting from herbicides you use.

You'll find a list of many commercially available herbicides on page 88. If you have a particularly bad weed problem, consider contacting a professional with a commercial applicator's license. He or she will have access to a larger arsenal of sprays and will know how to use them correctly.

SOME COMMON WEEDS

Some of the most common and hard-to-control garden weeds are profiled on the next few pages. For each, we first suggest nonchemical controls. Appropriate chemical controls are also noted; these may include pre-emergence herbicides, post-emergence products, or both. *Before using any chemical control, always check the label to make sure the product is safe for any desirable plants growing in or near the area to be treated.* For more on herbicides and a definition of terms, see page 88.

✍ BERMUDA GRASS *(Cynodon dactylon)*

A fine-textured and fast-growing perennial, Bermuda grass is frequently planted as a lawn in warm climates. In other sorts of lawns and in gardens, though, it can be a difficult weed. It spreads by underground stems (rhizomes), aboveground runners (stolons), and seed.

If you have a Bermuda grass lawn, use deep barriers or edging to prevent it from advancing into other parts of the garden. Dig up stray clumps before they form sod, being sure to remove all the underground stems; any left behind can start new shoots. Repeated pulling and digging are generally necessary to stop this weed; mulches will slow it down, but it eventually grows through most of them.

For chemical control, you can use a selective herbicide containing fluazifop-butyl or sethoxydim, which can be sprayed over some ornamentals. Spot-treat actively growing Bermuda grass with glyphosate, taking care not to get the chemical on desirable plants.

BINDWEED
(Convolvulus arvensis)

Also called wild morning glory, bindweed grows in open areas—usually in loam to heavy clay soil—throughout the United States. Its 1- to 4-foot-long stems crawl over the ground and twine over and around other plants. Bindweed is deep rooted, so pulling usually doesn't eradicate it—the stems break off, but the weed returns from the roots. To get rid of it, you'll have to dig the roots out repeatedly (persistence is required). It's important not to let bindweed set seed, since the hard-coated seeds can sprout even after lying dormant in the soil for 50 years!

For chemical control, you can use a pre-emergence herbicide containing trifluralin around ornamentals. In midsummer, when bindweed is at the height of its growth season but has not yet set seed, spot-treat isolated patches with glyphosate, taking care to avoid contact with desirable plants. If the weed is twined around desirable plants, detach it before treating. Repeated applications are usually needed to destroy the root system.

BLACKBERRY (Rubus species)

Wild blackberry can be a vexing weed almost anywhere in the United States, but it's particularly troublesome in the Northeast, the Southeast, and many areas of the West. The roots are perennial but the canes are biennial: they grow one year, then bloom and fruit the next. Plants spread rapidly by underground runners and by seed.

To control, pull young plants in spring, before they develop a perennial root system. To kill established clumps, repeatedly prune back the stems as they sprout; this eventually exhausts the roots. Or mow the tops and dig out the roots; repeat the process as new canes grow from roots left behind in the soil.

Bermuda grass

Bindweed

Blackberry

Common mallow

Crabgrass

For chemical control, cut stems to the ground and apply glyphosate to the stubs as soon as possible after cutting. Spot-treat any new shoots with glyphosate as they appear. Or spray triclopyr or glyphosate on mature leaves, taking care to avoid contact with desirable plants.

COMMON MALLOW
(Malva neglecta)

Also known as cheeseweed (thanks to the fruits, which resemble a round of cheese), common mallow is a widespread annual or biennial weed with broad, lobed leaves and pinkish white, five-petaled flowers.

Hoe or pull these weeds when they're young. Mature plants have a long, tough taproot that is difficult to extract from the soil, and they are of course more likely to have set seed.

For chemical control, use a pre-emergence herbicide containing isoxaben to prevent seedlings from becoming established in lawns and around ornamentals. For postemergence control in lawns, use a product containing MCPA, MCPP, and dicamba. Spot-treat young weeds with an herbicide containing glufosinate-ammonium or glyphosate, taking care to avoid contact with desirable plants.

CRABGRASS (Digitaria species)

This infamous summer annual thrives in hot, moist areas. It's a shallow-rooted weed that flourishes in underfed lawns, in poorly drained areas, and in lawns and flower beds that receive frequent surface watering. Seeds germinate in early spring in southern climates, later in northern areas. As the plant grows, it branches out at the base; stems can root where they touch the soil.

In flower beds, pull crabgrass before it sets seed. To thwart crabgrass in lawns, keep the turf well fertilized and vigorous, so it will provide tough competition for weeds. Also water your lawn deeply, but not frequently; this tactic will dry out crabgrass roots, killing the weeds or at least diminishing their vigor. Solarization can control crabgrass if high temperatures are achieved.

For chemical control in lawns and around ornamentals, use a pre-emergence herbicide such as trifluralin; apply it in late winter to early spring, depending on when crab-grass germinates in your zone (a local nursery or your Cooperative Extension Office can provide this information). For postemergence control around ornamentals, apply fluazifop-butyl or sethoxydim.

DANDELION
(Taraxacum officinale)

Familiar as a lawn weed everywhere in the United States, dandelion is particularly troublesome in cold-winter climates. It grows from a deep, fleshy taproot and spreads by windborne seeds. Flowering begins in spring and often continues until frost.

If dandelions are growing in your lawn, the turf is probably thin and undernourished. A healthy lawn can outcompete dandelions, so thicken the turf by overseeding and by proper fertilizing, watering, and mowing. Pull dandelions from lawns and gardens while they're small, before they produce a taproot and set seed. Once the taproot has formed, you must remove all of it to get rid of the plant, since new plants can sprout from even a small piece. A special dandelion weeder with a forked blade is helpful.

For chemical control, use a selective postemergence herbicide containing MCPA, MCPP, and dicamba in spring or fall.

KUDZU VINE *(Pueraria lobata)*

The woody kudzu vine spreads very rapidly: in some regions, it can cover as much as 60 feet each year. A deep-rooted perennial, it's most common in the Southeast, but it also grows in the mid-Atlantic states. Its heavy, hairy brown stems twine over shrubs and trees; it can kill the plants it climbs by blocking sunlight from them with its large leaves. It spreads by seed and by rooting stems.

Control is difficult. Cut the shoots back and cover the area with a dense mulch, such as several layers of landscape fabric, for several growing seasons.

For chemical control, apply an herbicide in late summer, using a product containing glyphosate or triclopyr (take care to avoid contact with any desirable plants).

NUTSEDGE, YELLOW *(Cyperus esculentus)*

Also known as yellow nutgrass, this perennial weed thrives in moist areas in much of the country. Its bright green leaves grow from the base in groups of three; grass leaves, in contrast, grow

Dandelion

Kudzu vine

Yellow nutsedge

Yellow oxalis

in sets of two. The flower head is golden brown. Small, roughly round tubers (nutlets) form at the tips of the roots; the weed spreads by these tubers as well as by seed.

Remove nutsedge when it's young—when plants have fewer than five leaves or are less than 6 inches tall. Older, taller plants are mature enough to produce tubers; when you dig or pull the plant, the tubers remain in the soil to sprout.

For chemical control, try glyphosate, being careful not to get the chemical on desirable plants. It is most effective when the plants are young; it will not kill tubers that have become detached from the treated plant.

OXALIS, YELLOW
(Oxalis corniculata)

A very aggressive perennial weed, yellow oxalis (also called yellow wood sorrel) thrives throughout most of North America. Happy in sun or shade, it spreads quickly by seed. Seedlings start out from a single taproot, which soon develops into a shallow, spreading, knitted root system. Tiny, five-petaled yellow flowers are followed by elongated seed capsules that can shoot seed as far as 6 feet.

Dig out small plants before they set seed. Keep lawns vigorous to provide tough competition; water deeply but infrequently, since frequent shallow watering encourages this shallow-rooted weed.

For chemical control, use a pre-emergence herbicide containing oryzalin or pendimethalin to prevent seeds from germinating and becoming established. Spot-treat oxalis in garden areas with glyphosate, taking care to avoid contact with desirable plants.

PLANTAIN *(Plantago species)*

Perennial weeds found in lawns and gardens throughout the United States, especially in damp, heavy soil, plantains form rosettes of dark green leaves marked from end to end with distinctive parallel veining. Leaves of *P. lanceolata* (buckhorn plantain) are long and narrow; those of *P. major* (broadleaf plantain) are broadly oval.

To reduce infestations in lawns, keep the turf thick through consistent fertilizing; aerating the lawn will help, too. Dig out plantains before they set seed. Be sure to remove as much of the roots as possible (a dandelion weeder is helpful here), since these weeds can regrow from any pieces of the fibrous rootstalk that remain in the soil.

For chemical control, use a pre-emergence product containing isoxaben. Spot-treat plantains in the garden with glyphosate, taking care not to get the chemical on desirable plants.

🌿 POISON OAK, POISON IVY
(*Toxicodendron diversilobum* and *T. radicans*)

Poison oak is most common in California, western Oregon, and western Washington. In the open or in filtered sun, it forms a dense, leafy shrub; in the shade, it's a tall-growing vine. Its leaves are divided into three leaflets with scalloped, toothed, or lobed edges. Poison ivy is quite similar in appearance; it's common east of the Rockies and also grows in eastern Oregon and eastern Washington. Usually found in shady areas and at the edges of woodlands, it sprawls along the ground until it finds something to climb; then it becomes a vine.

A resin on the leaves, stems, fruits, and roots of both poison oak and poison ivy causes severe contact dermatitis in most people. Both these plants are spread by birds, who eat the fruits and disperse the seeds. Poison oak and poison ivy are most effectively controlled with an appropriately labeled herbicide, such as triclopyr or glyphosate (take care to avoid getting these chemicals on desirable plants).

🌿 PUNCTURE VINE
(*Tribulus terrestris*)

With its sharp, thorny burs that poke into tires, paws, and bare feet, puncture vine is painfully familiar to gardeners in much of the country. An annual weed often found in dry areas, it forms a dense, low mat 5 to 15 feet in diameter.

Hoe or dig plants before they can set seed, cutting below the crown to prevent regrowth. Once you've removed puncture vine growing in lawns, improve the soil with compost and sow grass seed in bare spots to prevent the weeds from re-establishing.

For chemical control, pre-emergence herbicides containing trifluralin or pen-

Broadleaf plantain

Poison ivy

Puncture vine

ABOVE: Purslane
BELOW: Quack grass

dimethalin may be used on some lawn grasses and ornamentals. For postemergence control in lawns, use a selective herbicide containing MCPA, MCPP, and dicamba.

🌿 PURSLANE (*Portulaca oleracea*)

Nor to be confused with the large-flowered ornamental purslane sold in nurseries (the 'Wildfire' strain, variously ascribed to *Portulaca oleracea, P. umbraticola,* and *P. grandiflora*), weedy purslane is a low-growing summer annual found in gardens and orchards throughout the country. It thrives in moist conditions but can withstand considerable drought. Its fleshy, dark green leaves are edible, with a tart, lemony flavor.

Though purslane is easy to pull or hoe, pieces of stem can reroot readily, so be sure to remove them from the garden. Also remove plants that have begun to flower, since they can ripen seed even after they've been pulled—and a single plant can produce more than 50,000 seeds.

Purslane can be controlled with solarization. For chemical control, use a pre-emergence herbicide containing oryzalin or pendimethalin.

🌿 QUACK GRASS
(*Elytrigia repens*)

Also known as couch grass or devil's grass, quack grass is an aggressive perennial that invades lawns and gardens in most of the country. It can reach 3 feet tall, but it stays much lower in mowed areas. It produces an extensive mass of long, slender, yellowish white branching rhizomes (underground stems) that can spread laterally 3 to 5 feet.

Because it reproduces readily from even small pieces of rhizome left in the soil, quack grass is difficult to manage. Before planting, thoroughly dig the area and remove all visible pieces of rhizome; this will slow the weed's growth for a few years. You can also suppress quack grass by smothering (see page 82); leave the cover in place for at least a year.

For chemical control, use selective herbicides containing fluazifop-butyl or sethoxydim; these will suppress quack grass and most other grasses. Or use a nonselective herbicide containing glyphosate, taking care to avoid contact with desirable plants.

🌱 SPOTTED SPURGE
(Chamaesyce maculata; sometimes listed as *Euphorbia maculata)*

This annual weed is particularly aggressive: not only does it produce large quantities of seed, it also sets seed within just a few weeks of germination. It grows from a shallow taproot and forms a low mat of branching stems that exude a milky juice when cut.

Spotted spurge

Hoe or pull young seedlings early in the season, before they bloom and set seed. A vigorous, well-fertilized lawn competes well against spotted spurge. If chemical control is necessary, use a pre-emergence product containing isoxaben, oryzalin, or pendimethalin on lawn grasses and around ornamentals. Spot treat spurge plants with herbicidal soap when they are young. For spurge growing in cracks in pavement, apply a product containing glufosinate-ammonium or glyphosate, taking care to avoid contact with desirable plants.

SYNTHETIC HERBICIDES

Herbicides generally fall into the two classes discussed below: pre-emergence and postemergence. A number of widely used products are described here, listed alphabetically by common name (the name you'll find on the label under "active ingredients"). Trade names are given in parentheses. You'll find other herbicides on the market besides those listed.

When applying any herbicide, read the label carefully and follow the directions exactly. Also review the safety tips on page 66.

PRE-EMERGENCE. Pre-emergence herbicides work by inhibiting the growth of germinating weed seeds and very young seedlings. Before applying these chemicals in ornamental gardens, remove any existing weeds. Some pre-emergence products are formulated to kill germinating weeds in lawns; these may be sold in combination with fertilizers. Follow label directions carefully; some of these products must be watered into the soil, while others are incorporated into it.

ISOXABEN (Snapshot). Sold in combination with oryzalin, this herbicide effectively controls both grasses and broad-leafed weeds.

ORYZALIN (Surflan). Used to control annual grasses and many broad-leafed weeds in warm-season turf grasses and in gardens.

PENDIMETHALIN (Prowl). Controls many annual grasses and broad-leafed weeds in turf.

TRIFLURALIN (Treflan). Controls many annual grasses and broad-leafed weeds in ornamental plantings.

POSTEMERGENCE. Two types of herbicides act on growing weeds and other unwanted vegetation. Contact herbicides kill only the plant parts on which they are sprayed; regrowth may still occur from roots or unsprayed buds. Translocated herbicides must be absorbed by the plant, which they then kill by interfering with its metabolism. Many work best if you add a surfactant (spreader-sticker) to the mixture. Check product labels for specific directions.

FLUAZIFOP-BUTYL (Fusilade, Grass-B-Gon). Translocated. Controls actively growing grassy weeds. Can be sprayed over many broad-leafed ornamentals; check the label.

GLUFOSINATE-AMMONIUM (Finale). Translocated. A nonselective herbicide that kills most kinds of weeds. Take care not to apply to desirable plants.

GLYPHOSATE (Roundup, Kleenup). Translocated. A nonselective herbicide that kills or damages any plant it contacts. Effective on a broad range of troublesome weeds, but must be used with care to avoid damaging desirable plants.

HERBICIDAL SOAP (Superfast). Contact. Made from selected fatty acids, as are insecticidal soaps. Provides quick topkill on many annual weeds; regrowth may occur from the roots.

MCPA, MCPP, DICAMBA (Weed Away). Translocated. This combination of chemicals is used to control broad-leafed weeds growing in turf. Spray drift can injure nearby shrubs and trees.

SETHOXYDIM (Poast). Translocated. Controls many grasses growing in ornamental plantings.

TRICLOPYR (Brush-B-Gon, Brush Killer). Translocated. A nonselective herbicide that kills or damages any plant it contacts. Effective on hard-to-kill brushy weeds such as blackberry, poison oak, and poison ivy. Use with care to avoid damaging desirable plants.

MODIFYING CLIMATE: SUMMER HEAT AND WINTER COLD

Even if you're careful to choose plants well adapted to your climate, there are times when they may require protection from heat, cold, or wind. Seedlings and newly set-out transplants, for example, are vulnerable to both heat and cold. In mild-winter areas, tropical and subtropical plants (such as citrus trees) may need occasional protection from frost; where winters are very cold, certain shrubs and young trees may need protection all winter long. And some shade-loving plants must have sun protection and high humidity throughout the growing season.

Trees with high branches shelter shade-loving rhododendrons from the hot sun.

CREATING TEMPORARY SHADE

Just-planted transplants and newly germinated seedlings can be damaged beyond recovery by a sudden hot, sunny spell, especially if drying winds come along with the heat. To protect such vulnerable young plants, it's wise to set up temporary screens; these should be left in place until the weather cools at least slightly or until the plants have had time to develop strong root systems that can efficiently absorb water from the soil.

To shield a few plants from sun and wind, insert shingles or pieces of plywood about 6 inches wide and a foot tall in the ground on the sunny side of each plant. For larger plants, make a screen by draping burlap or shade cloth over a cylinder of ¾-inch mesh wire or by stapling either material to stakes set firmly in the ground.

Protect a young transplant from sun and wind by stapling burlap to three stakes driven firmly into the ground.

PROVIDING FOR SHADE LOVERS

Shade-loving plants such as tuberous begonia, fuchsia, and rhododendron have shallow root systems. If exposed to hot sun for long, they lose water faster than they can absorb it from the soil—and they sunburn, wilt, or wither as a result. To grow these plants successfully, you'll need to hold direct sun to a minimum and keep humidity high. If you live near the ocean, the cloud cover and natural humidity may do your work for you. Gardeners living farther inland should locate their shade plants under the shelter of high-branching trees, beneath lath structures or shade cloth, or on the north or east side of a building, fence, or wall.

In any area—whether coastal or inland—it's important to shield shade-loving plants from steady winds. Fences, louvers, and windbreak plantings all do the job nicely.

To provide the necessary high humidity, water often and be sure to mulch your plantings; a coarse, moist mulch releases a considerable amount of water into the air. On days when temperatures are especially high or humidity especially low, water with particular diligence and mist the plants' foliage as well; a drip irrigation system with mister-type emitters can help you here (see page 45).

FROST AND FREEZE PROTECTION

Wherever you garden, the best defense against cold damage is to choose trees and shrubs that are hardy in your climate zone (see pages 6–7 for more on climate). Plants that are more tender to frost should be restricted to summertime display in borders or grown in containers that can be moved to shelter when the weather turns cold.

It's also important to know your garden's microclimates—that is, to learn which areas are warmer, which are cooler (see page 6). The riskiest spots for marginally hardy plants are stretches of open ground exposed to air from all sides (particularly from the north). Other dangerous locations include hollows and low, enclosed areas that catch cold air as it sinks, then hold it motionless. The warmest part of the garden is usually next to a south-facing wall with an overhang; such a spot offers maximum frost protection and supplies the warmth needed to stimulate buds, blossoms, and fruit on vines, shrubs, and espaliered trees that might not thrive elsewhere in the garden.

You can, to some extent, condition your plants and soil for cold weather. Water and fertilize the garden regularly in late spring and early summer, while plants are growing fastest. Taper off nitrogen feeding in late summer: actively growing plants are more susceptible to cold than are dormant or semidormant ones, so you don't want to stimulate the production of new growth that won't have time to mature before cold weather arrives. Cutting back on water also helps harden growth—but

Cold air drains

Cold air pools here

GARDEN MICROCLIMATES

Garden microclimates are influenced by hills and hollows, sunlight, and structures. Cold air moves downhill to the lowest point, and will settle there if it encounters a fence, wall, or other structure.

be sure the soil is moist at the onset of frosty weather, since moist soil holds and releases more heat than dry soil.

Frosts that hit early in fall (before the growing season ends) or in spring (after growth is underway) are much more damaging than those arriving when plants are semidormant or dormant. Be on the lookout: warning signs include still air, clear skies, low humidity, and, of course, low temperatures. If you notice these danger signals in late afternoon or evening, move at-risk container plants under a porch roof or into the garage. Give plants in the ground temporary shelters; two types are shown below. Remove coverings during the daytime (unless the threat of frost continues), then replace them at night to retain heat. (For advice on protecting vegetables from frost and extending their productivity, see page 173.)

Don't hurry to prune frost-damaged plants. Cutting them back too soon may stimulate tender new growth that will be nipped by later frosts—and besides that, it's easy to mistake leafless but still-living stems for dead ones. Hold off on pruning until new growth begins in spring, when you can remove wood that is clearly dead.

ALL-WINTER PROTECTION

In very cold climates, some plants require protection all winter long to survive; examples include broad-leafed evergreens such as boxwood *(Buxus)*, euonymus, holly *(Ilex)*, pieris, and rhododendron. Evergreens suffer in winter because the leaves continue to transpire and thus lose moisture (especially on relatively warm, windy days)—but when the soil is frozen, the roots cannot take up water to replace what has been lost, and the plant becomes desiccated.

Continued >

PROTECTING PLANTS FROM OCCASIONAL FROST

1 Make a frame of four strong stakes around the plant. Lay plastic or burlap over the stakes; make sure the material does not touch the leaves, since this would cause them to freeze. To supply additional heat, you can place one or two trouble lights or a string of holiday lights in the shelter. Plug the lights into an extension cord or outlet intended for outdoor use, and make sure they are not in contact with the plastic or burlap.

2 For a quick cover for smaller plants, use a large cardboard box. Cut the bottom on three sides to make a lid you can open and close as needed.

1

2

ALL WINTER PROTECTION FOR BROADLEAVED EVERGREENS

1 Water thoroughly before the ground freezes, then apply a thick mulch of oak leaves, pine needles, wood chips, or ground bark around the plants. The mulch limits the penetration of frost into the ground, allowing the deepest roots to continue absorbing moisture; it also protects surface roots from alternate freezing and thawing.

2 Apply an antitranspirant around the time the first hard frost is due. Available from garden centers, this product forms a thin film on the leaves, sealing in moisture. You may need to make further applications later in winter; check the label.

3 Construct a windbreak in especially exposed locations, if needed. Drive three or four stakes into the ground around the plant and staple or nail burlap to them. Don't use plastic film for the windbreak; it cuts off needed air circulation.

1

2

3

WINTER PROTECTION FOR ROSES

Where winter lows regularly fall to 10°F/–12°C or below, some protection is needed for most modern roses. After a couple of hard freezes have occurred, cut canes back to a manageable height and tie them together; then mound soil at least 1 foot high over base of bush. After soil mound freezes, cover it with an insulating mound of straw, hay, cut conifer boughs, or other noncompacting organic material. For greater security, surround insulated bush with a wire mesh cylinder: this will hold soil mound and its covering in place while allowing water to drain away easily.

COLD FRAMES AND HOTBEDS

Used to protect tender plants or rooted cuttings during the colder months, a cold frame is simply a box with a transparent lid or cover. It acts as a passive solar energy collector and reservoir. During the day, the sun's rays heat the air and soil in the frame; at night, the heat absorbed by the soil radiates out, keeping the plants warm.

A cold frame is useful at other times of year as well. In spring, it provides an ideal environment for hardening off annual flower and vegetable seedlings started indoors. Seeds of many plants can be sown directly in the frame and grown there until it's time to transplant them to the garden. In sum-mer, you can replace the cover with shade cloth or lath, creating a nursery for cuttings.

Set up your cold frame in a site protected from harsh winds by trees, shrubs, a fence, or a wall. To ensure that the frame will receive as much sunlight as possible, orient it to face south or southwest. Sinking the frame 8 to 10 inches into the ground increases heat retention significantly. Make sure the location has good drainage, since you don't want water to collect around the frame after every rain.

To speed the germination of seeds and the rooting of some kinds of cuttings, you can convert your cold frame to a hotbed, as shown below.

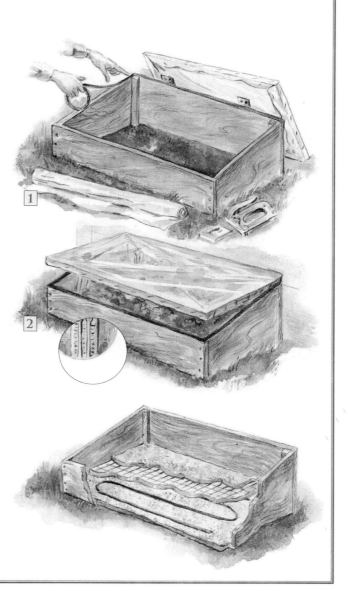

BUILDING A COLD FRAME

1 Start by selecting a cover, since its size will often determine the dimensions of the frame. Good choices include an old window sash or storm window; if you don't have one on hand, look for recycled windows at garage sales. You can also make a cover out of clear acrylic or fiberglass sheets sandwiched between narrow strips of wood and reinforced at the corners with metal corner plates. Polyethylene film stapled to a wooden frame is another option; it's quick and inexpensive, though it lasts only a year or so. Make sure the cover isn't too heavy to lift easily. Don't make it too wide, either, or you'll have a hard time reaching the plants inside the frame; a width of 2^1/$_2$ to 3 feet is ideal. A length of at least 4 feet will allow you to grow a variety of plants.

   Build the frame from lumber, such as rot-resistant red-wood or cedar or less expensive plywood or scrap lumber. The frame should slope from about 1^1/$_2$ feet high at the back to a foot high at the front; this traps the most heat and lets rainwa-ter run off. For strength, reinforce the corners of the box with vertical posts. Attach the cover with galvanized steel hinges and apply weather stripping around the top edges of the box.

2 Ventilation is vital to prevent overheating. A minimum-maximum thermometer is useful for keeping track of temperature fluctua-tions. Plan to prop open the cover when the temperature inside reaches 70° to 75°F/21° to 24°C. Close the cover in late after-noon to trap heat. (If you won't be around during the day, you can buy a nonelectric vent controller that will automatically open and close the cover at a preset temperature.) On very cold nights, drape the frame with an old blanket or piece of carpet to provide extra insulation.

MAKING A HOTBED

To convert your cold frame to a hotbed, add an electric heating cable. Make a base for the cable by spreading a 2- to 3-inch layer of sand or vermiculite. Lay the cable, spacing the loops 6 to 8 inches apart and keeping it 3 inches away from the sides of the frame. Add another inch of sand, then a sheet of window screen or hardware cloth to protect the cable. Most growers add another, 4- to 6-inch-thick layer of sand in which to sink pots of plants.

Selecting which plants you want to grow can be one of the most enjoyable aspects of gardening—and one of the most confusing, too, thanks to the thousands of possibilities.

A PRIMER OF

GARDEN PLANTS

Presented here is basic information to help you choose and care for plants in a number of basic categories, from trees and shrubs to annuals and perennials. For each group of plants, you'll find a sampler of good choices, complete with photographs.

The samplers present certain information in an at-a-glance format. Each entry begins with the plant's botanical name; any former botanical names (under which it may still be sold) appear in parentheses. Entries that contain references to a number of species and hybrids are headed simply by the plant's genus—*Acer*, for example. Other entries cover just one plant and are headed by genus and species, as in *Ginkgo biloba*.

After the botanical name comes the common name, if there is one. If the plant is popularly known by its botanical name—as for magnolia and zinnia, for example—no common name is noted.

Other information given in all entries includes climate adaptability, preceded by the symbol ✎ (see climate zone information on pages 8–11). Each plant's preferred exposure is also noted. ☼ indicates bright, unshaded sun; ● means no direct sun at all. ◐ describes plants that do equally well in partial shade (a spot that's sunny in the morning, shaded in afternoon) or light shade (no direct sun but plenty of light).

Moisture needs are identified, too. ◖ indicates a preference for regular water; the plant always needs moisture, but soil shouldn't remain saturated. ◖ describes plants that must have some moisture, but soil can become somewhat dry to quite dry between waterings. ◖◖ means the plant needs ample water and will flourish even in soggy soil.

Entries for some plants include other information. For trees, we note growth rate; for vines, we tell you just how each plant climbs. For many groups, we indicate whether the plant is evergreen, with foliage present all year; semievergreen, losing some leaves in fall; or deciduous, losing all its foliage each autumn. As you'll learn, certain plants are evergreen or semievergreen in the warmer parts of their range, deciduous where winters are colder.

An exuberant mix of ornamentals and edibles, this garden is a feast for all the senses.

T REES

Trees are the backbone of the garden. Besides providing shade and shelter, they bring year-round beauty to the landscape through their foliage, flowers, fruits, bark, and branch structure. They soften hard architectural lines; they frame special views and block out unattractive ones. And because the variety of available trees is so wide, you'll be able to find just the right one for your garden. Of course, the enormous range of possibilities also makes choosing the right tree a challenge, but there are several pointers you can follow to help narrow the field.

SELECTING TREES

To decide which trees are best for you, start by considering the points below. Also consult local nursery personnel and look carefully at the trees in your neighborhood to see which ones perform particularly well. For descriptions of specific trees, turn to page 99.

LANDSCAPE FUNCTION. What role do you want a tree to play in your garden? If you're looking for a source of shade, pick a tree with a wide canopy. Deciduous trees will give you shade in summer, then admit the sun after their leaves drop in fall. To block a view from a neighbor's second-story windows straight into your home or garden, choose relatively tall, dense trees and consider combining them with shrubs. If you want a specimen tree for a garden or patio focal point, look for interesting foliage or a striking display of flowers or berries. Fruit trees such as apple, pear, or plum do double duty, giving you delicious fruit as well as lovely form and flowers. (For more on selecting and growing fruit trees, see pages 182–188.)

CLIMATE ADAPTABILITY. Choose trees that will accept your local climate, including both winter lows and any extremes of summer weather, such as baking heat, dryness, or high humiity.

CULTURAL PREFERENCES. Match the needs of trees you choose to the conditions in your garden. Select those that will grow well in the sort of soil you have, with the amount of water they'll receive naturally or that you can provide.

DECIDUOUS VERSUS EVERGREEN. *Deciduous* trees start their growth with a burst of new leaves or flowers in early spring, then remain in leaf through summer. In autumn, the leaves drop to reveal the bare limbs. In many sorts of deciduous trees, the leaves change color before they fall.

Evergreen trees include both broad-leafed evergreens and conifers (there are a few deciduous conifers as well). Broad-leafed evergreens have the same sort of foliage as deciduous

trees; their older leaves may fall intermittently or in one season. Most conifers have leaves that are narrow and needlelike or tiny and scalelike. Because they keep their foliage year-round, both sorts of evergreens serve well as screens and windbreaks.

GROWTH RATE AND SIZE. Different trees grow at different rates. Speed (or lack of it) can be a crucial factor if you need a tree to shade a south-facing window or provide privacy: for quick results, select a fast-growing tree. If you're choosing a tree primarily for its beautiful flowers, however, you may be willing to wait a number of years for the tree to mature and begin blooming.

It's important to visualize the ultimate height and spread of any tree you consider. Not only is an overly large tree out of scale in most gardens, it eventually crowds other plants and may have to be removed—an expensive undertaking.

Autumn turns the Chinese pistache *(Pistacia chinensis)* on the left orange, the one on the right golden yellow. Such variation in color is normal in seed-grown plants of most species; to make sure of good color, select trees in fall leaf.

COMMON TREE SHAPES

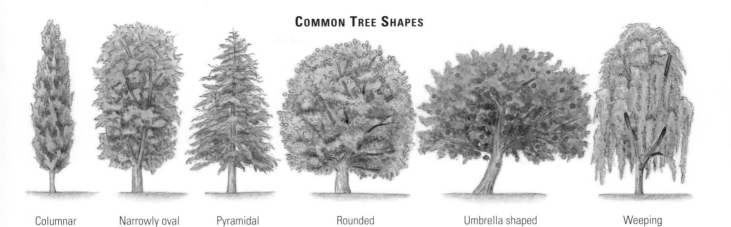

Columnar   Narrowly oval   Pyramidal   Rounded   Umbrella shaped   Weeping

ROOT SYSTEM. A tree with a network of greedy surface roots is a poor candidate for planting in your lawn or within the garden, since it will take more than its fair share of water and nutrients. But the same tree may be just right at the garden's fringes or along a country drive. Some trees have surface roots that can lift and crack nearby pavement, making them less-than-ideal choices for a patio, entryway, or parking strip.

MAINTENANCE. If a tree produces a fair amount of litter from falling leaves, flowers, or fruits, it's not a good selection for planting beside a patio, in a lawn, or near a swimming pool; you'd be spending far too much time cleaning up the debris. Such a tree is a better candidate for a background area, where the litter can remain where it falls. In regions with regular high winds or heavy annual snowfall, avoid trees with weak or brittle wood. They can be hazardous to people and property, and you'd probably have to remove broken branches frequently.

PEST AND DISEASE PROBLEMS. Make sure the trees you are considering are not overly susceptible to pests or diseases. Keep in mind that a tree that's trouble-free in one climate may be plagued with problems in other areas.

PLANTING AND CARING FOR TREES

Many deciduous trees are sold bare-root during the dormant season from late fall through early spring. Deciduous trees as well as conifers and broad-leafed evergreens may also be sold balled-and-burlapped from early fall into the following spring, or in containers throughout the year. For instructions on planting all types, see pages 36–39.

All trees—even the drought-tolerant kinds—need regular water during the first several years after planting, until the roots have grown deep enough to carry the plant through dry periods. Once established, however, most trees require only infrequent irrigation.

Regular fertilizing, too, is needed for a few years after planting. By ensuring a nitrogen supply for the springtime growth surge, you'll encourage young trees to get established quickly. Once a tree is well settled in, though, it may grow satisfactorily with no further feeding—and in fact, fertilizing a tree that continues to put out healthy, vigorous new growth is a waste of both time and fertilizer. But feeding may be in order if a tree's new growth is weak, sparse, or unusually pale, or if the tree has a fair amount of dieback that can't be ascribed to over- or underwatering.

FORMING A STRONG TREE TRUNK

Young trees develop a strong trunk more quickly if their lower branches are left in place for the first few years after planting; these branches also help shade the trunk. During this time, shorten the side branches only if they become too long or vigorous, pruning during the dormant season or just before spring growth begins. Once the trunk is at least 2 inches thick, begin removing the lower branches gradually, over a period of several years.

REMOVING A TREE LIMB

When removing larger branches, avoid ripping the bark by shortening the branch to a stub before cutting it off at the branch collar. Using a sharp pruning saw, make three cuts.

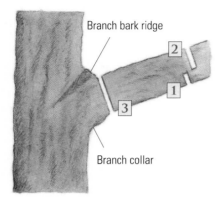

Branch bark ridge

Branch collar

1 Starting about a foot from the branch base, make a cut from the underside approximately a third of the way through.

2 About an inch farther out on the branch, cut through from the top until the branch rips off; it should split cleanly between the two cuts.

3 Make the final cut by placing your saw beside the branch bark ridge and cutting downward just outside the branch collar. If the crotch is very narrow, cut upward from the bottom to avoid cutting into the branch collar.

PROTECTING A YOUNG TREE'S TRUNK

Wrap the trunk of a newly planted tree to protect it from drying winds, hot sun, freezing temperatures, gnawing wild animals such as rabbits, deer and rodents, and damage from carelessly used lawn mowers or string trimmers. For wrapping, use loosely tied burlap or a manufactured trunk wrapping material. Remove the wrapping after a year, when the bark has become thicker and tougher. (Don't leave it in place longer than this, since it can eventually girdle a trunk.)

PRUNING MATURE TREES

In general, mature ornamental trees should be pruned just enough to maintain structure, health, and attractive appearance. This often amounts to minimal or only occasional pruning. Routine annual trimming is neither necessary nor advisable.

For large, potentially dangerous pruning jobs, such as removing heavy broken branches or limbs high in a tree, it's safest to hire a qualified professional.

Deciduous trees are usually pruned during the dormant season, while the tree is leafless and the branch structure is easy to see. In mild-winter regions, where one growing season blends into another, midwinter is generally the best time to prune. In cold-winter areas, late winter to early spring is the standard pruning period. When pruning a flowering tree, be mindful of when the flower buds form so that you won't inadvertently remove them. Trees that blossom early in the season, on the prior year's growth, should be pruned right after bloom. Those that flower later, on the current year's stems, should be pruned before spring growth begins.

Broad-leafed evergreens usually require very little pruning. When pruning is needed, do so during late dormancy or in summer; don't prune during or right after the spring growth flush. For flowering broad-leafed evergreens, timing is a bit more precise: like flowering deciduous trees, they should be pruned with an eye toward preserving flower buds. Prune after bloom for trees flowering on last season's growth; prune before spring growth begins for those that bloom on new growth.

For general pruning information and advice on pruning conifers, see pages 48–53.

STAKING YOUNG TREES

A young tree will develop a sturdier trunk if it grows unsupported and can sway in the breeze. Stake it only if it is planted in an extremely windy location or if the main trunk is too weak to stay upright on its own. Use ties that won't bind or cut into the bark, such as wide strips of canvas or rubber; fasten each tie around the tree and both stakes in a figure-8 pattern, as shown below. The tree should be able to move an inch in either direction.

To figure out where to attach the ties to a weak trunk, run your hand up the trunk until you find the point where the top no longer flops over. Cut off the stakes an inch or so above the ties. In a windswept site, a young tree's roots may need anchoring to keep them in firm contact with the soil; use stakes and ties only a foot above ground level for this kind of staking. In both cases, sink stakes at right angles to the prevailing wind. Remove them after about a year or as soon as the tree appears to be self-supporting.

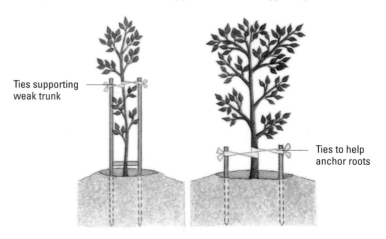

Ties supporting weak trunk

Ties to help anchor roots

A SAMPLER OF TREES

When you're deciding on basic trees for your garden, this sampler can help you choose. For an explanation of the at-a-glance information introducing each entry, see page 95.

SYMBOLS: These symbols indicate a tree's growth rate (▲) and whether it is evergreen (🌲) or deciduous (🌳).

ACER
🌳 MAPLE

⚡ ZONES VARY

☀ ◐ FULL SUN OR PARTIAL SHADE

💧 ○ REGULAR TO MODERATE

GROWTH RATE VARIES

The many maple species include small trees for patios as well as strong-growing shade trees. Maples of one type or another will grow in most zones, though none will really flourish in hot, dry areas. These trees prefer well-drained soil, but they must have regular moisture during the growing season. They are subject to anthracnose and verticillium wilt.

A. davidii. DAVID'S MAPLE. Zones 3–6, 15–17, 20, 21, 32–34. This 20- to 35-foot tree has distinctive shiny green bark with white stripes. Leaves are heart shaped, reaching 5 to 7 inches long. New growth is bronze tinted; autumn color is bright yellow, orange red, and purple.

A. palmatum. JAPANESE MAPLE. Zones 2–10, 12, 14–24, 31–41. The airiest and most delicate of all maples, this is a slow-growing, normally many-stemmed tree to 20 feet tall and wide. Leaves are 2 to 4 inches long, deeply lobed, carried in horizontal tiers. Autumn color is scarlet, orange, or yellow. Named varieties offer a range of tree sizes and foliage colors and shapes. Where summers are hot and dry, provide regular moisture, some shade, and shelter from wind.

A. rubrum. RED MAPLE. Zones 1–9, 14–17, 26, 28, 31–44. Fairly fast

Acer palmatum

ABOVE: *Acer rubrum* and birches
BELOW: *Betula platyphylla japonica* 'Whitespire'

growth to 60 feet or taller, 40 feet or wider. Lobed, 5-inch-long, shiny green leaves turn brilliant scarlet in autumn in frosty climates. Tolerates almost any soil type. Many named selections are sold, varying in habit (there are several columnar forms) and fall color.

BETULA
🌳 BIRCH

⚡ ZONES VARY

☀ ◐ FULL SUN OR PARTIAL SHADE

💧 AMPLE

▲ FAST

These familiar trees have fresh green, finely toothed leaves that turn to glowing yellow in autumn. After leaf drop, the trees' delicate limb structure and handsome bark lend beauty to the winter landscape. All are susceptible to aphids, which will drip honeydew onto anything beneath them. The two choices listed below are resistant to bronze birch borer.

B. nigra. RIVER or RED BIRCH. Zones 1–24, 26, 28–43. Eventually forms a pyramidal tree 50 to 90 feet high, 40 to 60 feet wide. Bark is apricot to pinkish on young trees, darker on older ones. Glossy green leaves with silvery undersides reach 3 inches long. Tolerates poor or slow drainage. 'Heritage' is a vigorous selection with larger, glossier leaves.

B. platyphylla japonica 'Whitespire'. JAPANESE WHITE BIRCH. Zones 2–11, 14–24, 31–41. This narrowly pyramidal, heat-tolerant selection grows 30 to 40 feet tall, 12 to 15 feet wide. Bark is white; leaves reach 3 inches long.

CEDRUS
🌳 CEDAR
- ✂ ZONES VARY
- ☼ FULL SUN
- 💧 MODERATE
- GROWTH RATE VARIES

These stately conifers look their best when given plenty of room; they are deep rooted and, once established, quite drought tolerant. Needles are borne in tufted clusters. Both species listed here stand up well to hot, humid weather.

C. atlantica. ATLAS CEDAR. Zones 2–24, 31, 32, 34. Slow to moderate growth to 60 feet or more, with a 30-foot spread. In Zones 2–7, branches can break in heavy snows. Needles are bluish green to light green, under an inch long.

C. deodara. DEODAR CEDAR. Zones 3–12, 14–24, 27–32, warmer parts of 33. Fast growing to 80 feet, with a spread of 40 feet at ground level; readily identified by its gracefully drooping branches and nodding tip. Softer in texture than Atlas cedar. Needles reach 2 inches long; they may be green or have a blue, gray, or yellow cast. To control spread in young trees, cut new growth of side branches halfway back in late spring.

CERCIS canadensis
🌳 EASTERN REDBUD
- ✂ ZONES 2–20, 26, 28–41
- ☼ ☽ FULL SUN OR PARTIAL SHADE
- 💧 REGULAR
- ▲ MODERATE

A round-headed tree 25 to 35 feet high and wide; branches form horizontal tiers with age. Rounded, rich green leaves with pointed tips are 3 to 6 inches long; autumn color is yellow. Early spring flowers are small and sweet pea shaped; colors include pink shades and white, depending on the variety. The selection 'Forest Pansy' has purple foliage borne on reddish branches.

Eastern redbud needs some winter chill to flower profusely. It makes an attractive patio, specimen, or understory tree.

Cedrus deodara

Cercis canadensis 'Forest Pansy'

Chionanthus retusus

Cladrastis lutea

CHIONANTHUS retusus
🌳 CHINESE FRINGE TREE
- ✂ ZONES 3–9, 14–24, 28–34, 39
- ☼ ☽ FULL SUN OR PARTIAL SHADE
- 💧 💧 REGULAR TO MODERATE
- ▲ SLOW TO MODERATE

Grow this one as a multistemmed shrub or a small tree. It reaches about 20 feet tall and wide, bearing broad, glossy green, 4-inch-long leaves that turn bright yellow in autumn. Beautiful 4-inch-long clusters of pure white flowers with fringelike petals appear in late spring or early summer. Plant in good soil. Tolerates city pollution.

CLADRASTIS lutea
🌳 YELLOW WOOD
- ✂ ZONES 1–9, 14–16, 31–43
- ☼ FULL SUN
- 💧 MODERATE
- ▲ MODERATE

Reaching 30 to 50 feet high, 40 to 55 feet wide, yellow wood has a broad, rounded crown and large leaves (8 to 12 inches long), each divided into seven to 11 oval leaflets. Foliage is yellowish green in spring, bright green by summer, brilliant yellow in fall. In late spring to early summer, branches are decorated with spectacular clusters of fragrant white flowers that look like wisteria blossoms (trees may not bloom until their tenth year). Mature trees have handsome smooth gray bark; the common name refers to the color of freshly cut heartwood.

Yellow wood is deep rooted, so you can grow other plants beneath it. Give young trees regular water; established trees withstand some drought.

CORNUS
🌳 DOGWOOD
- ✂ ZONES VARY
- ☼ ☽ FULL SUN OR PARTIAL SHADE
- 💧 REGULAR
- ▲ MODERATE

Dogwoods offer showy spring bloom and attractive foliage; their good-looking branch structure makes a nice display when trees are bare in winter. Give them well-drained, slightly acid soil and partial shade or full sun.

C. florida. FLOWERING DOGWOOD. Zones 2–9, 14–16, 26 (northern part), 28, 29, 31–41. Typically reaches 20 to 30 feet high and wide, though it sometimes attains 40 feet. Oval, bright green leaves to 6 inches long turn flaming red in autumn. True flowers are borne in small clusters, but they're surrounded by showy bracts that make a striking display, almost covering trees before the leaves expand. The basic species has white bracts; named selections offer pink to nearly red bracts. Clusters of small scarlet fruits follow flowers and last into winter. This species is subject to anthracnose and borers in its native territory.

C. kousa. KOUSA or JAPANESE DOGWOOD. Zones 3–9, 14, 15, 18, 19, 31–34. A big multistemmed shrub, or, with training, a small tree to 20 feet tall and wide. Branches form dense, horizontal tiers. Pointed-oval, lustrous medium green leaves to 4 inches long turn yellow or scarlet in fall. Creamy white bracts appear after the foliage emerges. Resistant to both anthracnose and borers.

CRATAEGUS
phaenopyrum
❀ WASHINGTON THORN, HAWTHORN

- ✂ ZONES 2–12, 14–17, 28, 30–41
- ☼ FULL SUN
- ◖ MODERATE
- ▲ MODERATE

Reaching 25 feet tall and 20 feet wide, Washington thorn has a graceful, open structure. The glossy leaves are 2 to 3 inches long, with three to five sharp-pointed lobes; foliage turns orange and red in autumn. Masses of white spring flowers are followed by clusters of small red fruits that attract birds. Needlelike thorns are sharp; to avoid snagging and scratching passersby, don't plant the tree too close to walkways.

Cornus florida 'Rubra'

Cornus kousa

Crataegus phaenopyrum

ABOVE: *Ginkgo biloba*
BELOW: *Koelreuteria paniculata*

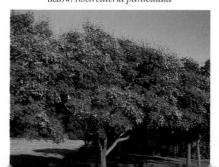

GINKGO biloba
❀ GINKGO, MAIDENHAIR TREE

- ✂ ZONES 1–10, 12, 14–24, 28, 30–44
- ☼ FULL SUN
- ◖◖ REGULAR TO MODERATE
- ▲ MODERATE

This graceful tree is attractive in any season, but it's especially lovely in fall, when the leathery, light green, fan-shaped leaves suddenly turn gold. They remain on the tree for a time, then drop quickly and cleanly. Most mature ginkgos are 35 to 50 feet tall, but they can reach 70 to 80 feet; spread ranges from a typical 30 to 40 feet to as much as 80 feet. Sometimes gawky in youth, they become well proportioned with age, with a narrow to spreading or umbrella-shaped silhouette.

Plant only male trees, since females produce messy, malodorous fruit if a male tree is nearby for pollination. 'Autumn Gold' is upright in youth, broader with age; 'Fairmont' is broadly pyramidal.

Ginkgo is tolerant of air pollution, heat, and acid or alkaline soil; it makes a good street or lawn tree.

KOELREUTERIA
paniculata
❀ GOLDENRAIN TREE

- ✂ ZONES 2–21, 28–41
- ☼ FULL SUN
- ◖ MODERATE TO LITTLE
- ▲ SLOW TO MODERATE

To 30 to 40 feet high and wide, with an open branching pattern that provides slight shade. The leaves are up to 15 inches long, divided into seven to 15 oval leaflets. Leaves emerge purplish in spring, turn bright green by summer. Very showy, fragrant yellow flower clusters appear in early to midsummer; these are followed by lanternlike fruits that mature from red to buff or brown. Goldenrain tree is not particular about soil and will perform well even in hot, windy regions. Give young trees regular water; established specimens tolerate considerable drought.

LAGERSTROEMIA indica
❀ CRAPE MYRTLE
- ✂ ZONES 7–10, 12–14, 18–21, 25–31, WARMER PARTS OF 32
- ☼ FULL SUN
- ⬦ MODERATE
- ▲ MODERATE

Crape myrtles vary in size—some are dwarf shrubs, others large shrubs or small trees. Habit is variable too, ranging from spreading to upright. But all types have 1- to 2-inch-long, dark green leaves that often turn orange or red in fall, and dense, showy clusters of crinkled, crepepapery flowers in white or shades of pink, red, or purple. Trained to a single trunk, crape myrtle becomes a rather vaseshaped tree with a rounded top; multitrunked specimens will develop a broader canopy. Smooth gray bark flakes off to reveal patches of pinkish inner bark. Best in hot-summer climates. Mildew can be a problem; if it's prevalent in your area, look for mildew-resistant strains.

LIQUIDAMBAR
styraciflua
❀ AMERICAN SWEET GUM
- ✂ ZONES 3–9, 14–37, 39
- ☼ FULL SUN
- ⬦ REGULAR
- ▲ MODERATE TO FAST

Narrow and erect when young, this tree becomes more rounded with age. It eventually reaches 60 to 75 feet tall. Spread is usually 20 to 25 feet, but trees may grow much wider in great age. Deep green, five- to seven-lobed, 3- to 7-inch-wide leaves turn purple, yellow, or red in autumn; fall color of seedling trees is variable, so select trees in fall leaf to be sure of good color. Branching pattern, furrowed bark, corky wings on twigs, and bristly fruits are showy in winter. Performs best in neutral or slightly acid soil; chlorosis in strongly alkaline soils is difficult to correct. Forms surface roots that can be a nuisance in lawns, planting beds, or narrow parking strips.

Lagerstroemia indica

Liquidambar styraciflua

Magnolia × soulangiana

Magnolia grandiflora

MAGNOLIA
❀ ❀ MAGNOLIA
- ✂ ZONES VARY
- ☼ ☼ FULL SUN OR PARTIAL SHADE
- ⬦ REGULAR
- ▲ SLOW TO MODERATE

These magnificent flowering trees and shrubs offer remarkable variety in color, leaf shape, and plant form. Below, we give just one example each of deciduous and evergreen kinds; many other species are available at well-stocked nurseries.

Plant magnolias in fairly rich, well-drained, neutral to acid soil. They have shallow, fleshy roots that are easily damaged by digging or soil compaction. Best locations are in a lawn (leave a wide grass-free area around the trunk) or shrub border. Stake single-trunked or very heavy trees to prevent them from being rocked by wind, which will tear the sensitive roots.

M. grandiflora. SOUTHERN MAGNOLIA. Zones 4–12, 14–24, 26–33. Evergreen. Reaching 80 feet tall and spreading to 40 feet wide, this statuesque tree offers year-round beauty. The thick, leathery, deep green leaves are ovals up to 8 inches long, often with rust-colored down on their undersides. Huge, pure white, powerfully fragrant flowers appear in late spring and summer (trees may not bloom until they are 10 years old or older). Surface roots will lift and crack nearby pavement, and the roots plus the dense shade cast by the canopy will eventually defeat lawn planted under the tree.

M. × soulangiana. SAUCER MAGNOLIA. Zones 2–10, 12–24, 28–41. Deciduous. Often erroneously called tulip tree, this magnolia grows slowly to 25 feet high and wide. The goblet-shaped blossoms are up to 6 inches across and vary in color from white to pink or purplish red, depending on the variety; they open before the green, rather coarse, 4- to 6-inch-long leaves expand. Late frosts can damage buds and blossoms; in cold-winter areas, plant late-flowering selections such as 'Lennei' or 'Alexandrina'.

MALUS
⚜ CRABAPPLE
- ✂ ZONES 1–21, 29–43
- ☀ FULL SUN
- ● ◐ REGULAR TO MODERATE
- GROWTH RATE VARIES

Crabapples are valued both for their white, pink, or red springtime flowers and for their showy (and sometimes edible) fruits. There are hundreds of cultivars. Most grow about 25 feet high, though heights range from as low as 6 feet to as tall as 40 feet. Pointed-oval leaves, often fuzzy in texture, vary in color from deep green to nearly purple; fall color is rarely noteworthy. Many varieties can be trained as formal or informal espaliers; see page 183.

Crabapples prefer good, deep, well-drained soil, but they'll grow in rocky or gravelly soils, including those that are acid to slightly alkaline. Though they adapt to a variety of climates, they aren't at their best in the humid lower South or low desert. Choose cultivars resistant to fireblight, scab, and rust.

PARROTIA persica
⚜ PERSIAN PARROTIA
- ✂ ZONES 3–6, 15–17, 31–41
- ☀ ◑ FULL SUN OR LIGHT SHADE
- ● ◐ REGULAR TO MODERATE
- ▲ SLOW

A single- or multitrunked small tree 20 to 40 feet high and from 15 to over 30 feet wide, Persian parrotia is attractive all year. Its ¾-inch, oval leaves unfurl reddish purple and mature to lustrous dark green; in autumn, they first turn golden yellow, then orange or rosy pink, and finally scarlet. Small flowers with conspicuous reddish stamens open in late winter, before new leaves emerge. In mature trees, the smooth gray bark flakes off to reveal lighter patches beneath.

Persian parrotia prefers slightly acid soil but tolerates alkaline soil; it will grow in sun as well as light shade. It's resistant to pests.

Malus 'Dorothea'

Parrotia persica

Picea pungens

Pinus nigra

PICEA pungens
⚜ COLORADO SPRUCE
- ✂ ZONES 1–6, 10, 14–17, 32–45
- ☀ FULL SUN
- ● ◐ REGULAR TO MODERATE
- ▲ SLOW TO MODERATE

This is a broadly pyramidal conifer with stiff, regular, horizontal branches; it eventually reaches 60 feet or higher and 25 feet across. Depending on the variety, the sharp needles vary in color from dark green through all shades of blue green to steely blue and silver. Colorado spruce is the only spruce that will succeed in the Southwest and lower Midwest.

PINUS
⚜ PINE
- ✂ ZONES VARY
- ☀ FULL SUN
- ● ◐ REGULAR TO LITTLE
- GROWTH RATE VARIES

These conifers display great diversity in size, habit, color and length of needles, and size and form of cones. They grow best in full sun and will thrive in just about any soil, as long as it is well drained. Following are just a few of the many pines available for gardens.

P. cembra. SWISS STONE PINE. Zones 1–7, 10, 32–45. Very slow growth (eventually to 70 feet tall, 15 to 25 feet wide) and dense, dark green needles make this pine a good choice for smaller gardens. Branches are short and spreading; the tree is a narrow, dense pyramid when young, becoming open and round topped with age.

P. nigra. AUSTRIAN BLACK PINE. Zones 2–11, 14–21, 32 (cooler parts), 33–41. Slow to moderate growth produces a stout, dense pyramid 40 to 60 feet high, 20 to 40 feet wide. Very dark green, stiff needles. Serves as a landscape accent or as a windbreak in cold regions. Tolerant of urban and seacoast conditions.

P. thunbergiana. JAPANESE BLACK PINE. Zones 3–12, 14–21, 28–37, 39. Growth is fast where climate is cool and moist, slow in arid regions. Height and spread vary considerably, depending on conditions: trees may be 20 to 100 feet tall, 20 to 40 feet wide. Spreading branches clothed in bright green needles form a broad, conical tree, irregular and spreading in age. This pine takes well to pruning, even shearing.

PISTACIA chinensis
❀ CHINESE PISTACHE

 ✎ ZONES 4–16, 18–23, 26, 28–33
 ☼ FULL SUN
 ◔ MODERATE TO LITTLE
 ▲ MODERATE

A reliable choice for street, lawn, patio, or garden, Chinese pistache forms a broadly rounded tree 30 to 60 feet tall and nearly as wide. Its foot-long leaves consist of 10 to 16 paired dark green leaflets. It has good orange to red fall color even in mild climates and tolerates a wide range of soils, including alkaline types. Very drought tolerant once established. Stake young trees; once they are established, prune to develop a head high enough to walk under.

PRUNUS
❀ FLOWERING PLUM, PEACH, NECTARINE, CHERRY

 ✎ ZONES VARY
 ☼ FULL SUN
 ◐ ◔ REGULAR TO MODERATE
 GROWTH RATE VARIES

These flowering trees—all members of the same genus—are valued for their showy springtime bloom; most also have appealing foliage and an attractive shape. Most produce few or no fruits; for fruiting varieties, see pages 186, 187, 188. Flowering peach, nectarine, and cherry require well-drained soil; flowering plum is less particular, but will fail if soil is waterlogged for long periods. A few of the many species and varieties are described below; check with local nurseries for others suited to your region.

Pinus thunbergiana

Pistacia chinensis

Prunus cerasifera 'Atropurpurea'

Prunus persica

P. cerasifera. FLOWERING PLUM. Zones 3–22, 28, 31–34, 39. The purple-leafed selections of flowering plum are widely grown; all are small and fast growing. 'Krauter Vesuvius', an upright tree to 18 feet high and 15 feet wide, has dark purple (almost black) leaves and light pink flowers. 'Thundercloud' grows 20 feet tall and wide; it has dark copper leaves and light pink to white blossoms, and may produce red fruits. 'Atropurpurea' grows 20 to 30 feet tall and wide and usually bears fruit.

P. persica. FLOWERING PEACH. Zones 2–24, 30–34, 39. Quickly reaching 15 to 20 feet high and wide, flowering peaches look much like the fruiting varieties. In areas where spring is early and hot, choose early-blooming varieties such as 'Early Double Pink'. Late-flowering kinds include 'Helen Borchers' (semi-double clear pink flowers) and 'Icicle' (double white); these are your best bet where late frosts might damage earlier-blooming sorts.

P. persica nectarina. FLOWERING NECTARINE. Zones 2–24, 30–34, 39. The one flowering nectarine, 'Alma Stultz', bears delicate, pink-tinted, fragrant, 2½-inch-wide blossoms with an azalealike form. It grows quickly to 20 feet high and wide.

P. sargentii. SARGENT CHERRY. Zones 2–7, 14–17, 32–41. Reaching 40 to 50 feet tall and wide, this fast-growing flowering cherry has a spreading, vase-shaped structure and glossy red-brown bark. In the spring, branches are covered with small clusters of single blush pink blossoms. 'Columnaris' is a narrowly upright selection.

Prunus sargentii 'Columnaris'

PYRUS calleryana

CALLERY PEAR

Zones 2–9, 14–21, 28, 31–41
Full sun
Regular to moderate
Moderate

Callery pear is grown for the clustered pure white blooms that appear in very early spring (and may be nipped by late freezes in cold areas). The dark green leaves are attractive, too: they're broad, scallop-edged ovals 1½ to 3 inches long. The tree reaches 25 to 50 feet tall and has a strong horizontal branching pattern.

The named selections offered by nurseries are improvements on the species, which tends to be thorny. One available variety is 'Aristocrat', a pyramidal tree (to 36 feet tall, 16 feet wide) with upward-curving branches and yellow to red fall color; it is susceptible to fireblight. A fireblight-resistant choice is 'Chanticleer', a narrow pyramid 40 feet tall and 15 feet wide, with fall color ranging from orange to reddish purple.

These trees aren't fussy about soil type, even growing well in heavy clay, but they don't do their best in shallow soil.

QUERCUS

OAK

Zones vary
Full sun
Water needs vary
Growth rate varies

Among the oaks are some of our most treasured large shade trees. But not all oaks are large; you'll find small and medium-size sorts as well. Many (but not all) have the typical lobed leaves; all produce acorns. In general, oaks grow best in deep soil that provides the anchorage their root systems need. A few widely adapted oaks are listed here.

Q. coccinea. SCARLET OAK. Zones 2–24, 31–41. Deciduous. Grows at a moderate to fast rate, reaching 60 to 80 feet tall, 40 to 50 feet wide. It has a high, light, open-branching habit and deep roots—features that make it a good choice for a lawn or garden tree. Bright green, 3- to 6-inch-long leaves turn scarlet where autumn weather is cold. Give moderate water.

Pyrus calleryana

Quercus coccinea

Quercus palustris

Tilia cordata

Q. ilex. HOLLY OAK. Zones 4–24, warmer parts of 32. Evergreen. A dense tree that grows at a moderate rate to 40 to 70 feet high and broad. Leaves are dark green above, yellowish or silvery beneath; they reach 3 inches long and may have smooth or toothed edges. Needs moderate watering; tolerates wind and salt air. A good street or lawn tree.

Q. palustris. PIN OAK. Zones 2–10, 14–24, 28–41. Deciduous. Reaches 50 to 70 feet tall, 25 to 40 feet wide, growing at a moderate to fast rate. Young trees are pyramidal, but their outline broad-ens with maturity; lowest branches droop almost to the ground. The glossy dark green leaves are 3 to 6 inches long and wide, deeply cut into bristle-pointed lobes. In brisk fall weather, leaves turn yellow, then red, then russet brown. Needs plenty of water; tolerates poorly drained soils. Widely used as a lawn and street tree.

TILIA cordata

LITTLE-LEAF LINDEN

Zones 1–17, 32–43
Full sun
Regular
Moderate

Forming a dense pyramid to 60 to 70 feet or taller and 35 to 60 feet wide, little-leaf linden is densely clothed in 1½- to 3-inch, irregularly heart-shaped leaves that are dark green above, lighter beneath. Drooping clusters of creamy white flowers appear in summer. An excellent medium-size lawn or street tree; very tolerant of city conditions.

Imposing rhododendrons and other well-placed shrubs bring beauty to a Pacific Northwest garden.

Shrubs

While trees are the focal points that give the garden its general character, shrubs typically form the framework that ties the landscape together. They are the constant, often unobtrusive plantings that create backgrounds, direct foot traffic, and provide a smooth transition from tree canopy to ground level.

It's not always easy to tell the difference between a tree and a shrub, especially since some shrubs can grow large enough to tower over smaller trees. One way to make the distinction (short of consulting a reference book) is to look at the main stems. Trees are likely to have just a single trunk, while shrubs typically have several to many, often equal in size. Also see how the foliage grows: trees usually carry their leaves on branches growing from

points fairly high on the trunk, while most shrubs carry foliage right down to the ground.

Hundreds of shrubs are good choices for the garden. To narrow the field, start by considering only those suited to your climate (see pages 8–11). Next, think about the role you want each shrub to play. If you're looking for a plant with a strong structure to act as a "filler" between taller trees or buildings and a stretch of lawn, try one of the many large, broad-leafed evergreen sorts, such as sweet olive *(Osmanthus fragrans)*. For an informal border to edge the back of the garden or a formidable barrier against wind or intruders, start by reviewing the sampler beginning on page 109; for a formal hedge to be clipped into a geometric shape, look first to the choices on page 118. Maybe you want a shrub that will grace the garden with exceptional blossoms each year, such as rhododendron or lilac *(Syringa)*. Or perhaps your goal is to find a shrub with interesting leaf color, such as gold dust plant *(Aucuba japonica* 'Variegata') or variegated tobira *(Pittosporum tobira* 'Variegata'), to complement a planting of flowering perennials.

Planting and caring for shrubs

Depending on the plant, shrubs are sold in containers, bareroot, or balled-and-burlapped. You'll find step-by-step instructions for planting all three kinds on pages 36–39.

WATERING AND FERTILIZING. The water and fertilizer needs of shrubs vary widely, so it's important to learn each plant's requirements before purchase. You'll find that some need little water once established, while others require regular moisture throughout the growing season. Likewise, many shrubs need little fertilizer when mature, but they grow better in the long run

---

SETTING OTHER PLANTS AMONG ESTABLISHED SHRUBS

Planting annuals and perennials among established shrubs can be tricky. If you're constantly setting in and removing plants, the shrubs' root systems will be disturbed. Tough, carefree shrubs may not be bothered by such intrusion, but less rugged individuals may be weakened. In some cases, it's the "intruders" that suffer—the shrubs take most of the available nutrients and water for themselves. If you want a mixed bed of flowers and shrubs, consider choosing perennial flowers; they'll thrive for several years before needing digging and dividing. It's also a good idea to set out fairly small plants—those in 4-inch or 1-gallon pots. These require smaller planting holes and so disturb shrubs' roots less.

If you're adding a ground cover near or beneath shrubs, make sure that both plants have similar water needs. For example, a thirsty lawn isn't the best companion for shrubs that prefer dry conditions.

if given a complete fertilizer each spring during their younger years. A few shrubs, especially those that prefer constantly moist, rich soil, do best with annual feeding throughout their lifetimes. For information on specific shrubs, see the sampler on pages 109–119 or consult *Sunset*'s *National Garden Book* or a local nursery.

When you do fertilize, you'll find that controlled-release granular products offer an efficient way to do the job, providing sufficient nutrients to last for an entire growing season. Apply the fertilizer beneath the shrub, spreading it in a wide circle (as directed below); then work it into the top few inches of soil. If the shrubs have extensive surface root systems (rhododendron and camellia, for example), don't cultivate the soil beneath the plants deeply; to avoid disturbing roots, just barely scratch the fertilizer in.

When you apply fertilizer and water, keep in mind that many shrubs have surprisingly extensive root systems. Gardeners frequently treat an area only as wide as the shrub's above-ground spread, but roots often reach much farther than that. As a general rule, water and fertilize in a circle two to three times wider than the plant's diameter at ground level, wider still for tall, narrow shrubs (see "The Drip Line," page 45).

MULCHING. To conserve moisture and discourage weeds, apply a mulch around and between shrubs. If you fertilize in spring, mulch after fertilizing. If you need to fertilize later in the season, use a liquid type that will soak through the mulch or a foliar spray.

MANAGING PESTS AND DISEASES. Though it's easy to forget those sturdy, uncomplaining shrubs at the back of the garden, it's important to check all shrubs periodically for signs of pests and diseases. Regularly rinse dust and debris from plants with strong blasts of water from a hose; you'll get rid of pests and disease spores at the same time.

Continued >

DEADHEADING

Some of the most popular garden shrubs, such as azalea, rhododendron, and pieris, require little or no pruning aside from deadheading (removing faded flowers before they can set seed). For all its simplicity, this job is an important one: failure to do it will greatly reduce the quantity of blossoms produced the next year. To deadhead, snap off spent flower clusters between your thumb and index finger, as shown below. Be careful not to damage growth buds just below the cluster.

PRUNING SHRUBS

By pruning shrubs regularly (yearly, in most cases), you'll hold them to the size you want and keep them from becoming too dense (and then dying out in the center as a result). The pruning method you follow depends on the way the shrub grows—from the base or from an established framework of branches. The appropriate technique for each is shown below. Refer to pages 48–53 for information on basic pruning cuts and tools.

NEW STEMS FROM THE BASE
Most deciduous shrubs and some evergreen ones grow by producing new stems, or canes, from the plant's base. Keep these plants vigorous by periodically removing the oldest and weakest stems.

A FRAMEWORK OF BRANCHES
Most evergreen shrubs and some deciduous ones form a permanent framework of branches. Often, the only pruning required is the removal of dead, damaged, diseased, or unattractively placed branches.

DRASTICALLY
If the shrub withstands severe pruning (see the list of examples below right), you can cut back the whole plant to rejuvenate it.

GRADUALLY
Remove about a third of the oldest growth annually for 3 years, pruning stems back to the ground before new growth begins in spring.

Periodic hosing also helps prevent the dry, dusty conditions that encourage summertime pests such as spider mites.

The leaves that fall naturally from shrubs may decompose and add humus to the soil. But some leaves drop because they're diseased—those afflicted with black spot, for example. Unless you're certain that natural debris is disease free, rake it up in the fall and discard it in the trash (don't compost it).

SALVAGING OLD SHRUBS. If you move into a home whose garden is filled with overgrown and tangled shrubs, your first inclination may be simply to dig them out. This can be a major undertaking, however, and the resulting bare spots may take years to fill. Before you seize your shovel, try a salvage operation. Shrubs that grow from a framework of branches can sometimes be transformed into small trees. You may also be able to rejuvenate shrubs (both those growing from a branch framework and those that grow from the base) to restore them to a well-grown yet under-control appearance.

Transforming an overgrown shrub to a small tree. If a shrub has one to several largely upright main stems and a framework of branches, you can convert it to a small tree by removing the lower branches.

If just one main stem is in good shape or well placed, cut the rest to the ground; the remaining main stem will become the trunk of the "tree." Remove side stems on the trunk up to the point where you want branching to begin.

If the shrub has several good stems, you can leave them all. Remove side stems up to the point where you want branching to begin; then thin out those that remain to form an uncluttered crown for your new tree.

Rejuvenating shrubs that grow from a framework of branches. If you do not want to transform an overgrown shrub into a tree, you can sometimes force it to grow to a lower height. To do this, cut the highest branches back halfway, making heading cuts (see page 52). Select about a third of the branches for such treatment each year. Some of them may die, but others often sprout new growth at the lower level. Once you've achieved a smaller shrub with vigorous young growth, thin out any weak, badly placed, or crowding shoots.

Rejuvenating shrubs that grow from the base (see illustration at left). Many of the shrubs that grow directly from the base, sending up stems (canes) from the roots, can withstand severe pruning. Some of the plants described in this chapter that take such treatment are glossy abelia (*Abelia* × *grandiflora*), barberry (*Berberis*), forsythia, oleander (*Nerium oleander*), mock orange (*Philadelphus coronarius*), cinquefoil (*Potentilla fruticosa*), and spiraea. Cut all growth back to the ground before new spring growth begins; if the treatment is successful, the plant will usually achieve its normal height within several years.

If you're not sure that the shrub can take such drastic pruning, implement a 4-year program. Do no cutting the first year—just water and fertilize well to make the plant as healthy as possible. Over the next 3 years, remove about a third of the oldest stems annually, pruning them back to the ground just before growth begins in spring.

A SAMPLER OF SHRUBS

This sampler includes a number of basic shrubs—some evergreen, some deciduous, some imposingly large, others that nestle close to the ground. The choices here play a variety of roles in the landscape, serving as anything from lovely flowering specimen plants to thorny barrier hedges. For an explanation of the at-a-glance information introducing each entry, see page 95.

SYMBOLS: These symbols indicate whether the shrub is evergreen (🍃), semievergreen (🍃), or deciduous (🍃).

ABELIA × grandiflora
🍃 🍃 GLOSSY ABELIA

    🌡 ZONES 4–24, 28–35

    ☀ ☼ FULL SUN OR PARTIAL SHADE

    💧 REGULAR

This mounding, arching shrub grows 6 to 8 feet tall, 4 to 5 feet wide. Oval, glossy, ½- to 1-inch leaves often turn dark maroon in winter in milder zones; where winters are colder, some leaves drop. The main attraction appears from early summer through fall—clusters of tubular flowers in pure white or pink-tinged white.

Glossy abelia grows best in sun but tolerates some shade. It does well in regular soil. Stems freeze at 0°F/−18°C, but plants usually recover to bloom the same year, though they reach just 10 to 15 inches (they'll attain normal size after several seasons). Shearing and heading ruin this shrub's graceful shape; to prune, selectively cut out some branches at ground level.

AUCUBA japonica
🍃 JAPANESE AUCUBA

    🌡 ZONES 4–24, 28–33

    ☼ ● PARTIAL TO FULL SHADE

    💧 MODERATE

Valued for its ability to thrive in deep shade, Japanese aucuba reaches 6 to 10 feet tall, 5 to 8 feet wide; tooth-edged

Abelia × grandiflora

Aucuba japonica 'Variegata'

Berberis thunbergii

leaves are 3 to 8 inches long. The solid green form is attractive, but many prefer the yellow-and-green cultivars. Among these, the widely planted 'Variegata', commonly called gold dust plant, has green leaves speckled in yellow. All forms can be grown in containers to decorate a shady patio or deck. If both male and female plants are present, small maroon flowers in spring will be followed by red berries in fall and winter.

While it prefers a shady location, Japanese aucuba will tolerate some morning or filtered sun. It has no special soil requirements. Prune in late winter or early spring; make heading cuts to control form, thinning cuts back to a main branch to lessen density.

BERBERIS
🍃 🍃 BARBERRY

    🌡 ZONES VARY

    ☀ ☼ FULL SUN OR PARTIAL SHADE

    💧💧 REGULAR TO MODERATE

Their ability to endure extremes of soil and weather makes the barberries, especially the deciduous sorts, good choices for harsh climates. Branches are spiny—one reason barberries are favored for barrier hedges. The plants described below have small leaves and bear yellow spring flowers followed by autumn berries.

Barberries grow vigorously and need regular pruning to keep inner branches from dying. They prosper in ordinary garden soil and will tolerate heat and dryness.

Continued >

B. julianae. WINTERGREEN BAR-
BERRY. Zones 4–24, 28–32. Evergreen.
A dense, very thorny green shrub to 6 to 8
feet tall and wide, wintergreen barberry is
often grown as a barrier hedge. Berries
are blue black. This species is hardy to
0°F/−18°C, but there's some cold damage
to leaves at low temperatures (unless they
are protected by snow). A dwarf form,
'Nana', grows just 4 feet high and wide.

B. thunbergii. JAPANESE BAR-
BERRY. Zones 1–24, 28–41. Deciduous.
Often grown for colorful fall foliage; used
as either a specimen plant or a barrier
hedge. The species grows 4 to 6 feet tall
and wide. Its dark green leaves turn yellow, orange, and red in fall; autumn
berries are red and beadlike. Popular
cultivars include 'Atropurpurea' (same
size as the species) and 'Atropurpurea
Nana' ('Crimson Pygmy'), to 1½ feet tall
and 2½ feet wide; both have red foliage
that turns gold in fall.

🌿 CAMELLIA

🌡 Zones 4–9, 12, 14–24, 26–31,
AND WARMER PARTS OF 32 FOR
MOST; HARDY TYPES THROUGHOUT
32

◐ PARTIAL SHADE

◖◖ ◖ REGULAR TO MODERATE

Camellias belong on the list of best-loved
shrubs in North America. Rounded, shiny
green leaves are 2 to 3 inches long; delicate but showy flowers in white and many
shades of pink and red reach 3 to 5
inches across. Buy and plant camellias
while they're in bloom. You'll be able to
choose just the flower type and color you
want—and strange as it may seem,
blooming plants are also at their most
dormant stage, so they'll suffer minimal
stress from planting.

Camellias prefer well-amended,
slightly acid soil. Their roots grow near
the surface, so it's better not to set out
other plants beneath them or cultivate the
soil near them. Apply a 2-inch-thick
mulch around the plants to protect roots
from extremes of heat and cold. Feed

Camellia japonica

Chamaecyparis obtusa 'Gracilis'

with specially formulated camellia fertilizer, following package directions for timing and amounts.

Prune camellias immediately after
bloom, making thinning cuts so flowers
aren't hidden and growth doesn't become
too dense. You can also make heading
cuts to keep shrubs from getting too lanky
on top. Camellia petal blight, evidenced
by brown spots on flowers, is a disease
unique to these plants. Control it by picking off infected blooms and buds, clearing
all infected petals from the ground, and
removing and replacing mulch.

C. japonica. The most familiar
camellias are cultivars of *C. japonica.*
For almost continuous bloom, plant
more than one kind. Some start blooming in November, others in early spring;
still others flower from midspring until
May. Flowers may be single, semidouble,
or double. Although they can attain great
size with age, most grow 6 to 12 feet tall
and wide.

C. oleifera. In recent years, hybrids
of *C. oleifera* have given gardeners in
colder zones a wider choice of camellia

flower colors and sizes: before the intro-
duction of these plants, small-flowered
species camellias were the only types able
to withstand the colder temperatures.
Given some shelter from winter sun and
wind, *C. oleifera* hybrids tolerate lows of
−15°F/−26°C.

C. sasanqua. Gardeners living in
mild-winter climates can include hybrids
of *C. sasanqua* among their camellias.
Most bloom from late autumn through
winter, bearing single to semidouble
blossoms. They tolerate more sun than *C.
japonica* and have more pliable stems,
making them good candidates for training against a wall. They range from 1½ to
15 feet tall, with equal spread.

CHAMAECYPARIS obtusa 'Gracilis' and 'Nana Gracilis'

🌿 HINOKI CYPRESS

🌡 Zones 4–6, 15–17, 32-34,
36–41

☼ ◑ FULL SUN OR PARTIAL SHADE

◖ MODERATE

Of the many available Hinoki cypress cultivars, 'Gracilis' and 'Nana Gracilis' are
the favorites of many gardeners. Both are
deep green, with flat, feathery-looking
foliage sprays. Thanks to their narrow
habit, they provide a contrast in form to
many other shrubs—and they add year-
round greenery to the garden without
taking up much space. 'Gracilis' can
reach 20 feet high, 5 feet wide. 'Nana
Gracilis' grows to 5 feet tall and just 1½
feet wide; it's good in rock gardens, containers, or wherever a low-growing
conifer is useful. Similar to 'Nana Gracilis' in size and shape is 'Nana Aurea',
with brilliant yellow foliage.

These plants grow slowly, so purchase them in 15- or 5-gallon containers.
They prefer sun but will take partial
shade. Well-amended, well-drained soil
is best, but ordinary garden soil will do.
In the first year or two after planting, you
may need to make some thinning cuts to
direct growth; otherwise, leave plants
unpruned.

FORSYTHIA × intermedia

🌿 FORSYTHIA, GOLDEN BELLS

✂ ZONES 2–16, 18, 19, 30–41

☼ FULL SUN

💧💧 REGULAR TO MODERATE

This long-time favorite is one of first shrubs to flower in spring, when each arching branch is completely covered in bright yellow blossoms. Oval, medium green, 5-inch leaves emerge after bloom. The biggest mistake gardeners make with forsythia is crowding it into too narrow an area. Plant it only if you have plenty of room: it rapidly forms a mound to 8 feet or taller, 12 to 15 feet wide. 'Fiesta' (to 3 to 4 feet tall and wide) is a better choice for small gardens.

Forsythia thrives in less-than-ideal conditions, tolerating poor soils and cold winters. (In the coldest zones, plant 'Northern Sun' or 'Meadowlark', with flower buds hardy to −25°F/−32°C.) After bloom ends in spring, prune tattered shoots to ground level; you can remove up to a third of the plant's wood each year.

KALMIA latifolia

🌿 MOUNTAIN LAUREL

✂ ZONES 3–7, 16, 17, 28 (NORTH-ERNMOST FLORIDA), 31–41

☼ PARTIAL SHADE; SOME SUN WHERE SUMMERS ARE COOL

💧 REGULAR

A favorite since colonial times, this East Coast native is a slow grower (to an eventual 10 feet tall and broad) that makes a good underplanting for taller deciduous trees. Flowers, each shaped like a pendent chalice with five starlike points, come in clusters to 5 inches across. The species has medium pink blooms; cultivars offer colors ranging from pale pink to dark rose. Leathery, 2- to 4-inch, elongated oval leaves turn from deep green to greenish gold in winter.

Mountain laurel thrives in conditions suitable for rhododendrons, though it will accept more sun where summers are cool. Give it moist, acid soil well

amended with organic matter; spread a 2-inch-thick organic mulch around plants each spring. To ensure a good flower show the next year, pinch off spent blossoms after the bloom season is over.

Note: Leaves and flowers of mountain laurel are toxic if ingested.

Forsythia × intermedia

Kalmia latifolia

ABOVE: *Nandina domestica*
BELOW: *Nerium oleander*

NANDINA domestica

🌿 HEAVENLY BAMBOO

✂ ZONES 4–33

☼ ◐ ● FULL SUN, PARTIAL SHADE, OR FULL SHADE

💧 REGULAR

Fine-textured, narrow leaflets on lightly branched, canelike stems give this shrub the look of bamboo. It grows slowly to 6 to 8 feet tall, 2 to 3 feet wide, with an upright habit that makes it a fine choice for narrow areas or for containers. It's also a good informal hedge. The leaves often turn from green to vivid scarlet during fall and winter. Small, creamy white spring flowers are followed by red berries that last from fall into the next spring. Because not all plants bloom and fruit equally well, buy them when either flowers or berries are present, choosing those that are heavily laden.

Heavenly bamboo does well in sun or shade, but fall color is more pronounced on plants grown in the sun. It prefers well-amended garden soil but will tolerate poorer soils. To control height, prune individual tall stems to the ground in spring; also cut any tattered stems to the ground.

NERIUM oleander

🌿 OLEANDER

✂ ZONES 8–16, 18–31

☼ FULL SUN

💧💧 REGULAR TO LITTLE

This extremely tough shrub thrives in areas with fairly mild winters (lows to 15°F/−9°C) and warm to hot summers. Flowers in bright shades of red, pink, and salmon, as well as in white and yellow shades, appear in clusters at stem tips and bloom throughout much of the year; some varieties bear fragrant blooms. Narrow, glossy dark green leaves grow 4 to 12 inches long. The plant grows rapidly to form a rounded mound to 6 to 12 feet tall and wide. Smaller oleanders—to 4 to 5 feet tall and wide—are also sold.

Continued >

Oleander stands up to difficult growing conditions, including heat, drought, alkaline soil, and wind. It's often used for screens, windbreaks, or borders along roads or driveways. It's a good large container plant and can be pruned to grow as a single-stemmed standard, with branches emerging from the trunk about 5 feet above the ground.

Prune oleander regularly by removing older stems to the ground; if unpruned, plants become too dense, resulting in thinner foliage and fewer flowers. To reduce height, pinch out individual stem tips.

Note: All parts of oleander are toxic if ingested. Smoke from burning branches and leaves is also toxic if inhaled, so do not burn oleander prunings.

OSMANTHUS fragrans
✿ SWEET OLIVE
- ✎ ZONES 8, 9, 12–24, 26 (NORTHERN PART), 28–31
- ☼ ◑ FULL SUN OR PARTIAL SHADE
- ◐◐ REGULAR TO MODERATE

Though it naturally forms a mound, this background shrub can be pruned to grow upright where space is limited. It is favored by many for the intense fragrance of its tiny white flowers; just one or two plants can scent the entire garden for months (bloom is heaviest in spring and early summer). Leaves are glossy green, pointed ovals to 4 inches long. Sweet olive grows moderately fast, reaching 10 feet tall and 8 feet wide (if not pruned) in just a few years. With age, it can reach 20 feet. Cold-winter gardeners will have best success with the hybrid *O. × fortunei*, which has a slightly wider range than *O. fragrans* (Zones 5–10, 14–24, 28, 31, and warmer parts of 32).

Sweet olive is an easy-care plant that performs well in all soil types. It enjoys sun but appreciates afternoon shade in the warmest zones. Pinch out stem tips after bloom to increase bushiness. Where space is limited, stems can be cut back to main branches or to the ground.

Osmanthus fragrans

Philadelphus coronarius

Pieris japonica

PHILADELPHUS coronarius
✿ MOCK ORANGE
- ✎ ZONES 2–17, 30–41
- ☼ ◑ FULL SUN OR PARTIAL SHADE
- ◐◐ REGULAR TO MODERATE

Like sweet olive *(Osmanthus fragrans)*, mock orange is a favorite of many gardeners for its sweet-scented blossoms. A fast-growing shrub with arching, fountainlike form, it reaches 10 feet tall and wide and fits especially well in corners. Oval, pale green, 1½- to 4-inch-long leaves emerge in early spring; showy white, 1- to 4-inch, single or double blooms follow in early summer. 'Minnesota Snowflake' is a 6- to 8-footer that survives colder winters (reported hardiness to −30°F/−34°C); a smaller cultivar of this hybrid is 'Miniature Snowflake', to 3 feet tall and broad.

Give mock orange partial shade in the warmest areas. It tolerates ordinary garden soil but must have good drainage. After bloom is over, thin and neaten plants by cutting older, tattered stems to the ground. To rejuvenate an entire plant, cut it to the ground in early spring, before leaves appear.

PIERIS japonica
✿ PIERIS, LILY-OF-THE-VALLEY SHRUB
- ✎ ZONES 3–9, 14–17, 31–35, 37
- ☼◑ PARTIAL TO FULL SHADE
- ◐ REGULAR

A useful shrub for shady parts of the garden, pieris is often grown under taller broad-leafed evergreen trees. Most striking when it is adorned with white, pink, or nearly red flowers in late winter to early spring, it stays attractive throughout the year thanks to its glossy dark green foliage. Since it is taller than it is wide (to an eventual 9 by 6 feet), it's a suitable choice for somewhat narrow spaces. It grows slowly, so start with plants in 15- or 5-gallon containers.

Flowers of all pieris resemble lily-of-the-valley *(Convallaria)*, hence the common name.

Give moist, well-drained, acid soil rich in humus. Attractive shape and lush appearance make pieris a good companion for rhododendrons or azaleas, which sometimes have less desirable leaf coloration and leggy growth. Prune by pinching off dead flowers.

Note: Leaves and flowers of pieris are toxic if ingested.

PINUS mugo mugo
✿ MUGHO PINE
- ✎ ZONES 1–11, 14–24, 32–45
- ☼ FULL SUN
- ◐◐ REGULAR TO LITTLE

Also called dwarf mountain pine, this little conifer eventually achieves a height and width of 4 feet, with branching, upright stems evenly covered in 2-inch-long needles of a deep, dark true green. Thanks to its low growth, mugho pine can be used at the front of a border or anywhere you want year-round greenery in conifer form. Because it grows very slowly, start with a plant in a 15- or 5-gallon container.

Mugho pine does not need special soil; in nature, it often grows in slightly rocky areas with shallow topsoil. It does require good drainage, however. Roots grow near the surface; cover soil with a 2-inch-thick mulch to protect them. It performs best if left to grow naturally, so pick a plant with a pleasingly rounded form rather than trying to shape it later through pruning.

PITTOSPORUM tobira

🍃 TOBIRA

 ✒ ZONES 8–31
 ☼ ◑ FULL SUN OR PARTIAL SHADE
 💧💧 REGULAR TO MODERATE

Tobira is a dependable background or low foreground shrub that requires little attention and is widely planted in warm-winter zones. It grows at a moderate rate, attaining full size in just a few years. The species reaches 10 to 15 feet high with a spread of 8 to 10 feet; equally popular is 'Wheeler's Dwarf' (to 2 to 3 feet high, 1½ feet wide). Both have thick, elliptical, glossy green leaves. Another favorite is 'Variegata' (to 4 to 5 feet tall, 3 to 4 feet wide), with leaves marbled in pale green and white. Foliage of all tobiras grows in whorls; leaves reach 5 inches long. All bear clusters of small, intensely fragrant white spring flowers that are followed by chick pea–size green berries that ripen to brownish orange.

This tough shrub grows well in sun or partial shade and thrives in all soils, including unamended clay; it also tolerates ocean spray. It has a naturally rounded form and needs little pruning, but if growth becomes too dense, cut entire branches to the ground or take branches back to a main trunk. If you want to shape tobira as a hedge, make

heading cuts with hand-held pruners rather than hedge shears (they make jagged, ugly tears in the thick leaves). Do any pruning in spring, after bloom is over.

Pinus mugo mugo

Pittosporum tobira 'Variegata'

ABOVE: *Potentilla fruticosa*
BELOW: *Pyracantha*

POTENTILLA fruticosa

🍃 CINQUEFOIL

 ✒ 1–21, 32 (COOLER PARTS), 34–45
 ☼ ◑ FULL SUN OR PARTIAL SHADE
 💧 MODERATE

Its manageable size, long bloom season, and adaptability to many climates make cinquefoil one of the more popular deciduous shrubs. From summer to fall, branches are covered with 1-inch single flowers in white, yellow, or dark reddish orange. You'll find a dozen or more named cultivars with various blossom colors and heights of 1, 2, 3, or 4 feet; spread is slightly less than height in each case. Narrowly oval, green to gray-green leaves that reach less than an inch long clothe the random-growing, somewhat stiff branches.

Growth rate varies by cultivar; initial growth is often rapid, tapering off to a more moderate pace.

Cinquefoil grows best in well-drained soil. It prefers sun but needs some afternoon shade in the warmest regions. Prune each year after bloom to remove crossing, damaged, and older branches. To keep plants compact, you can cut them to the ground every few years as dormancy is ending in late winter.

PYRACANTHA

🍃 FIRETHORN

 ✒ ZONES VARY
 ☼ ◑ FULL SUN OR PARTIAL SHADE
 💧 MODERATE

Grown for its bright red, orange, or yellow fruits and its deep green foliage, fast-growing firethorn ranks high on the list of popular shrubs. All its forms have small, glossy leaves, and most have needlelike thorns; creamy white spring blossoms are followed by thick clusters of pea-size berries that provide vivid color in fall and winter and attract birds. Limber branches make firethorn a good candidate for growing against a fence, mounding over uneven terrain, or espaliering. Cold resistance varies, so purchase plants locally or ask about hardiness if you're buying by mail.

Firethorn takes ordinary soil and grows well in sun or partial shade. It is prone to fireblight (see page 78), especially in humid areas. For best success, buy disease-resistant varieties such as 'Apache'.

RHODODENDRON

🌿🌿 RHODODENDRON
AND AZALEA

- 🌿 ZONES 4–6, 15–17, 34, 37, AND
  39 FOR BEST PERFORMANCE
- ◑ LIGHT SHADE
- ◆ REGULAR

Both azaleas and rhododendrons belong to the same genus: *Rhododendron*. The group as a whole includes over 800 species, and countless cultivars have been developed from these.

These shrubs have exacting requirements. They prefer light shade or filtered sun (a good planting location is the area underneath high-branching trees). They need acid soil that's well drained but constantly moist; to meet this need, you must either add large quantities of organic matter to planting beds or—if the native soil can't be adequately amended—grow plants in containers. As a rule, they must have moist air and don't thrive in hot, dry climates, though some handle such conditions better than others. They perform most consistently in the zones listed above, but some cultivars and species also thrive in other areas; for best success, consult local nurseries or your Cooperative Extension Office for advice on rhododendrons and azaleas that do well in your region.

Deadhead shrubs after bloom (as shown on page 107) to ensure a good flower show the next year. Individual stems may be cut back to main branches in late winter if plants are becoming too dense or too tall.

RHODODENDRONS. The most popular rhododendrons are medium to large

Rhododendron

Spiraea japonica

evergreen shrubs with rounded clusters (trusses) of blooms in white and many shades of pink, red, purple, yellow, salmon, and peach. Elliptical, leathery, deep green leaves reach 5 inches or longer. Your selection will depend on your climate (some rhododendrons are hardier to cold than others), the flower color appropriate for your garden, and the plant's ultimate size. The most widely available rhododendrons grow slowly to 6 to 8 feet high and wide, but you'll also find choices in the 3-foot range. A common mistake is to plant a rhododendron too close to a house or walkway, where it soon outgrows the space.

AZALEAS. The many azaleas include both evergreen and deciduous kinds; all of them typically bear small (1- to 2-inch), pointed-oval leaves. Deciduous sorts are typically showier than evergreen types, and they're less particular about soil as well. They bear masses of blooms in shades of yellow, orange, and flame red; you'll also find some bicolors. Fall

foliage is often brilliantly striking, ranging from orange red to plain red to maroon.

Evergreen azaleas are an excellent choice where year-round greenery is wanted. Many do best in warmer climates, though new cultivars are extending the range. These plants offer a variety of sizes and flower colors. The smaller growers are often used as borders for shady pathways; they're also popular as flowering gift plants (you'll see these sold in nurseries, florists' shops, and supermarkets).

🌿 SPIRAEA

- 🌿 ZONES VARY
- ☀ ◑ FULL SUN OR PARTIAL SHADE
- ◆ REGULAR

Two distinctly different sorts of these easy-to-grow shrubs are commonly planted. The bridal wreath type has long, arching branches that grow from the ground to form a vaselike shrub; in early spring, branches are covered with small white flowers. Also popular are summer-blooming spiraeas that form smaller, rounded mounds and bear white or pink blossoms, often in flat-topped clusters. Both types are unfussy about soil and moderately fast growing. In the warmest areas, they appreciate afternoon shade.

S. japonica. Zones 2–9, 14–21, 32–41. Ranging from 1½ to 4½ feet tall depending on variety, this spiraea has a naturally mounding form and a long summer bloom season. Oval, serrated leaves range from 1½ to 4 inches long. One widely grown form is 'Shirobana', a neat 2- to 3-foot mound with flower clusters in white, light pink, and deep rose—all on the same plant.

Prune *S. japonica* and its varieties by removing older branches to ground level in late winter to early spring, just before the dormant period ends.

S. vanhouttei. Zones 1–11, 14–21, 29–43. This is the classic bridal wreath spiraea. From mid- to late spring through early summer, the leafy branches are covered with circular, flattened clusters of small (½-inch) single white blossoms. Dark green, slightly oval, serrated leaves grow 1 to 1½ inches long. Allow plenty of room for this shrub; it can reach 6 to 8 feet tall and just as wide. To prune, cut old or oversized branches back to the ground after bloom is over.

SYRINGA
🌿 LILAC
✿ ZONES VARY
☀ ◑ FULL SUN OR PARTIAL SHADE
💧 REGULAR

These multistemmed shrubs are cherished for the showy, usually fragrant flowers that cluster at their stem tips. While their foliage and overall appearance are somewhat less than striking, many gardeners consider the bland out-of-bloom looks a small price to pay for the blossoms. Be patient when you buy a lilac: plants usually don't bloom until they reach 2 to 5 years old.

Lilacs do best in climates with winter chill, since they need cold to set blossoms. They prefer sun but need some shade where summers are hot. Give them regular water and well-drained, well-amended, neutral to slightly alkaline soil. If soil is acid, adjust the pH before planting as discussed on page 23.

Rejuvenate old, overgrown plants by cutting a few of the oldest stems to the ground each year. Prune to shape during bloom, cutting currently flowering or spent stems back to a main branch.

S. patula 'Miss Kim'. Zones 1–9, 14–16, 32–43. Several smaller species lilacs are gaining popularity; *S. patula* 'Miss Kim' is one of the most widely grown. It stays at about 4 feet tall and 3 feet wide for many years. Flowers are pale lavender blue and very fragrant; dark green leaves turn purple in fall.

S. vulgaris. Zones 1–11, 14, 32–45. This species and its hybrids are among the most fragrant of all lilacs. The species eventually reaches a height of 20 feet, with nearly equal spread. Flowers are pinkish lavender, bluish lavender, or white. Over the years, many hundreds of varieties (often called French hybrids) have been developed from *S. vulgaris*; they vary in form and size and bear flowers in pink, lavender, purple, wine red, or white.

Note: If you live in a warm-winter climate and can't get lilacs to bloom, choose one of the Descanso Hybrids of *S. vulgaris*. Developed in Southern California, these are especially well suited to winters with little or no frost.

🌿🌿 VIBURNUM
✿ ZONES VARY
☀ ◑ FULL SUN IN WINTER AND SPRING, LIGHT SHADE IN SUMMER
💧 REGULAR

This is a large, diverse group, including more than 150 species and countless cul-

Syringa vulgaris

Viburnum tinus

tivars. Some are evergreen, others deciduous; all bear clustered, sometimes fragrant flowers followed by fruits (often brightly colored) much appreciated by birds. We describe just two popular choices below.

While they generally prefer slightly acid soil, most viburnums are very tolerant of various soil types and conditions. They do, however, need good drainage. Mulch well to keep the root area moist and cool. For best performance, give plants full sun in winter and spring, light shade in summer.

V. carlesii. KOREAN SPICE VIBURNUM. Zones 2–11, 14–24, 31–41. Deciduous. The spice viburnums are noted for their 2- to 3-inch clusters of sweet-scented white flowers that open from pink buds. Dull green, 2- to 3-inch-long leaves turn reddish purple before dropping in autumn. Most varieties of this species reach 4 to 5 feet tall and wide; 'Compactum' is a round ball to 3 feet tall and wide. 'Cayuga' is noted for its attractive foliage as well as its dense blossom clusters.

V. tinus. LAURUSTINUS. Zones 4–10, 12–23, 26, 28–31; 33 with some risk of frost damage. Evergreen. One of several popular evergreen viburnums, laurustinus has lightly scented white flowers opening from pink buds; the bloom period runs from late winter to early spring, when little else in the garden is in flower. Bright metallic blue fruits follow the flowers and last through summer. Leathery, dark green, oval leaves are 2 to 3 inches long. Laurustinus grows 6 to 12 feet tall and 3 to 8 feet wide, making it a good choice for spots where you want a tall, fairly narrow shrub. It can also be grown as an informal hedge (it has dense foliage right to the ground). The species is susceptible to mildew; a resistant variety, 'Lucidum', is available, but it's less cold hardy than the species, growing only in Zones 8, 9, 12–23, 26, 28, 29. 'Spring Bouquet' ('Compactum') is shorter than the species (to 6 feet); 'Dwarf' is shorter still, to 3 to 5 feet.

ROSES

Roses are perhaps the most beloved of all flowers, esteemed throughout history for their form, color, and fragrance. Until fairly recently, gardeners tended to focus on hybrid teas, elegant modern roses featuring a stylish bud on a long stem. Lately, though, old roses— historic classes such as alba and damask, Bourbon and China—have made a strong comeback. Popular, too, are the shrub roses developed by modern breeders, rugged plants that function as shrubs in the landscape and offer the bonus of beautiful, long-lasting bloom.

Of course, you don't need to study the history of roses or distinguish between the many forms to appreciate these marvelous flowers. To enjoy them to the full, though, do aim to include an assortment of types in your garden. The choices shown on these pages—just five varieties out of the thousands available!—give a hint of what you'll find at nurseries and in catalogs. (For a few possibilities among ground cover and climbing roses, see pages 138 and 146.) Most nurseries carry a fair selection of hybrid teas and other modern roses. Old roses, too, are being offered ever more frequently; if your local nursery doesn't stock them, ask for the names of mail-order suppliers.

Rose hips

In the descriptions that follow, the date given in parentheses after the name of each rose indicates the year in which it was introduced or first recorded.

PLANTING AND CARING FOR ROSES

The best time to buy roses is in late winter, when they're available as dormant bare-root plants, or during the first bloom flush of spring, when they're sold as flowering container plants (shop early for the widest possible selection). For planting instructions, see pages 36–38.

Roses appreciate well-amended soil. If you know you'll be planting bare-root roses at some time in winter, clean up the area and amend the soil in fall. That will leave you with less work to do come planting time, when the weather is often cold and

'BALLERINA' (1937)

is a mounded shrub to 4 feet high and wide (sometimes larger in warmer climates), covered throughout the growing season in single, white-centered pink blossoms. The glossy, elongated leaflets are disease resistant. Classed as a hybrid musk, 'Ballerina' is considered by many to be just the type of rose more and me gardeners are looking for today—a plant with an attractive shrubby shape as w as profuse bloom.

unpredictable and you may be rushing to set in a bare-root pl between storms.

Because most modern roses put out new growth and flow throughout the growing season, they need regular water and c sistent fertilizing during that time. In general, a rose needs c stantly moist (but not soggy) soil to the full depth of its roots. T can take up to 5 gallons of water per rose in sandy soil, almo gallons in loam, and up to 13 gallons in clay. Water again when top few inches of soil are dry—usually within a week for sa soil, 10 days for loam, and up to 2 weeks for clay. Mulch arou plants to enhance moisture retention.

Roses are heavy feeders. Many gardeners prefer to wor controlled-release complete fertilizer into the top few inches soil at the start of the growing season (before applying a mulc If you don't go the controlled-release route, plan on feeding yo repeat-flowering roses every 6 weeks (with a dry granular fer izer) or every month (with a liquid fertilizer). Stop fertiliz about 6 weeks before the first frost date—or in September, if y live in a mild-winter climate.

With repeat-flowering kinds, deadhead spent blooms re larly, cutting back several inches to a five-leaflet leaf. If the r bears attractive hips, stop deadheading in September. You'll able to enjoy the brightly colored hips during autumn, and yo also be sending a signal to the plant that it's time to slow do and prepare for dormancy. There's no need to deadhead ros that flower just once a year.

'GRAHAM THOMAS' (1983)

is one of the first—and still one of the most popular—of the group called English roses, plants bred to combine modern rose colors and repeat bloom with old rose floral style. Some feature globular, ultra-double blossoms, while others have single flowers reminiscent of wild roses. 'Graham Thomas' has plump, red-tinted yellow buds that open to large, cupped blossoms filled with butter yellow petals. Blooms are carried at the ends of arching canes that can reach 10 feet or longer.

'ICEBERG' (1958)

If you think you can't grow roses, try easy-to-grow 'Iceberg'. It's a vigorous, sparsely thorned plant that is rarely bothered by pests and diseases. It belongs to the floribunda class, a complex group of roses that typically range in height from 2½ to 4 feet; some bear large clusters of single or semidouble, rather informal blossoms, while many have blooms resembling small hybrid tea flowers. 'Iceberg' is also available in a climbing form.

'MISTER LINCOLN' (1964)

For many, a long-stemmed red rose is the one rose to have. 'Mister Lincoln' is among the best , boasting perfectly formed buds, beautiful open blossoms, and a wonderful fragrance. And although many hybrid teas form rather ungainly bushes, this one is an attractive urn-shaped shrub.

'PEACE' (1945)

is so well known it hardly needs description. Full, ovoid buds of yellow touched with pink or red slowly unfurl to glorious extra-large blossoms with pink-rimmed yellow petals. A vigorous hybrid tea, 'Peace' has large, strong-growing canes; it can reach 4 feet tall and wide (even taller if pruned only lightly each year). Leaves are large, glossy, and disease resistant.

PRUNING ROSES

When should you prune? Repeat-blooming roses are usually pruned just before dormancy ends in late winter or early spring. Roses that bloom only once a season are traditionally pruned just after the bloom period ends; strong new growth produced after bloom will bear flowers the following spring.

The amount of pruning you'll do depends on the rose. Most old garden and modern shrub roses need little pruning; you'll prune simply to remove dead or damaged limbs or to lightly control growth.

Other roses, such as hybrid teas and grandifloras, usually get more extensive pruning; they tend to produce larger blooms on longer, stronger stems if a portion of the previous year's growth is shortened and weak and old wood is removed. When you prune, first remove any weakened or winter-damaged stems; then cut out those growing at odd angles (see illustrations at left).

After you have removed all unwanted growth, reduce the length of the remaining stems. In mild-winter regions, cut them back by about one-third to one-half. In cold-winter regions, cut out dead and damaged stems after you remove protection (see page 92); the final size of the bush depends on the severity of the past winter.

Ready for pruning, a dormant bush will be leafless or nearly so (in mild-winter climates, you may need to strip off some leaves). You will see many stems and twigs of varying thicknesses, ages, and health.

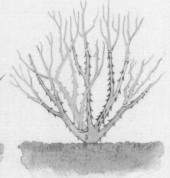

Entirely remove old canes that produced no strong growth during the last year, branches that cross through bush's center, and twiggy, weak stems. Shorten growth that remains.

FORMAL HEDGES

While many shrubs are suitable for formal clipping and shearing, just a handful of plants are the most popular choices. Most are available in various sizes, and some offer both deciduous and evergreen forms. The plants described below are evergreen unless otherwise noted.

ENGLISH YEW *(Taxus baccata)* is the classic choice for a formal hedge: it's the conifer you see bordering garden beds on palace grounds, forming mazes, and trimmed into fanciful topiary. It succeeds in Zones 3–9, 14–24, 32, 33, and the warmest parts of 34; it's not suitable for very cold or very hot regions. As its uses make plain, it easily tolerates frequent shearing and pruning. It grows slowly, so you'll need to be patient if your goal is to replicate the hedges you've seen in famous English gardens.

LEYLAND CYPRESS *(Cupressocyparis leylandii)* is an excellent choice for gardeners who want the lush look of a neatly pruned conifer but don't want to wait for a yew hedge to grow. It's suited to Zones 3–24, 26, 28–34, 39. In 5 years, it will reach 15 to 20 feet high—and because it isn't bothered by strong winds, the hedge can double as a windbreak. To keep it manageable, prune it moderately to severely on a regular basis.

JAPANESE OR WAX-LEAF PRIVET *(Ligustrum japonicum)*, successful in Zones 4–31 and the warmer parts of 32, is another alternative to English yew. You might try this one if you want a

faster-growing evergreen than yew or live in a warm-winter climate where yew won't thrive. Like yew, Japanese privet can be clipped as a formal hedge or into forms such as globes and pyramids. Leaves are 2- to 4-inch ovals, but new growth rapidly covers cuts made by shearing. Japanese privet's normal height is 10 to 12 feet, but you can prune it lower or choose lower-growing cultivars.

COMMON PRIVET *(Ligustrum vulgare)*, suitable for Zones 2–24, 30–41, is another popular hedge privet. It's deciduous; the 1- to 3-inch leaves turn from dark green to purplish green before falling in autumn. If left unpruned, it reaches 15 feet tall and 20 feet wide. A more compact form is *L. vulgare* 'Lodense' ('Nanum'), a dense-growing dwarf to just 4 feet high and wide.

COMMON BOXWOOD *(Buxus sempervirens)*, adapted to Zones 3–6, 15–17, 31–34, 39, is a classic hedge shrub. It can reach 15 feet high and wide, but you'll usually see it pruned smaller. When lightly pruned, bushes spill and mound over each other; clipped into boxy, straight-edged geometrical shapes, they line pathways and define the edges of formal plantings. The matte green, oval leaves are just 1 inch long; the small size makes the plant a good candidate for shearing, since cut marks are inconspicuous. Common boxwood cannot tolerate alkaline soils or hot summers.

JAPANESE BOXWOOD *(Buxus microphylla japonica)* is a popular alternative to common boxwood; it grows in Zones 3–24, 26–34, 39. It does fine in alkaline soils and hot weather, but looks shabby during winter in the colder parts of its range. It's similar in leaf size and plant shape to common boxwood but much smaller overall, slowly growing to 3 to 6 feet tall and wide. It has shiny (rather than matte), yellowish green leaves.

COMMON MYRTLE *(Myrtus communis)* is suited to Zones 8–24, 26–28. It naturally forms a rounded shrub (to 5 to 6 feet tall) but also takes well to formal clipping. It has small, pointed leaves and fragrant white spring or summer flowers. 'Compacta' has even smaller leaves and reaches just 2 to 3 feet high, making it a good choice for an edging or a low formal hedge. In general, myrtles grow wider than they're high.

JAPANESE HOLLY *(Ilex crenata)* is an alternative to myrtle or boxwood for colder zones; it flourishes in Zones 2–9, 14–24, 28, 31–35, 37. It looks more like boxwood than holly, with small, oval leaves and a naturally mounding habit. Many cultivars are available, differing mainly in size; those most commonly used for hedges reach 3 to 4 feet high and wide. When you prune Japanese holly, it's best to make individual cuts with hand-held pruners rather than shearing the plant.

HOW TO GROW A FORMAL HEDGE

To plant a formal hedge, space shrubs more closely than usual, typically setting them only one-half to one-third as far apart from each other as the planting directions indicate. However, do leave the full recommended spacing between plants and a walkway or other permanent barrier. Otherwise, you'll end up doing more than the desirable amount of pruning to keep the plants in bounds, and the hedge will show a lot of bare wood.

In most cases, you'll prune shrubs at planting time to force branching and encourage a thick hedge that's foliaged to the ground. Cut back larger deciduous plants by about a third, smaller ones to within several inches of the ground. Also cut back fast-growing broad-leafed evergreen plants, but less severely than deciduous sorts. Don't

Sheared boxwood *(Buxus)* makes a good low edging for beds of ornamentals.

head back slow-growing broad-leafed evergreens or conifers; just shorten their lateral branches.

During the rest of the first year, don't prune again except to trim overly vigorous shoots. In subsequent years, cut back new growth by about half to encourage dense branching. Prune after the initial spring growth flush, then again later in the season if needed. In regions where plants are subject to frost damage, don't prune after midsummer.

No matter what the hedge's shape, slope the sides so that the bottom is wider than the top. This allows sunlight to reach the entire hedge surface, stimulating growth all over the plant.

REJUVENATING A FORMAL HEDGE

You're faced with a horrid-looking formal hedge. Perhaps it's a tangled thicket looming over your head; perhaps it's spindly and full of bare wood. What to do now? Before you resort to the Herculean task of digging the whole thing out, try to rejuvenate it, returning it to a more informal look. If the shrubs grow from a framework of branches, do the job gradually; don't remove more than a third of the growth each year. Begin by thinning out dense outer clusters of twigs throughout the crown; cut each cluster back to a lateral branch. Also remove weak or crossing branches. The next year, continue to remove more twiggy clusters; also remove new growth that's poorly placed. By the third year, the hedge should begin looking more natural.

If the shrubs grow from the base, you can try pruning the hedge right down to the ground, then letting it regrow. Fast-growing deciduous shrubs such as common privet *(Ligustrum vulgare)* are good subjects for this treatment. Consult a local nursery or your Cooperative Extension Office to find out if a particular hedge can take severe cutting back (if it can't, follow the steps described on page 108 for rejuvenating such shrubs gradually).

To begin the process, cut back all growth to about 6 inches above ground just before plants break dormancy in spring. Remove debris and dig out weeds and other plants that have taken root in the area. When new growth emerges, feed with a controlled-release complete fertilizer; then water thoroughly and apply a mulch. Each month for the rest of the growing season, reduce new growth by half to encourage side branching and make the renewed hedge dense. As you cut back, take care to slope the hedge's sides as shown below.

Until the hedge reaches its desired height, cut growth back by half each month during the growing season, starting when plants begin growth in spring. Once the hedge is as tall as you want it, clip it at least twice a year, in late spring and midsummer, to maintain size, shape, and density.

WRONG   **RIGHT**

SLOPING THE SIDES OF A HEDGE

Slope the sides of a clipped or sheared hedge so that the bottom is wider than the top, allowing sunlight to reach the entire hedge surface. Without adequate light, the lower leaves and stems will die. In snowy climates, a peaked or rounded top will keep snow from accumulating on the hedge and possibly damaging it.

LAWNS

Lawns are one of the most important elements of the traditional garden landscape, and they remain popular today. But the scale has changed—instead of wide expanses of turf, you're likely to find cool, green pockets that share the garden equally with other plants.

THE CONTEMPORARY LAWN

Once upon a time, much of the available garden space was devoted to lawn. In recent years, however, there has been a grass-roots movement (pun intended!) to make lawns smaller. In parts of the country where substantial summer watering is needed just to keep lawns alive, local officials urge gardeners to reduce the area planted with grass in an effort to bring down water use (some experts suggest that current lawn coverage should be reduced by 25 to 30%). Shrinking lot sizes, too, have forced many gardeners to rethink the value of a lawn. It was once rare to see a home with no front lawn—but more and more, the green turf is giving way to shrubs, flowers, ground covers, or even vegetable beds.

Ringed by trees and low-growing plants, this small circle of lawn provides both a pretty patch of green and a play area.

In this California garden, flowers and vegetables fill the space once occupied by a front lawn.

Smaller lawns also mean less time spent on upkeep and maintenance. New, lightweight push mowers make it easy to keep a small lawn trimmed. Among power mowers, battery-operated models are quiet and non-polluting, require less maintenance than gas mowers, and eliminate the annoyance of tripping over electric cords while mowing. Hybrid grasses are being developed for every climate that grow more slowly than their predecessors—and thus require less frequent mowing.

Of course, lawns continue to play a useful role, providing a pleasant setting for outdoor activities and a safe place for children to play. But one study suggests that just 600 square feet of lawn is sufficient for most activities. Reducing the size of your lawn is easily accomplished by extending the beds surrounding the grass farther into the lawn by a few feet, then filling the reclaimed area with appropriate plants of your choice. You can also convert the center of the lawn to a planting bed as shown on the facing page, using a garden hose as your design tool.

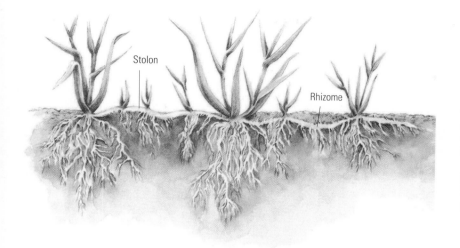

Stolon

Rhizome

LAWN GRASSES

Most lawn grasses spread by creeping stems growing either aboveground (stolons) or below ground (rhizomes). As the stems advance, they send up shoots, ultimately producing a thick, carpetlike turf.

Unlike almost all other plants, grasses grow from the base, not the tip. After you mow the lawn, the grass blades renew their length from the root end, or new blades sprout from the base.

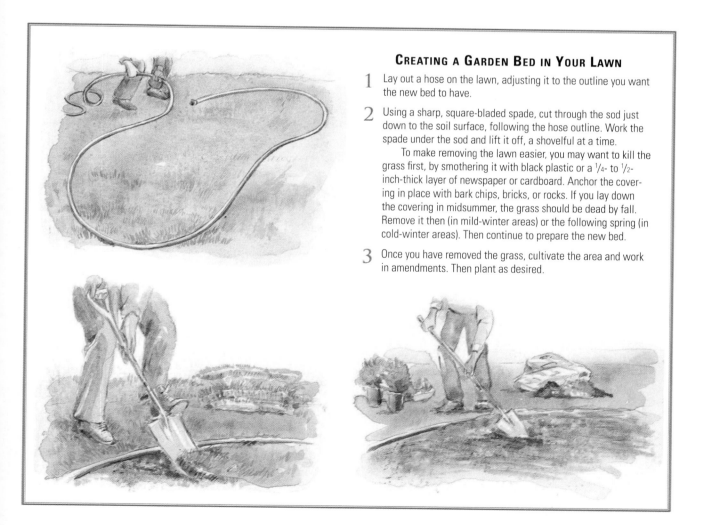

CREATING A GARDEN BED IN YOUR LAWN

1 Lay out a hose on the lawn, adjusting it to the outline you want the new bed to have.

2 Using a sharp, square-bladed spade, cut through the sod just down to the soil surface, following the hose outline. Work the spade under the sod and lift it off, a shovelful at a time.

To make removing the lawn easier, you may want to kill the grass first, by smothering it with black plastic or a $1/4$- to $1/2$-inch-thick layer of newspaper or cardboard. Anchor the covering in place with bark chips, bricks, or rocks. If you lay down the covering in midsummer, the grass should be dead by fall. Remove it then (in mild-winter areas) or the following spring (in cold-winter areas). Then continue to prepare the new bed.

3 Once you have removed the grass, cultivate the area and work in amendments. Then plant as desired.

A blend of perennial rye and Kentucky blue grass makes an attractive play surface—one that easily cushions falls and handles toddlers' rough-and-tumble games.

HANDLING SHADE

Like many other plants, grasses prefer a sunny location. If you're considering planting lawn in a deeply shaded area, think first about alternatives. Could the area be covered with nonplant material, such as decorative bark or stone? Would a shade-loving ground cover be a satisfactory substitute for grass? If a lawn is still your top choice, decide how to let as much light as possible into the area; you may be able to thin the canopy of a tree or remove low-growing branches, for example. Given more sunlight, the lawn will be thicker, have fewer weeds, and be better able to resist diseases and pests.

Some grasses handle shade better than others; tall fescues and St. Augustine are good choices. Consult a local nursery that carries a wide variety of grasses (both seed and sod) for a list of hybrids best suited to shade.

Let grass in shady conditions grow about an inch higher than you would if it were in sun; this compensates for the plants' reduced ability to manufacture nutrients in low-light conditions. Be sure to water regularly and fertilize at the rate recommended for the particular grass.

Tall fescue *(Festuca elatior)*

GRASS TYPES

Lawn grasses fall into two general categories: cool-season and warm-season. Each group comprises a wide variety of grasses. Water and fertilizer needs differ between the two groups, and susceptibility to some pests and diseases varies as well. Where you live usually dictates the type of grass you can grow, although cool-season sorts succeed in many areas if given sufficient water.

COOL-SEASON GRASSES. Most widely grown in the northern parts of the United States, these grasses can retain their color all year round if they receive enough water from rain or irrigation. They aren't recommended for very hot climates (whether dry of humid). You will, however, find hybrids intended especially for the warmer, more southerly parts of the range; for extremely cold-winter areas; and for regions with particular needs (high-elevation areas or those where grasses do better if resistant to specific diseases, for example).

Cool-season grasses include the "premier" lawn grasses: *blue grass* (the all-time favorite lawn grass), *perennial rye grass, bent grass,* and *fine fescue.* All have narrow blades and good color, and make lush-looking lawns. Many of the blue grass hybrids are very cold tolerant. Bent grass has the finest texture of all; you'll see it most often on putting greens or used as a garden accent in a rarely-walked-on spot. *Tall fescue* is another cool-season choice.

Perennial rye grasses are famed for their toughness; they're a top choice for playgrounds and for football and other playing fields.

Tall fescues, too, do well on playing fields. They're also good on unstable slopes. Compared to many other cool-season choices, they are more shade tolerant, less thirsty, and slower growing (so need mowing less often). In recent years, they have become an increasingly popular alternative to blue grasses and fine fescues.

Many of the cool-season grasses on the market are blends. One common mixture combines blue grass (for color and lushness) with perennial rye (for toughness). Bent grass, too, is often included in blends to give the lawn a lusher look. These blends are developed by seed manufacturers and sod producers to suit specific situations; some take more wear and tear and others more shade, for example.

WARM-SEASON GRASSES. Unlike cool-season grasses, warm-season sorts go partially to completely dormant during winter (depending on how cold the weather gets) whether water is available or not. The group includes *common Bermuda* and *hybrid Bermuda, zoysia, St. Augustine, bahia, centipede,* and *buffalo* grasses. All grow most vigorously during hot weather, and most are grown in the warm climates of the South and Southeast, as well as in some parts of the Southwest and Far West. Buffalo grass has so far been most widely used in Texas and parts of the Great Plains states.

Common and hybrid Bermuda are among the most popular warm-season grasses. Both are relatively drought tolerant and very resistant to wear and tear. Hybrid Bermuda is finer textured than common Bermuda and and doesn't turn brown in winter as readily.

Perhaps the toughest and most drought tolerant of all the warm-season grasses is zoysia. It's also one of the most attractive, but it tends to go dormant sooner and stay dormant longer than the others.

Note that both Bermuda and zoysia are so tough and vigorous that it's hard to eliminate them should you ever want to replace them with a different type of grass. Both are invasive, as well: they'll travel into other parts of the garden via underground or above-ground runners. Be sure to monitor them and remove stray growth regularly.

St. Augustine is another tough (and invasive) variety; it tolerates shade and seaside conditions. It's moderately drought tolerant but looks quite shabby during winter.

Drought-tolerant bahia grass is a good choice where soil is sandy or acid; it's popular in Florida. Centipede grass is widely used throughout the South in regions where soil is infertile, acid, or both. It needs regular water and doesn't take heavy foot traffic.

This informal buffalo grass lawn needs only minimal attention to watering and mowing.

Gaining in popularity is our native buffalo grass. It forms the sort of even-looking, "classic" lawn we associate with cool-season grasses, but it survives intense summer heat and retains its color for much of the summer with little additional water (though it does tend to turn brown as summer draws to a close). It thrives in many parts of the country, even in areas where cool-season grasses are grown—but gardeners in those regions prefer grasses that stay green year-round. However, new hybrids are being developed that hold their green color longer, giving buffalo grass a wider appeal.

One drawback to warm-season grasses is that they're difficult to establish from seed (with the exception of bahia and centipede grass) and must be started from sod, plugs, or sprigs (see page 131). Of those started from plugs or sprigs, St. Augustine and Bermuda initially spread and fill in faster than the others.

St. Augustine is one lawn choice for warm, humid climates. It prefers close cutting (to about 1½ inches), as shown here.

Oscillating sprinkler

Dual-arm revolving sprinkler

Rotary sprinkler

Pulsating sprinkler

Walking sprinkler

WATERING

Though lawns do need lots of water, many gardeners are *too* generous, often providing twice the amount the lawn really needs. Overwatering does more than just waste water. It leaches fertilizer and natural soil nutrients from the root zone; it creates perpetually wet conditions that can encourage disease. And a heavily watered lawn grows faster and requires more mowing.

In general, warm-season grasses require less moisture than cool-season types; the tall fescues are among the least needy of the cool-season sorts. On average, however, most of the grasses described on pages 122–123 need 1 to 2 inches of water per week (except when rainfall makes up the difference). To encourage roots to grow deep, it's best to water infrequently, adding the 1 to 2 inches all at one go. If you simply sprinkle on a little water each day, the roots will stay near the surface. If there is then a prolonged dry spell or if you forget to water, the root system won't be able to draw enough water from deeper in the soil to survive.

After watering, wait until the top inch or two of soil has dried before watering again. To check, probe the soil with a thick piece of wire or a long screwdriver: it will move easily through moist soil but stop when it reaches firmer, dry soil. You can also use a soil sampling tube (see page 41). An even faster way to tell if a lawn needs watering is simply to walk across it. If your footprints remain for several minutes, it's time to water (a well-watered lawn springs right back).

Water early in the day, when there's less moisture loss due to heat evaporation and wind is less likely to blow water away. If you need to water later in the day, do so well before dusk, so the grass will dry before nightfall; grass that stays damp for long periods is typically more susceptible to disease.

SPRINKLERS

Most lawns are watered by sprinklers—either the hose-end sort or those that are part of a fixed system.

HOSE-END SPRINKLERS. Available hose-end sprinklers include oscillating sprinklers, "machine-gun" pulsating types, revolving-arm sprinklers, and "walking" sprinklers that move along a laid-out hose. Delivery patterns and amounts vary from one model to another. The shape and slope of your lawn will affect the type you choose; kinds that deliver water relatively quickly may cause runoff on slopes, for example.

Be aware that all hose-end sprinklers have some uneven distribution, providing more water to some areas than to others. If you end up overwatering most of the lawn just to get enough moisture to those few areas that receive less water, consider changing the type of sprinkler or where you place it. This may be all that's needed to conserve a fair amount of water each week.

Space straight-sided containers evenly over the lawn and water for a set amount of time. Check the water level in each container; then move the sprinkler as needed to compensate for uneven distribution.

A well-designed underground sprinkler system distributes water evenly over the entire lawn and frees you from the chore of dragging hoses and hose-end sprinklers from place to place.

To get a good idea of your current setup's water distribution pattern, follow the method described on page 42.

UNDERGROUND SPRINKLER SYSTEMS. If lawns in your area require regular watering—or if you'd just rather not bother with manually placing and moving sprinklers—consider installing an underground sprinkler system. If planned carefully, these systems virtually eliminate the problem of uneven water delivery. In fact, the design is the most important part of the job: you'll need to determine the placement of pipes and sprinkler heads, making sure that the water patterns from each head overlap for even coverage. Many gardeners hire a licensed landscape contractor to plan and install such systems. If you want to do the job yourself, consult *Sunset*'s *Garden Watering Systems* or the booklets provided by the major component manufacturers.

MOWING

Even if you are somewhat cavalier in the care of your lawn, you'll probably be able to maintain it fairly well if you water regularly, then follow this one rule: *never mow off more than the topmost third of a blade of grass at one time.* Even if the lawn is overgrown, mow off just a third; then wait a few days and mow another third. Because each blade of grass provides food for the entire plant, continual scalping will compromise the health of the lawn. Some of its roots may die; it will be less able to withstand extremes of temperature, lack of water, and incursions by pests and diseases.

The optimum heights of various grasses differ. Under normal conditions, these heights are:

Common Bermuda, hybrid Bermuda, and colonial bent grass: ½ to 1 inch
Zoysia and centipede: 1 to 2 inches
Perennial rye and St. Augustine: 1½ to 2 inches
Fine fescue: 1½ to 2½ inches
Bahia, blue grass, and tall fescue: 2 to 3 inches
Buffalo grass: 2 to 4 inches

Warm-season grasses grow fastest in hot weather, cool-season grasses in spring. At the peak of the growing season, mowing may be needed more than once a week. At other times of year, every 2 weeks or even once a month may be enough.

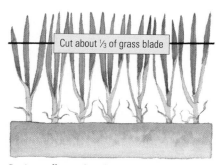

Cut about ⅓ of grass blade

Don't cut off more than the top third of a grass blade when you mow. Leave the clippings to decompose on the lawn.

Self-propelled electric mower

Self-propelled gas-powered mower

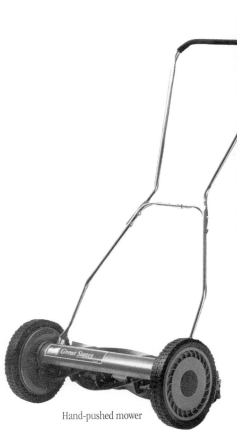

Hand-pushed mower

Brick edging highlights the curve of a garden bed, draws the eye to the patio in the distance, and serves as a mowing strip.

LAWN MOWERS. Hand-pushed mowers were once the only type of mower sold. The original models were cumbersome, and their popularity declined with the advent of self-propelled gasoline and electric mowers, which are easier to use: you just walk along behind them, guiding their direction. But gas mowers—like car engines—require regular maintenance, can be fussy about starting, and spew fumes into the air. And the standard electric mowers, though fume-free, can cause problems too: you need to have an outdoor outlet and, in order to mow a large yard, a very long cord.

In recent years, improvements have been made in all types of mowers. The new hand-pushed types, suitable for small to medium-size lawns, are more compact and lighter in weight than their predecessors; many can easily be carried in one hand. Their blades cut cleaner and stay sharper longer than those of self-propelled mowers. (Most models have four or seven blades; a four-bladed mower is a good choice for most home lawns, while a seven-bladed model will cut a bent-grass lawn to putting-green perfection.) And, of course, these mowers don't fill the air with gas fumes.

The pollution problem is certainly one drawback of gas mowers: it has been postulated that they contribute significantly to poor air quality, and in many cities gardeners are asked not to use them on "spare the air" or "ozone action" days. Still, the newest gasoline mowers offer an improvement over older types. The simple two-cycle kinds have more efficient engines and require less mechanical know-how to stay in running order. Many are fairly light and small, good choices for maintaining a medium to large lawn.

Electric mowers have changed dramatically. They still offer self-propelled power without gas fumes or noise, but the cord is gone, replaced by a battery with enough power to cut most lawns on a single charge.

Most gasoline and electric mowers include so-called mulching mowers that chop the cut grass blades into tiny pieces and deposit them back on the lawn. While it's always a good idea to leave grass clippings on the lawn—they decompose and return nutrients to the soil—mulching mowers result in a neater look (since the clippings are so fine) and speed up the decomposition process.

Mower blades should be sharpened at least once a year, more frequently if the grass begins to look chewed rather than sharply cut.

EDGING

Edging a lawn can take as much time as mowing it. Concrete or brick mowing strips like those shown on the facing page reduce the need for edging; where such a design isn't feasible, hand-held shears are effective for edging small areas. For larger lawns, however, battery-operated or gas-powered edgers are more efficient. Some gardeners use string trimmers ("weed whips") for edging lawns. These are an unwise choice for edging around large shrubs or trees, since the nylon string can easily whip into the bark and damage it badly. They're also risky around annual and perennial beds: angle the trimmer the wrong way for even a split second and you'll decapitate your plants.

FERTILIZING

Lawns need some fertilizing to grow well each year. If unfed, they'll grow sparsely, allowing weed seeds to germinate and flourish. Grass that's insufficiently nourished is also more susceptible to pests and diseases.

What your lawn *doesn't* need, however, is year-round, over-enthusiastic feeding. In fact, some say the greatest threat to our water supply comes not from pesticides or industrial runoff, but from excess nitrogen applied to lawns by home gardeners and landscape maintenance companies. Extra nitrogen fosters algal overgrowth in lakes and rivers, thus upsetting their ecosystems. Beyond this, it doesn't even help the lawn that much in the long run. More thatch develops, roots don't grow as well, and more water is needed.

Fertilizing just once or twice a year is sufficient for most lawns. If you're growing a cool-season grass, fertilize in fall; roots will be nourished and the stored nutrients will give new growth a boost in spring. Depending on the lawn's overall health and growth, you may want to fertilize again in late spring or early summer. Warm-season grasses should be fertilized in summer, at the height of their growth period. Fertilize once in June, a second time in August.

For any grass, use a fertilizer formulated especially for lawns, choosing a controlled-release formula. Some fertilizers are mixed with herbicides to control weeds in the lawn; such a product may be a good choice if your lawn is infested with a weed susceptible to the particular herbicide (check the label to see which weeds the product kills).

To ensure even distribution, use an applicator to fertilize your lawn. Uneven distribution often results in fertilizer burn or unevenly green grass (see page 128).

Spreaders make it easy to distribute fertilizer evenly over a lawn.

Hand-held grass shears (sheep-shearing type)

Battery-operated grass shears

Standard hand-held grass shears

DETHATCHING AND AERATING

Controlling thatch is one of the most important—and most overlooked—parts of lawn care. Thatch is simply the layer of dead grass, roots, and debris that accumulates between the soil surface and the green grass blades above. Over time, it forms a thick mat, hindering water and air from reaching the soil and providing an environment that can encourage pests and diseases. Dethatching can help prevent these problems.

Almost every lawn needs dethatching about once a year, or whenever the thatch reaches a thickness of about ½ inch. To check, just work your fingers into the grass and note the depth of the thatch layer. Dethatch cool-season grasses in fall, warm-season types in early spring.

If your lawn is small, you can dethatch it with a special dethatching rake. The sturdy, very sharp, crescent-shaped tines slice into the thatch, then rake it up. For larger lawns, you may prefer to rent a dethatching machine. Similar in appearance to a large, heavy gas mower, it has knifelike blades that slice the turf vertically. Make several crisscrossing passes to cut and loosen the thatch, then rake up and remove all debris. Dethatching machines have several settings. For most grasses, adjust the blades to a high setting and 3 inches apart; for tougher grasses, such as Bermuda and zoysia, set the blades lower and about an inch apart.

Aeration, a method of punching holes into the lawn to allow moisture, oxygen, and nutrients to penetrate the soil, also helps break up thatch. Its primary goal is to loosen compacted soil; it's often needed for lawns grown in clay soils and those subject to heavy foot traffic. You can do the job more than once a year, if

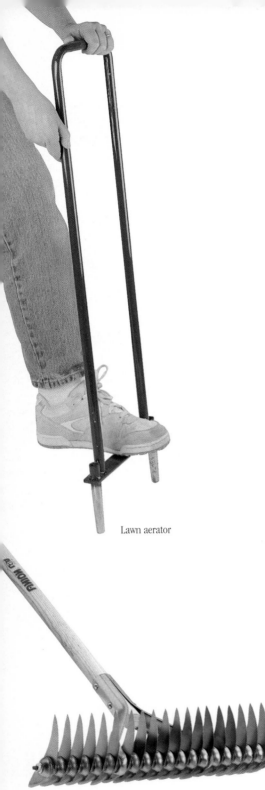

Lawn aerator

Dethatching rake

necessary. If you aerate once annually, do it in fall for cool-season grasses, in spring for warm-season sorts.

You can aerate soil with a hand tool—you press the cutting end into the soil with your foot, then lift it out along with a 2-inch, cylindrical plug of sod. Hand aeration is certainly good aerobic exercise, but it can be time consuming if you have a large lawn. For good-sized areas, a gas-powered aerator does the job faster; you can rent one from supply centers offering garden-machine rentals. (You may also see spike-soled sandals sold as aerating tools; when you walk back and forth over the lawn wearing this footgear, the spikes will supposedly penetrate the soil. Unfortunately, the spikes are both too short and too thin to do an efficient job. Save your money.)

Once the lawn has been aerated, clear away the plugs, spread a layer of organic matter such as compost or soil conditioner over the lawn, and water it in. The organic matter seeps into the holes left by the plugs, improving the soil's texture.

LAWN PROBLEMS

The best way to solve many lawn problems is to prevent them from occurring in the first place, by watering, mowing, fertilizing, aerating, and dethatching regularly. Some of the more common problems are described below. If you're not sure what's causing the symptoms you see, consult a local nursery or your Cooperative Extension Office, or hire a professional to inspect your lawn and make an assessment.

GASOLINE SPILLS OR DOG URINE. Round patches of dead grass can be caused by gasoline spills (did you fill the mower while it was sitting on the grass?) or dog urine. To remedy the problem, leach the area thoroughly with water; then gently rake away the dead grass. If the bare patch doesn't fill in on its own, reseed it or replace it with a patch of sod.

UNEVEN FERTILIZER APPLICATION. Dead or yellow patches can also result from uneven fertilizer application. Parts of the lawn that received the right amount of fertilizer turn dark green; areas that didn't get enough are pale green or yellow, while those that received too much burn and turn brown. Remove the dead patches and water well. If the grass doesn't come back on its own, reseed or resod.

CHINCH BUGS. Chinch bugs are ¼-inch-long, gray-black insects that suck juices from grass blades. They cause brownish-yellow patches in lawns, primarily in St. Augustine and zoysia grasses (and sometimes in blue grass and creeping bent grass), especially in hot or drought-stressed conditions. To diagnose, sink an empty can (open at *both* ends) into the ground at the edge of a patch. Fill the can with water. If chinch bugs are present, they'll float to the surface. To minimize spread, keep the area well watered. Chemical controls include chlorpyrifos and diazinon (see page 75).

SOD WEBWORMS. Sod webworms aren't worms at all, but small, hairless gray caterpillars—the larval form of tiny, buff-colored moths that, if present, can be seen flying close to the lawn's surface in the evening. Sod webworms feed on grass blades. Symptoms are small dead patches of lawn that appear in spring and enlarge during summer. To make a diagnosis, drench an area of lawn near the dead spots with a solution of 1 tablespoon liquid dishwashing detergent diluted in 1 gallon water. The larvae will come to the surface. If you find more than 15 larvae in a square yard, treat the lawn. For chemical control, use chlorpyrifos or diazinon (see page 75). If you don't want to use chemicals, you may be able to reduce the pest population by improving lawn care. Don't overwater or overfertilize; maintain a regular dethatching and aeration schedule.

WHITE GRUBS. "White grubs" is a catchall name for the soil-dwelling larvae of various kinds of beetles, including June bugs (named for the month when they are usually noticed), rose chafers, and Japanese beetles. All these larvae feed on lawn roots. They're typically white with brown heads; when exposed, they curl up in a C-shape. Signs of their presence include distinct, irregularly shaped brown patches in the lawn; damage is usually most severe in late summer. Because the roots have been eaten, the dead patches pull up easily. Remove a patch and dig into the soil; if you find more than one grub per square foot, treat the soil. Correct identification of the grubs will help you choose the best means of treatment; for assistance in identifying them, take a few to a local nursery or your Cooperative Extension Office. For information on controls for Japanese beetles and rose chafers, see pages 71 and 72.

FAIRY RINGS. Fairy rings are small circular patches of dark green grass surrounding areas of dead or light-colored grass; mushrooms may or may not be present at the perimeter of the green area. The rings result from a fungal disease common in lawns growing in soil high in organic matter. To control the problem, aerate the soil; then apply a nitrogen fertilizer formulated for lawn care and keep the lawn wet for 3 to 5 days.

RUST. Rust (see page 79) is a fungal disease. Among lawns, it affects primarily blue grass and rye grass. Grass blades turn yellowish to reddish brown throughout; small reddish pustules form in groups on older blades and stems, and the blades eventually die. The best solution for rust is to apply a nitrogen fertilizer formulated for lawn care, water regularly, and mow more frequently.

WEEDS. Chances are that any weeds infesting the rest of your garden will also attempt to establish themselves in the lawn. A healthy lawn isn't at high risk: its grass stems grow thickly together, making it difficult for weed seeds to reach soil, germinate, and take root. But if the lawn is in poor condition and patchy soil is exposed, weed infestation is likely. Making the wrong grass choice (growing a type that can't tolerate shade in a semishaded area, for instance) also leads to sparse turf and invites weed invasion.

Some warm-season grasses—Bermuda and zoysia, in particular—can themselves be weeds if accidentally introduced into a lawn of a different grass type. The controls noted for Bermuda grass on page 84 are also effective against zoysia.

Other lawn weeds include common mallow (page 85), crabgrass (page 85), dandelion (page 86), oxalis (page 86), plantain (page 86), quack grass (page 87), and spotted spurge (page 88).

RENOVATING AN OLD LAWN

At some point, you may move into a home with a tired, worn lawn. Before you decide that you need to remove it and start over from scratch, see if it can be renovated.

As a first step, just give the lawn good care. Check for diseases and pests and control any you find; get rid of weeds. At the best time of year for the type of grass, dethatch and aerate, being sure you do a thorough job: you want to be certain that grass seed will be able to reach the soil to germinate. Rake up and remove all debris.

Buy a grass seed compatible with your climate and the use the lawn will receive (see pages 122–123). Apply both seed and a complete dry granular, controlled-release fertilizer over the lawn. Topdress the area with an organic amendment such as compost or soil conditioner; it will seep into the holes made during aeration, improving the soil, and will also provide some protection for the germinating grass seeds.

Water the lawn lightly and evenly; then continue to water often enough to keep it constantly moist until the seeds are fully sprouted and the new blades are about one-third taller than their optimum height (this usually works out to 2 to 3 inches tall). You may need to water three, four, or more times a day if the weather is warm. Once the new grass is tall enough, you can mow it, taking off only the top third. At this time, begin a

Dog urine

Uneven fertilizing

Chinch bugs

Sod webworms

White grubs

regular watering program, but avoid walking on the lawn for another 4 to 6 weeks.

PLANTING A NEW LAWN

Establishing a new lawn takes advance planning and work. Sowing seed or laying sod is only the final step.

Start by determining what type of lawn is needed. Will it be heavily used for group sports, play by children, or exercise for dogs? Or is it intended not for foot traffic, but simply as a lush, fine-textured green plot in the overall landscape? Once you've made these decisions, choose the appropriate cool-season or warm-season grasses (see pages 122–123) that can provide the characteristics you need. The most appropriate choices will probably be those stocked by local nurseries or lawn specialists. Read grass-seed package labels and descriptive information; ask for flyers or brochures that describe the grasses in various sods.

When preparing the area to be planted, make sure it has a gentle slope away from buildings and other areas that could be damaged by standing water. In general, allow a 1-foot slope for every 100 feet of distance. As you measure for slope, you may find that some areas are higher or lower than others; grade these for an overall even appearance. If you need to bring in additional soil, buy the same type as the existing soil (to the extent this is possible) and mix it with the existing soil as you work.

Test and amend the soil as you would in any other garden area, following the advice in "Managing Soil" (pages 18–27).

Many warm-season grasses are sold as sprigs or plugs. Shown here are buffalo grass plugs; they are planted about 8 inches apart.

Because grass forms a thick mat about 1 inch high, the prepared planting area should finish out at about an inch lower than surrounding areas.

If you are installing an underground sprinkler system, allow enough time in your schedule to design it carefully for complete, even coverage; or have a licensed landscape contractor do the design and/or installation for you. The system should be installed after the lawn area has been graded.

STARTING FROM SEED. Seeding applies primarily to cool-season grasses; most warm-season kinds are started from sprigs or plugs.

Lawns started from seed are best planted in fall, early enough in the season to give the grass time to establish before cold weather comes. The next best time is spring, after all danger of frost is past and before weather turns hot.

When you prepare the soil, don't cultivate it too finely—it may crust, forming a hard surface which emerging seedlings cannot penetrate. Ideally, aim for pea-size to marble-size soil particles. Do final leveling with a garden rake.

Pick a windless day and sow seed evenly, using a drop or rotary spreader.

Apply a complete dry granular fertilizer, also using a spreader. Several manufacturers offer fertilizers formulated especially for starting new lawns.

Cover seeds by dragging the back of a lightweight leaf rake over the area or applying a thin (½-inch) mulch. Mulching is the better option if you expect hot, dry weather or drying winds.

READING A LAWN SEED LABEL

When you buy grass seed, read labels carefully. Look for a product with a high germination rate and a low percentage of weed seeds and other crop seeds in relation to the percentage of grass seed.

Use an organic mulch, but not peat moss or sawdust—both of these tend to crust over, making it hard for seedlings to penetrate them. Note that it's not necessary to roll the new lawn's surface with a water-filled roller. Doing so can actually inhibit germination, since the roller packs down the soil surface and causes it to crust over.

Water thoroughly, taking care not to wash away the seed. Then keep the seeded area moist for about 3 weeks or until all grass is sprouted, watering briefly (in 5- to 10-minute spells) and frequently. You may need to water three, four, or more times a day during warm periods.

Mow for the first time when the grass is one-third taller than its optimum height. Mow slowly to keep from disturbing the barely set roots. After the initial mowing, continue to water frequently; the top inch of soil should not be allowed to dry out until the lawn is well established (this usually takes about 6 weeks and four mowings).

If weeds emerge, don't attempt to control them until the young lawn has been mowed four times. By this stage, many weeds will have been killed by mowing or crowded out by the growing lawn. If weeds are still a problem after four mowings, many gardeners prefer to treat the lawn with an herbicide; unlike hand pulling, it kills weeds without the risk of disturbing the root systems of the grass.

Try to avoid walking on the lawn too much during the initial 4 to 6 weeks.

STARTING FROM SOD. Sod lawns can be started almost any time of year, except when weather is very cold. It's also best to avoid installation during a summer heat wave.

Water the planting area thoroughly the day before the sod is delivered.

Time the delivery of sod so you can sod the area in a single day, beginning early in the morning.

When you lay out strips, stagger them so ends aren't adjacent; butt sides tightly together. Use a sharp knife to cut sod to fit it into odd-shaped areas.

Roll the entire lawn with a roller half-filled with water to smooth out rough spots and press the roots of the sod firmly against the soil. (Rollers can be rented at garden and tool supply centers.)

Water once a day (more often if the weather is hot), keeping the area thoroughly moist for at least 6 weeks.

Mow for the first time when the grass is one-third taller than its optimum height. When mowing during the initial 6 weeks, be very careful not to disturb the seams. Also try to avoid walking on the lawn too much during the initial 4 to 6 weeks.

STARTING FROM SPRIGS OR PLUGS. Many warm-season grasses are sold as sprigs or plugs. A sprig is a piece of grass stem with roots and blades. A plug is a small square or circle cut from sod. Early spring is the best time to plant sprigs and plugs.

Sprigs are usually sold by the bushel; the supplier can tell you how much area a bushel will cover. The fastest way to plant them is to scatter them evenly by hand over the prepared area, then roll them with a cleated roller (this tool is usually available for rent from nurseries that sell sprigs).

Plugs are usually 2 to 3 inches across and are often sold 18 to a tray—enough to plant 50 square feet. Plant the plugs in the prepared area, spacing them 8 to 12 inches apart.

SEED OR SOD?

The greatest advantage seeding has over sod is cost. Though improved growing, harvesting, and distribution has made sod less expensive than in years past, seeded lawns remain much cheaper to plant. And while sod offers a wider choice of grasses than it once did, seed still provides the most variety. You can easily find hybrid seed mixtures that thrive in shade, for example, but these are harder come by in sod. Sod also has occasional problems with bonding to the soil beneath; if it fails do so properly, you'll get a shallow-rooted lawn at best—or, at worst, one that completely fails.

On the other hand, many gardeners can't stay at home to keep a seeded lawn constantly moist for weeks, and not everyone has an automatic sprinkler system that allows for watering several times per day. Sodded lawns must be kept moist, too, of course, but they don't dry out as fast as seeded lawns; watering just twice a day (before and after work, for instance) is often enough to do the job.

Sod also provides an instant reward for your labors—a morale booster if the entire garden is brand new, with only small trees and shrubs dotting the landscape.

Japanese spurge *(Pachysandra terminalis)* is an invaluable ground cover for shady places.

GROUND COVERS

Ground covers are dependable plants that we count on to blanket the soil with dense foliage, adding beauty and variety to the garden and suppressing weeds at the same time. Lawn is the best-known ground cover, unsurpassed as a surface to walk or play on. But in areas where foot traffic is infrequent and in sites inhospitable to lawn grasses—in the shade under large trees or on hot, steep banks, for example—ground covers offer the neatness and uniformity of a lawn for considerably less maintenance and water.

Ice plant
(Delosperma nubigenum)

These plants run the gamut of foliage textures and colors, and many are noted for their bright flowers. Height varies, too: some are low mats, while others are knee-high or even taller. Some spread by underground runners or root on top of the ground as they grow. Others form clumps and should be planted close together to produce a tight cover. For a sampler of ground cover choices, turn to page 135.

PLANTING GROUND COVERS

Where winters are cold, plant in spring; this will give the ground cover an entire season to become established before it must face the rigors of winter. In areas with hot, dry summers and mild winters, plant in fall; the winter rains will help get the plants off to a good start.

Though ground covers are tough, they'll grow and spread more quickly if you prepare the planting area carefully. Dig out weeds, amend the soil with compost or well-rotted manure, and broadcast a complete fertilizer over the area (follow the package directions for amounts). Work in amendments and fertilizer with a shovel or tiller, then rake to level the soil. (*Note:* Shrubby plants from gallon containers are an exception to the above advice; these are often planted in the native soil, without amendments.) Install landscape fabric (see page 83), if desired.

Ground cover plants are sold in small pots, cell-packs, or 1-gallon containers, or as rooted cuttings in flats. Before setting out flat-grown plants, separate them by cutting between them with a putty knife. For information on spacing, see page 134.

When planting ground covers purchased in smaller pots or flats, set them in holes just deep enough for and slightly wider than the root ball. To plant from gallon containers, follow the steps described on page 37: dig a hole that tapers outward at the bottom to accommodate the loosened roots, leaving a "plateau" of undisturbed soil in the middle. The root ball rests on the plateau; the crown of each plant should remain slightly above the soil surface to prevent rot.

After planting, water the plants thoroughly. As they become established over the next several weeks, water every few days, keeping the soil moist but not soggy. To help maintain soil moisture and prevent weed seeds from growing, spread a 2- to 4-inch-thick layer of an organic mulch between the young plants, taking care not to cover the plants' crowns.

Tough, dependable, and attractive, Aaron's beard *(Hypericum calycinum)* grows vigorously even in poor soil.

CARING FOR GROUND COVERS

Most ground covers require little attention beyond routine watering, mulching, fertilizing, and grooming. In many cases, maintenance takes very little time—especially when compared to the hours typically invested in lawn care.

WATERING. Ground covers, like any other plants, vary in their moisture needs, depending on the type and age of the plant. Soil texture and climate influence water needs as well. In general, however, most ground covers require regular water when young but may do very well with only occasional irrigation or with rainfall alone once they are mature and established.

A hose-end sprinkler is often sufficient for applying water to small areas of ground cover. But for large areas or sloping sites that may be subject to erosion, you'll find it more efficient to install a permanent watering system. Drip systems (see pages 44–45) are well suited to ground covers.

FERTILIZING. The kind of plant and the soil texture determine a ground cover's need for fertilizer. As a rule of thumb, assume that woody, shrubby ground covers (especially drought-tolerant sorts) have fairly low nutrient needs and may get along with no additional fertilizer after planting. Perennial ground covers, with softer, lusher growth, generally have higher nutrient requirements and should receive an annual feeding.

As far as soil goes, heavier (claylike) soils contain more nutrients and hold dissolved nutrients from fertilizers longer than do lighter, sandier ones—so ground covers in lighter soils are more likely to need periodic feeding. Ground covers that must compete with trees or shrubs often benefit from added fertilizer as well.

It's best to fertilize just before the growing season begins, so that nutrients are available for the year's major growth push. Use a complete fertilizer in the amounts directed on the label.

WEEDING. One of the primary reasons for planting a ground cover is to eliminate weeding. However, don't expect to be freed from the job starting from the moment the plants are in the ground; until they fill in, some weeding is usually necessary. Getting rid of weeds before they set seed is important to prevent ongoing problems. Replenishing the mulch as it decomposes also aids in weed control. For serious weed problems, you may

Use hedge shears to cut back vigorous ground covers. This removes old growth and keeps plants from spreading out of bounds. Rake up the clippings and compost them.

A heavy-duty power mower (set at 3 to 4 inches) makes fast work of trimming large expanses of spreading ground covers such as periwinkle *(Vinca),* Aaron's beard *(Hypericum),* and ivy *(Hedera).*

Installing a permanent barrier of wood, brick, stone, or concrete prevents creeping ground covers such as carpet bugle *(Ajuga)* from invading an adjacent lawn or flower bed.

PLANTING GROUND COVERS ON A SLOPE

When setting plants on a steep slope where erosion may occur, arrange them in staggered rows. Make an individual terrace for each plant and create a basin or low spot behind each one to catch water. Set the crowns of the plants high, so they won't become saturated and rot after watering.

be able to use a selective herbicide—one that will kill weeds but not your ground cover. Read the label of any such product carefully to determine which weeds it kills and which ornamental plants it leaves unaffected. For more on herbicides, see pages 84 and 88.

EDGING. If not restricted, many ground covers will advance beyond the area you've allotted for them. If the plant spreads by underground stems or by rooting along stems that touch the soil, you may be able to control it by trimming the planting's edges with pruning or hedge shears or with a rotary mower. But if growth is progressing significantly out of bounds, you may have to dig out the portions that have gone too far. Installing a permanent barrier of wood, brick, stone, or concrete will save you a great deal of hand edging. To keep persistent ground covers from creeping under the barrier, check the plant's root depth and be sure the barrier extends deeper than that distance below ground.

PRUNING. Some shrubby ground covers that are normally low growing may occasionally send out upright stems that spoil the evenness of the planting; cotoneaster is one example. When you see such stems, cut them back to their point of origin or to a horizontally growing lateral within the foliage mass.

Woody ground covers—especially junipers and cotoneasters—are sometimes planted too close to paths, making frequent pruning necessary. Because constant cutting back usually ruins the shape of the plants, it's often better simply to replace them with more suitable plants.

MOWING. Ground covers that root as they spread, as well as those that spread by underground stems to form dense patches, may eventually become so thick and matted that only mowing will restore their good looks. Plants like ivy *(Hedera)* accumulate thatch beneath the foliage; others, such as winter creeper *(Euonymus)* and Aaron's beard *(Hypericum)*, may become rangy and untidy. Mow these ground covers just before the start of the growing season, using a heavy-duty power mower set at 3 to 4 inches. Then fertilize to encourage rapid new growth.

SPACING GROUND COVER PLANTS

The spacing to allow between ground cover plants depends on the particular plant and, to some extent, on how quickly you want the area covered with growth. The descriptions beginning on the facing page give guidelines for spacing; for ground covers not discussed there, consult knowledgeable nursery personnel. Check the chart below to calculate the area that will be covered by a specified number of plants set out at various spacings.

SPACING between plants	48 plants*	64 plants*	72 plants*	100 plants*
6 in.	10 sq. ft.	13½ sq. ft.	15½ sq. ft.	21½ sq. ft.
8 in.	18 sq. ft.	24½ sq. ft.	27½ sq. ft.	38 sq. ft.
10 in.	28½ sq. ft.	38½ sq. ft.	43 sq. ft.	60 sq. ft.
12 in.	41½ sq. ft.	55½ sq. ft.	62½ sq. ft.	86½ sq. ft.
15 in.	64½ sq. ft.	86 sq. ft.	97 sq. ft.	135 sq. ft.
18 in.	92 sq. ft.	123 sq. ft.	138 sq. ft.	192 sq. ft.
24 in.	165½ sq. ft.	220½ sq. ft.	248 sq. ft.	344½ sq. ft.

*Plants per flat

A GROUND COVER SAMPLER

When selecting ground covers, be mindful of your soil and climate; plants that need constant coddling aren't suitable for this role. For an explanation of the at-a-glance information introducing each entry, see page 95.

SYMBOLS: These symbols indicate whether the plant is an evergreen perennial (🌿), a deciduous perennial (🌿), an evergreen shrubby ground cover (🍃), a semievergreen shrubby ground cover (🍃), a deciduous shrubby ground cover (🍃), or an evergreen woody vine (🌿).

AJUGA reptans
🌿 CARPET BUGLE

- ✂ ZONES 1–24, 26–45
- ☀ ◐ FULL SUN OR PARTIAL SHADE
- 💧 REGULAR

Spreading quickly by runners, carpet bugle makes a mat to 4 inches high of dark green (or, in some kinds, purple or variegated) leaves that grow 2 to 4 inches wide, depending on exposure and on the particular variety. Six-inch-tall spikes of blue flowers appear in spring. Mow or trim off old spikes after flowering. Carpet bugle may escape into lawns or other plantings if not confined by an edging or path. It is subject to root rot and fungus in heavy soils. Space 6 to 12 inches apart.

ARCTOSTAPHYLOS
uva-ursi

🍃 BEARBERRY, KINNIKINNICK

- ✂ ZONES 1–9, 14–24, 34, 36–45
- ☀ ◐ FULL SUN OR PARTIAL SHADE
- 💧 MODERATE

Good looking all year, bearberry spreads widely at a moderate rate to form a dense, foot-tall mat; stems root as they spread. Small white or pink spring flowers are followed by red berries in fall. Does best in well-drained soil. Establishes slowly; mulch heavily between plants to keep down weeds until

Ajuga reptans

Arctostaphylos uva-ursi

Cerastium tomentosum

Ceratostigma plumbaginoides

branches provide cover. Many named selections are available. Space 2 feet apart.

CERASTIUM tomentosum
🌿 SNOW-IN-SUMMER

- ✂ ZONES 1–24, 32–45
- ☀ ◐ FULL SUN; PARTIAL SHADE IN HOT CLIMATES
- 💧 REGULAR FOR FASTEST GROWTH

Reliable everywhere except in the hot, humid South, snow-in-summer grows 6 to 8 inches high, bearing silvery gray foliage and masses of small, snow white flowers from late spring into early summer. It takes any soil as long as drainage is good; it tolerates drought once established, but spreads fastest with regular water. It is not long-lived. When plantings start to look shabby after several seasons, replant with divisions or cutting-grown plants. Space 1 to 1½ feet apart.

CERATOSTIGMA
plumbaginoides

🌿 DWARF PLUMBAGO

- ✂ ZONES 2–10, 14–24, 29–41
- ☀ ◐ FULL SUN OR PARTIAL SHADE
- 💧 MODERATE

Vivid blue flowers bloom from midsummer to midautumn, carried at the ends of wiry 6- to 12-inch stems. Bronzy green, 3-inch-long leaves turn reddish brown in fall. Dwarf plumbago spreads by underground stems; it grows best in areas where the growing season is long. It takes a wide range of soils, from claylike to sandy. Stems die back after bloom; shear or mow plantings before new growth starts in spring. Space about 1½ feet apart.

🌿🌿 COTONEASTER

🌿 ZONES VARY
☼ ◐ FULL SUN OR PARTIAL SHADE
🌢 MODERATE

Rugged and undemanding, cotoneasters provide clusters of small white or pale pink flowers in spring and bright red fruits (enjoyed by birds) in fall and winter. They grow well in good soil with regular moisture, but also tolerate poor soil and moderate water. Give them room to spread, since frequent pruning spoils their shape. The species listed below have small (½- to 1-inch) oval leaves. Space all three 3 to 5 feet apart.

C. adpressus. CREEPING COTON-EASTER. Zones 1–24, 29–43. Deciduous. Good as a bank cover, this species hugs the ground, spreading slowly to 4 to 6 feet and remaining under 1 foot tall.

C. dammeri. EVERGREEN BEAR-BERRY COTONEASTER. Zones 2–24, 29–41. Fast growing, forming a prostrate mat 3 to 6 inches tall and 10 feet wide.

C. horizontalis. ROCK COTON-EASTER. Zones 2–11, 14–24, 31–41. Deciduous. A moderately fast grower, reaching 2 to 3 feet tall and 15 feet wide. Its stiff, horizontal branches form a flat herringbone pattern.

DUCHESNEA indica

🌿 INDIAN MOCK STRAWBERRY
🌿 ZONES 1–24, 29–43
☼ ◐ ● FULL SUN, PARTIAL SHADE, OR FULL SHADE
🌢 MODERATE

It looks like a strawberry plant: the stems are trailing and rooting, the leaves bright green, with three leaflets. But unlike true strawberry, Indian mock strawberry has yellow flowers rather than white ones, and its red fruits—edible but insipid—are carried above the foliage rather than under the leaves. It is best used among open shrubs or small trees, since it can be invasive in well-watered gardens. Tidy up plantings by mowing them in early spring. Space 1 to 1½ feet apart.

Cotoneaster horizontalis

Duchesnea indica

Euonymus fortunei

Galium odoratum

EUONYMUS fortunei

🌿 WINTER CREEPER
🌿 ZONES 3–17, 28–41
☼ ◐ ● FULL SUN, PARTIAL SHADE, OR FULL SHADE
🌢 MODERATE

Some forms of winter creeper are compact shrubs—but the ground cover sorts are trailing and vinelike, rooting as they spread and climbing upward when they encounter a vertical surface. Common winter creeper, *E. f. radicans,* has thick, oval dark green leaves up to an inch long. Foliage of purple-leaf winter creeper, *E. f.* 'Coloratus', turns dark purple in fall and winter. Numerous other varieties are available, some with variegated leaves.

These plants are tolerant of a wide range of soils. Scale can be a problem. Space 3 to 5 feet apart, depending on the plant's ultimate size and on how fast you want the planting to fill in. When plantings begin to look rangy or untidy, mow or shear in late winter or early spring.

GALIUM odoratum

🌿 SWEET WOODRUFF
🌿 ZONES 1–6, 15–17, 31–43
◐ ● PARTIAL TO FULL SHADE
🌢 REGULAR

Spreading to form a mat of 6- to 12-inch stems bearing whorls of dark green leaves, sweet woodruff is a good choice for covering the ground under trees and tall shrubs. Clusters of tiny white flowers appear from spring into summer. May spread too rapidly in rich soil; dig or cut back excess growth. Space plants 1 foot apart.

HEDERA

🌿 IVY
🌿 ZONES VARY
☼ ◐ FULL SUN; SOME SHADE IN HOT AREAS
🌢 🌢 REGULAR TO MODERATE

Spreading at a moderate to fast rate, rugged, adaptable ivy makes a ground cover that always looks neat and uniform. Its deep roots hold the soil, discouraging erosion on banks; its branches root as they grow, further knitting the soil. When the branches reach a vertical surface, they will ascend it, clinging with aerial rootlets.

Trim around the edges of ground cover plantings to keep them tidy and in bounds. Plantings may build up a thick thatch of stems after several years; shear or mow them back in early spring. Set plants about 1½ feet apart.

H. canariensis. ALGERIAN IVY. Zones 8, 9, 12–28. Glossy, shallowly lobed leaves are especially large—up to 8 inches across.

H. helix. ENGLISH IVY. Zones 3–34, 39; hardiest varieties in 35, 37, and warmer parts of 38 and 41. Three- to five-lobed leaves up to 4 inches across are a matte dark green with paler veins. Many named varieties are sold, varying widely in foliage shape, color, and size.

HYPERICUM calycinum
🌿 AARON'S BEARD, CREEPING ST. JOHNSWORT
- 🌱 ZONES 3–24, 31–34
- ☀ ◐ ● FULL SUN, PARTIAL SHADE, OR FULL SHADE
- 💧 MODERATE

Good looking and indestructible, Aaron's beard forms a dense, even cover to 1 foot high. The arching stems bear pairs of 4-inch, oval leaves that are rich green in sun, yellow green in shade. Showy, 3-inch-wide yellow flowers that look rather like single roses bloom from late spring to early summer. The plant spreads aggressively by underground stems and may invade other plantings unless confined by a barrier. It takes poor soil, competes well with tree roots, and helps prevent erosion on sloping ground. To renew growth and maintain an even surface, mow or shear plantings about every 3 years in late winter or early spring. Space 1½ feet apart.

Hedera canariensis

Hypericum calycinum

ABOVE: Ice plant *(Delosperma cooperi)*
BELOW: *Juniperus conferta*

🌿 ICE PLANT
- 🌱 ZONES VARY
- ☀ FULL SUN
- 💧 MODERATE TO LITTLE

Included under the common name "ice plant" are a number of succulent perennials. All have thick, juicy foliage, often with a powdery gray surface; most produce showy, daisylike flowers, often in brilliant colors. These plants aren't particular about soil and require only enough water to keep the leaves from wilting. Three of the many available ice plants are described here.

Carpobrotus edulis. Zones 12–27. Grows 1 to 1½ feet tall, with curved, 4- to 5-inch-long leaves and pale yellow to rose flowers in summer. Space 1½ to 2 feet apart.

Delosperma. Two species are especially adaptable; space 1 to 1½ feet apart. *D. cooperi* succeeds in Zones 3–24, 28–31, and warmer parts of 32; it grows 5 inches high, bearing glistening purple flowers all summer. *D. nubigenum,* hardiest of cultivated ice plants, grows in Zones 2–24, 28–41. Barely 1 inch high, it has fleshy cylindrical leaves and bright golden late spring flowers.

JUNIPERUS
🌿 JUNIPER
- 🌱 ZONES VARY
- ☀ ◐ FULL SUN; MOST TOLERATE LIGHT SHADE
- 💧 💧 REGULAR TO MODERATE

So many juniper species and varieties are available that you'll find ground cover choices for almost any climate. These adaptable plants vary in height from a few inches to 2 to 3 feet; their foliage color ranges from silvery blue through many shades of green to nearly yellow, and there are variegated kinds as well. They thrive in most soils—from light to heavy, acid to alkaline—but they won't tolerate waterlogged soil, which can lead to root rot.

Continued >

Most junipers grow at a slow to moderate rate, but it's best to space them 5 to 6 feet apart to avoid future overcrowding. Mulching will help keep weeds under control while the plants are filling in. A few of the most widely sold junipers are described below; check with local nurseries for other species and varieties.

J. chinensis procumbens. JAPANESE GARDEN JUNIPER. Zones 1–24, 28–43. Blue-green, feathery foliage comes on a plant that reaches 3 feet high and spreads 12 to 20 feet.

J. conferta. SHORE JUNIPER. Zones 3–9, 14–24, 26–28, 31–34, 39. A trailing plant to 8 feet across and 1½ feet high; soft, bright green foliage. 'Blue Pacific' has blue-green leaves.

J. horizontalis 'Bar Harbor'. Zones 1–24, 28, 31–45. Spreads quickly to 10 feet, but grows no more than a foot high; feathery blue-gray foliage turns plum purple in winter. Foliage of *J. h.* 'Wiltonii', blue carpet juniper, is a striking silver blue; the plant is a very flat grower (just 4 inches tall), creeping to 8 to 10 feet across.

J. sabina 'Calgary Carpet'. Zones 1–24, 31–45. Extremely cold hardy, with soft green foliage. Grows 6 to 9 inches tall, 10 feet wide.

LAMIUM maculatum
DEAD NETTLE
- ZONES 1–24, 32–43
- PARTIAL TO FULL SHADE
- REGULAR

A nice choice for lighting up shady areas, the variegated varieties of dead nettle have grayish green leaves with silvery markings; they're evergreen where winters are mild, deciduous elsewhere. Plants reach 6 inches tall and spread 2 to 3 feet wide. Short spikes of small, hooded flowers bloom in late spring or early summer. Among available varieties, 'Beacon Silver' has pink flowers; 'White Nancy' has clear white blossoms. Space 1½ to 2 feet apart.

Lamium maculatum 'White Nancy'

Pachysandra terminalis

Rosa 'Flower Carpet'

PACHYSANDRA terminalis
JAPANESE SPURGE
- ZONES 1–10, 14–21, 31–43
- FULL SHADE
- REGULAR

Widely used as an elegant ground cover under trees, Japanese spurge forms an even, 10-inch-high carpet of shiny dark green leaves. Spikes of small white flowers appear in late spring or early summer. To add extra sparkle to heavily shaded spots, try the variety 'Variegata', with white leaf margins. Plants spread at a moderate rate by underground stems and grow best in good, somewhat acid soil. Fertilize in early spring. Space 1 foot apart.

ROSA
ROSE
- ZONES VARY
- FULL SUN
- REGULAR

In recent years, breeders have developed low-growing shrub roses (usually to about 2 feet tall) that are vigorous, disease resistant, and long blooming, perfect for covering slopes or forming a trafficproof cover on level ground. Four good choices are 'Flower Carpet' (with clusters of semidouble dark pink flowers); 'White Flower Carpet' (with white blooms); 'Magic Carpet' (profuse clusters of small, semidouble lilac pink blossoms); and 'Red Ribbons' (clustered semidouble flowers in lipstick red). Beyond these, many other varieties are available; for more complete listings, consult a specialty catalog. These can be grown in all zones, but they'll need winter protection in the coldest areas. Space 8 feet apart.

Among species ground cover roses is *Rosa wichuraiana,* known as memorial rose. It's deciduous in Zones 3, 34, 35, and 39, evergreen or semievergreen in Zones 4–32. Trailing, prostrate stems root when they contact moist soil, spreading 10 to 12 feet in a single season.

Single white flowers bloom only in late spring. Several hybrids between this species and various garden roses are also useful ground covers; among them are 'Alberic Barbier', with creamy white flowers, and 'Max Graf', with large pink blooms. Plant *R. wichuraiana* and its hybrids 10 feet apart.

TEUCRIUM chamaedrys

GERMANDER

- ZONES 3–24, 28–34, 39
- FULL SUN OR PARTIAL SHADE
- MODERATE TO LITTLE

Even in poor soil and with little water, germander forms a dark green carpet that grows 1 foot high and spreads at a slow to moderate rate to about 2 feet. The many upright, woody-based stems are densely clothed in toothed, 3/4-inch leaves. Spikes of small pinkish purple or white flowers appear in summer. A lower-growing variety is 'Prostratum', which reaches just 4 to 6 inches tall.

If plants become straggly, shear them back to encourage new branching growth. Space 1½ feet apart.

Teucrium chamaedrys

Vinca minor

VINCA

PERIWINKLE, MYRTLE

- ZONES VARY
- FULL SUN, PARTIAL SHADE, OR FULL SHADE
- MODERATE

These useful ground covers have trailing, arching stems, shiny oval leaves, and phloxlike spring blossoms; they'll grow in any soil, even competing well with surface tree roots. If plantings mound too high or become layered with old stems, shear or mow in late winter or early spring to encourage fresh new growth.

V. major. Zones 5–24, 28–31, warmer parts of 32 and 33. This species mounds 1 to 2 feet high and bears lavender blue blooms; it spreads rapidly and can be extremely invasive in sheltered, wooded areas. Space 2 to 2½ feet apart.

V. minor. Zones 1–24, 28–43. Known as dwarf periwinkle, *V. minor* has smaller leaves and flowers than *V. major;* it reaches just 6 inches high and is less likely to invade adjacent plantings. There are sorts with flowers in white and various blue shades, as well as some with variegated leaves. Space 1½ feet apart.

WALK-ON LAWN SUBSTITUTES

While they won't tolerate as much foot traffic as a lawn, a few low-growing ground covers can take some traffic.

Chamomile (*Chamaemelum nobile*, Zones 1–24, 30–43) forms a soft-textured evergreen mat of aromatic leaves in bright, light green. Stems root as they spread, forming a solid cover. Small yellow flowers appear in summer. Space 1 foot apart.

Lippia (*Phyla nodiflora*, Zones 8–29) creeps and spreads to form a sturdy mat of 3/4-inch, gray-green leaves. Tiny lilac to rose flowers bloom from spring to fall; these attract bees and can be mowed off, if desired. Dormant in winter. Space 1 to 2 feet apart.

Scotch moss (*Sagina subulata*) and the very similar Irish moss (*Arenaria verna*) both grow in Zones 1–11, 14–24, 32–43. Good choices for planting between stepping-stones or to cover a small area, they form dense, compact, mosslike masses of slender leaves on slender stems. They grow best in good, well-drained soil. Space 6 inches apart.

Arenaria verna

Twining stems

Tendrils

Suction (holdfast) discs

Aerial rootlets

Scrambles; no means of attachment

VINES

Vines play garden roles no other plant can fill. They cover arbors and screen porches, creating shady oases on hot summer days. They hide unattractive sheds and tree stumps; they cloak stark chain-link fences with greenery and bloom. And with neatly trimmed vines framing its doors and windows, an ordinary house facade can become a standout.

Gardeners with space limitations often turn to vines as way to include more plants in a pocket-handkerchief garden. Many choices grow happily in containers, adding color and privacy to decks and patios.

Other than the fact that all have long, pliable stems (when they're young, in any case), vines differ greatly. They may be evergreen, semievergreen, or deciduous; they may be modest in size or rampant enough to engulf trees or scale high walls. Many grow well in ordinary garden soil with an annual springtime application of fertilizer, but a few need rich, well-amended soil and regular fertilizer throughout the growing season. Some require ample moisture, but a great many perform well with little additional water once established.

Climate preferences vary too, so always match your climate zone (see pages 8–11) to the vines you want to grow. Many are native to semitropical parts of the world and cannot tolerate cold temperatures—or they may remain lush and green all year where winters are mild, but drop their foliage or die to the ground during winter in colder areas. Some vines are well behaved in temperate zones but grow with great vigor in warmer regions, overwhelming their support (and possibly the entire garden, too!).

Though most vines are quite easy to grow, they do need an appropriate support structure and some attention to training while young. Once they obtain the right size for their location, they'll usually require periodic pruning to stay in bounds.

HOW VINES CLIMB

The particular way each vine climbs determines what sort of support you'll need to provide.

TWINING VINES. As these vines grow, their stems twist and spiral. They coil too tightly to grasp large supports such as posts, so give them something slender, such as cord or wire. To cover a wood fence with chocolate vine *(Akebia quinata),* for example, string wire up and down the fence through eyescrews attached at 6- to 8-inch intervals. Twining vines with moderate growth habits are also good choices for growing on fan-shaped or rectangular trellises with narrow vertical members. If you want a twining vine to spill over the top of an arbor, you can sink a narrow pole into the ground beside the structure and train the vine around the pole; when it reaches the top, it will twine along horizontally, with streamers of stems and leaves trailing downward.

Besides Carolina jessamine, twiners include include Dutchman's pipe *(Aristolochia macrophylla),* honeysuckle *(Lonicera),* and wisteria.

VINES WITH TENDRILS OR COILING LEAFSTALKS. Tendrils are specialized plant parts growing from the end of a leaf or the side of a stem. They grow straight until they contact something they can grasp—wire or cord, another stem on the same vine, another plant—then reflexively contract into a spiral and wrap around the support.

Vines that climb by tendrils include grape and sweet pea *(Lathyrus odoratus)*.

Some plants (clematis is the best-known example) ascend by coiling leafstalks: as a stem grows and puts out foliage, the leafstalks of young leaves encircle anything slender they encounter, behaving more or less like tendrils.

Like twiners, vines that attach by tendrils or coiling leafstalks need slender supports; if the support is too thick, the vine will merely attach to its own stems, growing into a tangled mess. These vines are excellent choices for latticework supports such as chain-link fences and lath trellises.

CLINGING VINES. If there's any kind of vine that gives the whole group a bad name, it's the clinging sort, which let them adhere tenaciously to almost any flat surface. Specialized structures let them grip their supports. Some, such as trumpet vine *(Campsis)* and ivy *(Hedera)*, have stems equipped with aerial rootlets; others, like Boston ivy *(Parthenocissus tricuspidata)*, have tendrils that terminate in suction (holdfast) discs.

Clinging vines are a good choice when you need to cover a wide wall. If you grow them on a fence or pergola, the stems will first attach to the surface; subsequent growth will pile up on itself, often resulting in the look of a twining vine.

SCRAMBLING VINES. Some vines have no means of attachment; they climb only in the sense that their stems will proceed on a vertical path if secured to a support as they grow. Left to themselves, they'll simply mound, sprawl, and scramble, though a few, such as climbing roses and most bougainvilleas, can hook themselves through adjacent shrubs or trees with their thorns. These vines will grow on almost any support as long as you provide appropriate attachment. Many gardeners cover flat surfaces with eyescrews and wire, then tie the plant in place at various points as it grows.

TRAINING AND PRUNING VINES

Until a vine gets a firm hold on its support, you may need to tie it in place with twine or plastic garden tape. (For heavy vines, you can use thin rope or strips of canvas or rubber.) For clinging vines, you might tack plastic mesh over the stems until you see the aerial rootlets or holdfast discs adhering. Once the stems of twining and scrambling vines gain some length, you can weave them through any openwork support, such as a trellis or wire fence.

To encourage bushy growth on young vines, pinch out the stems' terminal buds. If you want just a few vertical stems, though (for a tracery of growth around a column, for example), don't pinch. Instead, remove all but one or two long stems at the base.

Once a vine is established, you'll need to prune it periodically to keep it in bounds or to clear out unwanted or dead growth. The job is often done late in the dormant season, just before new growth begins, though you may want to wait to prune early-spring bloomers such as Carolina jessamine *(Gelsemium sempervirens)* until flowering has finished. Some vines are so vigorous they can pruned at any time; see the sampler on pages 143–147 for some of these.

Continued >

It's probably best known for cloaking buildings, but Boston ivy *(Parthenocissus tricuspidata)* is just as attractive spilling over fences and low walls.

The stems of vigorous twiners like this clematis tend to become snarled. Often the best way to sort out the problem is just to snip through the tangles. Resultant dead growth will be easier to identify and remove later on.

Vines that twine, climb by tendrils or coiling leafstalks, or scramble are pruned by similar methods. Start by removing dead and damaged growth. If the stems are so tangled that can you can't tell what to remove, snip through the mat of stems here and there; later on, remove those that have died (see photo at left). If the problem is really severe—if the vine is such a haystack of growth that you can hardly find the support, for example—make heading cuts low enough to reduce the vine's length by half. Once you've done that, you can usually untangle the stems and make thinning cuts to remove unwanted growth at ground level. As a last resort, cut the entire vine to the ground in late winter or early spring and start training it all over again.

Clinging vines need regular monitoring. If you don't keep them under control, they'll crawl under eaves and wood shakes, causing structural damage; if removed, they'll take paint and plaster with them. Prune out any stems you see extending into eaves, windows, shingles, and so on. Once every few years, prune more extensively: cut out wayward branches and any that have pulled away from their support (once aerial rootlets and holdfast discs have come loose, they won't reattach). Cut branches away from windows and doors; reduce the bulk of protruding or unruly growth.

SUPPORTING WISTERIA VINES

Wisteria is heavy. Its main stems eventually reach several inches thick—and in great age, they may be as large as a small tree trunk. Think about the future when you plant: if you don't allow for your wisteria's ultimate weight, you'll end up with a vine that overwhelms its support.

Most gardeners choose to grow wisteria up a wall or on a sturdy arbor or pergola. To establish it against a house wall, begin by screwing a series of 6- to 8-inch L-brackets to the support. One row of brackets, spaced at 1-foot intervals, runs vertically up the center of the wall; the other rows run horizontally, spaced 2 to 3 feet apart. Attach the top row 3 feet below the eaves to keep vines from growing into them.

Run galvanized wire between the brackets, then attach the young wisteria vine to the wire with string; its stems will twine around the wire as they grow. (Because the wire is positioned 6 to 8 inches away from the wall, there's plenty of room for air circulation and growth.)

To grow a wisteria up an arbor or pergola, make sure that the structure's support posts are at least 4 by 4 inches. The main stem can be twined around a post or grown straight against it; keep the stem firmly attached with heavy-duty garden twine until it has grown over the top of the structure and is attached there.

A single wisteria vine is vigorous enough to cover a sturdy arbor. This one's stem was hand-wrapped around one post and then allowed to twine on its own once it reached the arbor top.

While the wisteria is becoming established—especially during the first year or two—leave the lateral branches on the main stem. Once the plant is growing well, gradually begin pinching or pruning off lateral growth at the plant's base. Continue to remove some lateral growth each year as the vine ascends the post, then heads along the arbor or pergola roof.

Once the vine has reached the roof, direct its growth horizontally, tying it in place. As it matures, its own weight and its twining side branches will hold it in place. If you want to keep it lashed down for extra security, check annually to be sure the ties aren't girdling the branches.

A SAMPLER OF VINES

The vines in this sampler vary from modest to rampant, heat loving to frost tolerant; some bear bright flowers, while others are grown for their foliage alone. For an explanation of the at-a-glance information introducing each entry, see page 95.

SYMBOLS: These symbols indicate whether the vine is evergreen (🍃), semievergreen (🍃), or deciduous (🍃).

AKEBIA quinata
🍃 🍃 🍃 CHOCOLATE VINE, FIVELEAF AKEBIA
- 🌿 ZONES 3–24, 29–41
- ☼ ◐ FULL SUN OR PARTIAL SHADE
- 💧 REGULAR
- CLIMBS BY: TWINING

Gardeners choose chocolate vine for the lush yet delicate look it brings to the landscape. Foliage is fine textured, with each leaf consisting of five small leaflets radiating from the stem tip. The small, purplish spring flowers are a bonus (some say they smell like chocolate). The vine ascends rapidly to 15 to 30 feet, providing shade and hiding less-than-lovely structures from view. It can also provide a tracery of growth on walls or columns; to achieve this effect, remove all but 2 or 3 stems as the vine grows.

Chocolate vine grows in ordinary garden soil, but it must have good drainage. It thrives in sun or partial shade. Be sure to provide a sturdy support for its many twining stems. It can be pruned severely; do the job just before plants break dormancy in spring, cutting stems back to five to nine growth buds from ground level and thinning out tangling stems. During the growing season, cut back wayward stems as needed.

This plant is evergreen to semievergreen in the milder parts of its range; where winters are colder, all leaves drop in fall.

Akebia quinata

Aristolochia macrophylla

ARISTOLOCHIA macrophylla (A. durior)
🍃 DUTCHMAN'S PIPE
- 🌿 ZONES 1–24, 29–43
- ☼ ◐ ● FULL SUN, PARTIAL SHADE, OR FULL SHADE
- 💧💧 AMPLE
- CLIMBS BY: TWINING

This attractive vine has long been a favorite for shielding a porch from hot summer sun or covering an ugly building. It grows rapidly, reaching 15 to 20 feet in a season and easily attaining an ultimate size of 30 feet. The deep green,

kidney-shaped, 8- to 14-inch-long leaves slightly overlap each other, making for a thick, shingled-looking cover. The flowers appear in late spring to early summer. They're often hidden in the foliage, but worth a look for their interesting structure, which gives the general impression of an old-fashioned pipe.

Dutchman's pipe tolerates summer heat well, but it does require winter chill to thrive—making it a good choice for zones with hot summers and frosty winters. Because it grows so rapidly, it can cover a large area in a short growing season. This vine easily twines up a trellis.

Provide protection from strong winds. You can prune back heavy growth just before the end of dormancy in late winter; during the growing season, pinch back new growth to encourage a thick foliage mat.

🍃 BOUGAINVILLEA
- 🌿 ZONES 12, 13, 15–17, 19, 22–28
- ☼ ◐ FULL SUN OR PARTIAL SHADE
- 💧 💧 REGULAR TO MODERATE
- CLIMBS BY: SCRAMBLING; USES THORNS AS HOOKS

Covering walls and scrambling over hillsides, vivid bougainvillea is a much-loved vine for warmer zones. The bright color comes not from the true flowers, which are tiny and inconspicuous, but from the bracts surrounding them. Bloom reaches its peak in midsummer, but flowers may appear from spring through fall and even into winter. Stems are outfitted in rich deep green, 1- to 2-inch leaves and equipped with needlelike thorns; they have no real means of attachment (though the thorns do help them scramble through other plants), so you'll need to tie them to the support you provide. The vines reach 15 to 30 feet.

Handle bougainvillea carefully while planting, since roots are fine and break easily. To plant, cut off the container's bottom; then set plant and container in the planting hole. Slide the container up over the plant, filling in with soil as you go. (Don't worry about damaging plants when you remove the container; they have pliable stems and little horizontal growth.)

Prune bougainvillea after the season's first bloom flush to keep its size under control, cutting back any stems that are growing beyond your desired limits. Don't be afraid to cut it to the shape you want.

CAMPSIS

🌿🌿 TRUMPET VINE, TRUMPET CREEPER

✎ ZONES VARY
☼ ☽ FULL SUN OR PARTIAL SHADE
◖◗ REGULAR TO MODERATE
CLIMBS BY: CLINGING WITH AERIAL ROOTLETS

Covered with trumpet-shaped flowers from early summer through late fall, these fast-growing vines are a popular choice for the garden—and a favorite of hummingbirds, too. Many withstand colder zones; though they die to the ground in hard freezes, they make a rapid recovery. The flowers, carried in clusters of six to 12, are long tubes that flare open to five-part lobes; leaves are divided featherwise into seven to 11 leaflets.

It's important to keep trumpet vines well pruned as they mature. Left untended, the heavy top growth can weaken the hold of the aerial rootlets and bring the whole vine tumbling down. After a plant has established itself, cut many of the stems to the ground; cut others back by half.

Bougainvillea

Campsis radicans

Clematis terniflora

C. grandiflora. CHINESE TRUMPET VINE, CHINESE TRUMPET CREEPER. Zones 4–12, 14–21, 29–32. This one is slightly less hardy than common trumpet vine; its flowers are somewhat larger, with more open lobes, and their color is more scarlet than orange. The plant reaches 30 feet.

C. radicans. COMMON TRUMPET VINE, COMMON TRUMPET CREEPER. Zones 2–21, 26–41. Native to the United States, this is the most widely sold trumpet vine, flourishing throughout most of the country. It easily reaches 30 to 50 feet (and can weigh up to 100 pounds) in the milder parts of its range. Flowers of the

species are 3-inch-long orange tubes that flare open to scarlet lobes; 'Flava' has yellow flowers.

C. × tagliabuana. Zones 3–24, 26–34. Many gardeners prefer this hybrid to common trumpet vine for its somewhat larger flowers and more modest growth: while it can reach 30 feet, pruning often easily holds it to 15 to 20 feet. Most widely sold is 'Mme. Galen', with salmon red blooms.

CLEMATIS terniflora (C. dioscoreifolia, C. maximowicziana, C. paniculata)

🌿 SWEET AUTUMN CLEMATIS

✎ ZONES 3–9, 14–24, 26, 28–41
☼ ☽ FULL SUN FOR TOPS, PARTIAL SHADE FOR ROOTS
◗ REGULAR
CLIMBS BY: COILING LEAFSTALKS

Sweet autumn clematis is covered with billowy masses of extremely fragrant, inch-wide white flowers from late summer to early fall, at a time when many other garden plants are finishing their bloom. Carefree and easy to grow, it's a vigorous vine that can reach 30 feet per season in milder zones. Medium to dark green leaves are divided into three to five oval, 1- to 2½-inch-long leaflets. Tightly coiling leafstalks allow the plant to climb by grasping its own stems and any fairly slim vertical support. Nurseries and catalogs offer sweet autumn clematis under various botanical names; to make sure you're getting the right plant, look for the common name as well.

Sweet autumn clematis is happy with regular garden soil, but like all clematis, it performs best with its roots in shade, its leaves and stems in sunlight. Because it grows so vigorously, be sure you provide it with sufficient support.

The best time to prune and thin this vine is from late fall to early spring, before new growth begins. You can cut back stems heavily, leaving as little as 1 to 1½ feet of the previous year's growth.

GELSEMIUM sempervirens

🌿 CAROLINA JESSAMINE, CAROLINA JASMINE

⬦ ZONES 8–24, 26–33
☀ ◐ FULL SUN OR PARTIAL SHADE
💧 REGULAR
CLIMBS BY: TWINING

In late winter and early spring, when little else is blooming, Carolina jessamine is covered in brilliant yellow, fragrant, tubular flowers 1 to 1½ inches long. It's good looking out of bloom too, thanks to its cloak of shiny light green, 1- to 4-inch, oval leaves.

Growing to about 20 feet, this vine twines easily up all kinds of supporting structures, including trellises and chain link fences. Individual stems are long streamers; they can be trimmed back, woven into their support, or left to sway in the breeze from the top of an arbor or pergola.

Carolina jessamine is a carefree plant, little bothered by pests and diseases. It performs well in ordinary soil but grows faster and more luxuriantly in rich, well-amended soil. It grows best in full sun but will tolerate some shade. It can be pruned at any time of the year, though the best time for the job is after the bloom period ends. At this time, thin out tangled stems and superfluous growth, if necessary. Vines have a tendency to become topheavy; you can prune them back severely when this happens.

Note: All parts of Carolina jessamine are toxic if ingested.

LONICERA

🌿🌿🌿 HONEYSUCKLE

⬦ ZONES VARY
☀ ◐ FULL SUN OR PARTIAL SHADE
💧 MODERATE
CLIMBS BY: TWINING

Honeysuckle is an old-fashioned favorite, beloved for its casual charm and (in many species) the sweet perfume of its tubular spring-to-summer blossoms. The twining stems are outfitted in oval, 2- to

3-inch long leaves in dark to bluish green. Give the vines support in the form of a trellis or a wall strung with wire. Prune as flowering tapers off (usually in late summer), cutting vines to a manageable size. Badly overgrown plants can be cut back to the ground any time; they'll regrow rapidly.

Japanese honeysuckle, *L. japonica*, is the most commonly grown species—but it has become an invasive pest in much of the Southeast, overrunning the native flora. To avoid contributing to its spread in

Gelsemium sempervirens

ABOVE: *Lonicera × heckrottii*
BELOW: *Mandevilla* 'Alice du Pont'

the wild (its seeds spread from backyard gardens to cover an enormous radius), consider one of the other honeysuckles.

L. × heckrottii. GOLD FLAME HONEYSUCKLE, CORAL HONEYSUCKLE. Zones 3–24, 30–35. Evergreen in mild-winter zones, deciduous in colder regions. Many honeysuckles have blooms in modest shades of cream, white, or pale yellow, but this one is different. Coral pink buds open to 1½-inch-long, bright coral pink flowers that are rich yellow inside. The vine reaches 12 to 15 feet. It is often trained on a trellis against a wall or on wires along house eaves to form an embroidery of leaves and blossoms.

Gold flame honeysuckle prefers rich, well-drained soil and shade for its roots. It rarely sets seed, so it generally is not invasive.

L. sempervirens. TRUMPET HONEYSUCKLE. Zones 2–41. Semievergreen in milder areas; deciduous elsewhere. Though this species lacks the famed honeysuckle perfume, its blooms do offer eye-catching color, ranging from bright orange-yellow to scarlet. The flowers are 1½- to 2-inch trumpets, carried in whorls at stem tips. The vine is a fairly modest grower, reaching 10 to 20 feet.

Trumpet honeysuckle isn't particular about soil, but it does need good drainage. It may set some seed, but it's unlikely to be as invasive as Japanese honeysuckle.

🌿 MANDEVILLA 'Alice du Pont'

⬦ ZONES 21–25; MAY GROW AS A ROOT-HARDY PERENNIAL IN ZONES 26, 27
☀ ◐ FULL SUN OR PARTIAL SHADE
💧 REGULAR
CLIMBS BY: TWINING

If it were grown exclusively outdoors, this lovely vine would be found in only the mildest zones. But because it thrives in pots on porch or deck, it's one of the most widely sold vines in the country.

Continued >

Pure pink, 2- to 4-inch-wide flowers shaped like flaring trumpets usually bloom from spring into fall, carried against a backdrop of glossy green, 3- to 8-inch leaves. And unlike many other vines, this one blooms happily at a small size—plants in 4-inch containers regularly produce flowers.

You'll often find this plant identified simply by its cultivar name—'Alice du Pont'—rather than by genus and cultivar (*Mandevilla* 'Alice du Pont').

This vine does best with rich soil. It likes sun but needs some afternoon shade in the hottest areas. Grown outdoors in its preferred warm climates, it can reach 20 to 30 feet; container-grown plants stay much lower. For in-ground as well as containerized plants, provide a trellis or similar support. Feed container plants with a complete fertilizer every 2 weeks until the end of bloom; then trim the stems back by half and bring the plant indoors or to a sheltered spot. Water regularly throughout winter. If you're growing the plant outdoors, do any necessary pruning during the growing season.

PARTHENOCISSUS
tricuspidata
🌿 BOSTON IVY
- ❚ ZONES 2–24, 31–41
- ☼ ◑ ● FULL SUN, PARTIAL SHADE, OR FULL SHADE
- ◗ REGULAR
- CLIMBS BY: CLINGING WITH HOLDFAST DISCS AT ENDS OF TENDRILS

Though it isn't an ivy, this is the vine that gave the Ivy League its nickname: English ivy *(Hedera helix)* froze in the colder northern climates, so gardeners ended up planting *Parthenocissus* instead. It soon became a favorite, especially appreciated for its brilliant fall color. It clings tightly to its support by holdfast discs, quickly climbing as high as 30 to 50 feet.

Leaves are up to 8 inches wide, with three distinct lobes or three leaflets; they're glossy green from spring through

Parthenocissus tricuspidata

Rosa 'Blaze'

summer, then turn to red, yellow, or orange in autumn. For a finer-textured, smaller-leafed vine than the species, look for 'Veitchii'; its foliage is burgundy red when new, and many believe it has the finest fall color.

Boston ivy does well in ordinary garden soil. In intensely hot regions, plant it only on walls that have a northern or eastern exposure. It naturally forms a matlike foliage cover. Prune to control and train at any time during the growing season; thin vines heavily and routinely if you want just a fine tracery of growth.

ROSA
🌺 🌺 ROSE
- ❚ ZONES VARY
- ☼ FULL SUN
- ◗ REGULAR
- CLIMBS BY: SCRAMBLING; USES THORNS AS HOOKS

A climbing rose trained on a trellis, decorating a wall, or clambering into a tree is one of the most delightful sights in the garden. Climbing roses are almost as popular as their shrubby counterparts, and they likewise need regular water and fertilizer to thrive. We describe just three popular climbers, but countless choices are available; for a more complete selection, consult *Sunset*'s *Roses* (1998).

R. banksiae 'Lutea'. LADY BANKS' ROSE. Native to China, this spring-blooming species rose is a favorite in many parts of the country. It grows in Zones 4–33 and is evergreen in all but the coldest parts of its range. Though it isn't hardy below 0°F/−18°C, it does survive the heat and humidity of the Gulf Coast, Florida, and the Deep South. Very double, primrose yellow blossoms are small (just 1 inch across), in pendent clusters; leaves are small, too, and highly resistant to pests and diseases. The virtually thornless canes can reach 25 feet long and are quite pliable, easy to twine around a support structure; they are best displayed over an arbor, where they can form a thick canopy. They don't require formal training. If you need to thin growth or prune to limit spread, do it right after flowering.

R. 'Blaze'. A long-time favorite for its plentiful bright red blooms, 'Blaze' tolerates both cold and heat and is grown throughout the country. Though cane length varies by region, it's typically a fairly restrained climber that will grow happily on a low fence or over a small arbor. The double, 2- to 3-inch blossoms are often borne in clusters; they typically don't appear in profusion until the plant is 2 or 3 years old.

'Blaze' is rarely troubled by pests or diseases; it tolerates tough conditions but appreciates regular water and fertilizer, rewarding you with an almost continuous display of bloom throughout the growing season. Prune and thin as needed during dormancy.

R. 'New Dawn'. One of the most popular climbing roses, fast-growing 'New Dawn' is cold hardy in all but the northernmost parts of the United States. Make sure you give it plenty of room: its many canes can reach 15 to 25 feet, with vigorous side branching. Plump pink buds open to scented semidouble blossoms that age to a lighter, creamier pink. The glossy green foliage is seldom troubled by pests, but in humid climates it may be afflicted by mildew or black spot late in the season.

'New Dawn' is attractive scrambling atop an arbor, engulfing a dead tree trunk, or tumbling over a wall. To contain growth, cut back some of the the oldest canes to the bud union each year; this also keeps the plant from getting too dense.

🌿 WISTERIA

🌡 ZONES VARY
☀ FULL SUN; *W. SINENSIS* TAKES
   SOME SHADE
💧 REGULAR
CLIMBS BY: TWINING

Breathtaking in full bloom, wisteria is the queen of flowering vines. The sweet pea–shaped flowers grow in elongated clusters; violet blue is the most common color, though you'll see white and even pink wisterias as well. Leaves often reach 1 foot or longer, bearing seven to 15 or more leaflets arranged featherwise along a central leafstalk.

Most wisterias don't bloom right away. To shorten the flowerless period, buy the largest plant possible: a wisteria started from a 5-gallon container may bloom in 1 to 2 years, several years sooner than a 1-gallon plant.

Wisteria is easy to grow, but you will need to choose the planting location carefully. For Japanese wisteria, make

Wisteria floribunda

sure vines will be in sun; they rarely bloom in shade. Chinese wisteria prefers sun, too, although it will flower even in some shade. Be sure to provide sturdy support (see page 142).

These vines aren't fussy about soil, but they do need good drainage. In alkaline soils, they may suffer from chlorosis; treat the problem with iron chelates or iron sulfate.

Wisteria needs little to no fertilizer—and in fact, feeding often curtails bloom. If a wisteria that you've been fertilizing fails to flower, stop the feeding; since buds for next spring's bloom are started early in the summer, you'll need to withhold fertilizer an entire growing season to see if excess fertilizer was responsible for the lack of flowers. If the vine again fails to bloom, try pruning roots in the spring (after you're sure no flowers are forthcoming): plunge a sharp spade vertically into the plant's root zone, cutting into the soil 1 foot away from the main trunk on all sides for each inch of the trunk's diameter. This treatment may shock the wisteria into blooming the following year.

Prune wisteria twice a year. During the summer months, numerous long

streamers will emerge from all over the vine. Cut back most of these to side branches before they can tangle up in the main body of the vine; save those you want to use to extend the vine's height or length, and tie them to the underlying support. (You may need to repeat this chore 4 to 6 weeks later.) At the end of winter dormancy, check the vine again and remove additional tangling side streamers; also remove any dead or poorly placed stems.

W. floribunda. JAPANESE WISTERIA. Zones 2–24, 26, 28–41. Intensely fragrant blooms grow in clusters about 1½ feet long. The typical color is violet to violet blue, but you'll find named cultivars in various other purple shades as well as in white or pink. Blossoms appear just as leaves emerge in spring. After the initial spring flush, vines continue to bloom off and on throughout summer, though flowering is less profuse than in spring. In autumn, leaves take on yellow to gold shades (even in mild-winter climates). The vine can reach 50 feet, but 30 feet is a more typical size.

'Texas Purple' starts flowering sooner than many other Japanese wisterias—usually the first season after planting.

W. sinensis. CHINESE WISTERIA. Zones 3–24, 26, 28–35, 37, 39. Chinese wisteria's blossom clusters are somewhat shorter than those of Japanese wisteria (to about 1 foot) and not as fragrant, but its floral display is more striking—it blooms before leaves emerge, with all flowers in a cluster opening at once. There's a second, less profuse bloom in fall. The usual flower color is violet blue. 'Alba' is a white form; 'Cooke's Special' has longer-than-average clusters of medium-violet blooms..

Chinese wisteria is smaller than Japanese wisteria, typically attaining about 20 feet. Though it excels as a vine, it is sometimes pruned and trained as a single-stemmed weeping shrub, providing a dramatic focal point in the landscape. In warmer zones, provide protection from hot afternoon sun.

ANNUALS AND BIENNIALS

Annuals fill the garden with quick, dependable color in every imaginable hue. These are plants that germinate, flower profusely, set seed, and die, all in the course of a single growing season. In contrast, biennials (see page 152) take two seasons to complete their life cycle, while perennials (see pages 154–163) can live and bloom for many years. Though the annual-biennial-perennial distinction seems clear on paper, in gardens it's somewhat blurred. For example, some tender perennials—such as geranium (Pelargonium), some kinds of salvia, and verbena—flower year after year in mild-winter climates, but are grown as annuals where winters are cold.

PLANTING ANNUALS

The best time to plant annuals depends on the specific plant and your climate. Annuals are designated as "cool-season" or "warm-season," based on their hardiness and ability to grow in cool soils.

Cool-season annuals, such as pansy *(Viola),* primrose *(Primula),* and calendula, grow best in the cool soils and mild temperatures of spring and fall. Most withstand fairly heavy frosts. When the weather turns hot, they set seed and deteriorate. If you live in a cold-winter area (Zones 1–6, 32–45), plant these annuals in very early spring, as soon as the soil can be

ABOVE: A bright mix of zinnias, globe amaranth *(Gomphrena globosa),* salvia, and marigolds *(Tagetes)* sparkles in this summer garden.

BELOW LEFT: A raised bed showcases pansies *(Viola)* and snapdragons *(Antirrhinum majus),* two annuals that thrive in cool weather.

worked. To bloom vigorously, they must develop roots and foliage during cool weather.

In mild-winter regions (Zones 7–31), many cool-season annuals can be planted in fall for bloom in winter and early spring; or plant them in late winter or very early spring for spring flowers.

Warm-season annuals include marigold *(Tagetes),* zinnia, and impatiens. These plants grow and flower best in the warm months of late spring, summer, and early fall; they're cold tender and may perish in a late frost if planted too early in spring. In cold-winter climates, set out warm-season annuals after the danger of frost has passed. In warm-winter areas, plant them in midspring.

Careful soil preparation will help get your annuals off to a good start and keep them growing well all season. Dig out any weeds on the site and add a 3-inch layer of compost, well-rotted manure, or other organic amendment. It's also a good idea to add a complete fertilizer; follow the package directions for amounts. Dig or till amendments and fertilizer into the soil, then rake the bed smooth.

You can start annuals from seed sown in pots or directly in the garden (see pages 54–57), or you can buy started plants at a nursery. Nursery plants may be sold in flats, cell-packs, peat pots, or gallon containers; see page 34 for planting instructions. For best results, choose relatively small plants with healthy foliage. Plants with yellowing leaves and those that are leggy, rootbound, or too big for their pots will establish only slowly in the garden, and they'll usually bloom poorly.

After planting, water the bed thoroughly. Young seedlings or transplants may need water once a day in warm weather, but as they become established, you can gradually cut back. Apply a 2- to 4-inch layer of mulch (such as compost, ground bark, or pine needles) to conserve moisture and help prevent weeds from becoming established.

Mixing a complete fertilizer into the soil before planting will generally supply your annuals with nutrients sufficient for at least half the growing season. In cold-winter areas, an additional feeding after bloom begins will carry the plants through their season. Where winters are warmer and the growing season correspondingly longer, apply fertilizer again in late summer.

| RECOMMENDED SPACING | AREA PLANTS WILL COVER | |
between plants	48 plants*	64 plants*
4 in.	4 1/2 sq. ft.	6 sq. ft.
6 in.	10 sq. ft.	13 1/2 sq. ft.
8 in.	18 sq. ft.	24 1/2 sq. ft.
10 in.	28 1/2 sq. ft.	38 1/2 sq. ft.
12 in.	41 1/2 sq. ft.	55 1/2 sq. ft.

*Plants per flat

BEDDING PLANTS

Many annuals are suitable for massing in beds to produce a swath of color. Set out bedding plants in offset rows, so that groups of four form diamonds; space them as recommended in the sampler (pages 150–152) or at the nursery. For even spacing, measure the distance between plants with a piece of wood of the desired length. The chart above show the area that will be covered by a particular number of plants set out at various spacings.

PINCHING, STAKING, AND DEADHEADING

A little extra care will keep your annuals looking attractive all season long.

PINCHING. Though most annuals are bred to be compact and well branched, some, including petunia and geranium *(Pelargonium)*, benefit from pinching. With your thumb and forefinger, nip off the tips of the stems; this forces side growth, making the plant denser and more compact.

STAKING. A few very tall annuals, such as sunflower *(Helianthus),* may require staking to keep them from falling over. Use a single stake and tie the stem to it with plastic tape or soft twine; or support the plant with a cylinder of wire fencing.

DEADHEADING. As their flowers fade, annuals put their energy into ripening seeds. If you regularly "deadhead"—remove dead flowers and any seedpods—the plant will typically bear more flowers in a continued effort to produce seeds. Deadheading also keeps the garden tidy. Large-blossomed annuals such as zinnia are easy to deadhead: just pinch or cut flowers back to the next branch. With smaller-flowered plants like floss flower *(Ageratum)*, it's easier to shear the flower heads off with pruning or hedge shears. Take care not to cut back too far: don't remove more than a third of the plant.

A SAMPLER OF ANNUALS AND BIENNIALS

Annuals can be grown in all climate zones, but you'll still need to pay attention to the time of year: choose annuals suitable to warm or cool seasons, depending on when you're planting. Also take care to select plants that fit the intended site, keeping in mind the ultimate size each plant will attain. For an explanation of the at-a-glance information introducing each entry, see page 95.

WARM-SEASON ANNUALS

AGERATUM houstonianum
FLOSS FLOWER

☼ ☽ FULL SUN OR PARTIAL SHADE
💧 REGULAR

Fluffy flower tassels come in azure blue, lavender, pink, or white on plants 1 to 2½ feet tall. Blooms from early summer to fall. Space dwarf varieties 6 inches apart, tall ones 1 to 1½ feet apart.

CATHARANTHUS roseus (Vinca rosea)
MADAGASCAR PERIWINKLE

☼ ☽ FULL SUN OR PARTIAL SHADE
💧 MODERATE

Phloxlike flowers bloom in shades of pink, rose, lavender, and white on plants 4 to 24 inches tall, depending on the variety. Thrives in hot conditions, whether dry or humid. Space 8 to 12 inches apart.

COSMOS

☼ ☽ FULL SUN OR PARTIAL SHADE
💧 MODERATE

Showy daisylike flowers nod above lacy foliage from summer through fall. Plants are fast growing, with heights ranging from 2 to 7 feet; tall sorts are good for

Ageratum houstonianum

background planting. *C. bipinnatus* has flowers in white, bicolors, and shades of pink, lavender, purple, and crimson. *C. sulphureus,* called yellow cosmos, has bold yellow to deep orange blossoms. Both species grow best in soil that is dry and not very fertile. Space 1 foot apart.

GOMPHRENA
GLOBE AMARANTH

☼ FULL SUN
💧 MODERATE

Cloverlike blossoms in red, pink, orange, purple, and white are borne on plants 9 inches to 2 feet tall. Easy to dry for winter bouquets. Space plants 8 to 12 inches apart.

HELIANTHUS annuus
SUNFLOWER

☼ FULL SUN
💧 REGULAR

Huge, radiant blooms in yellow, orange, maroon, creamy white, and bicolors. Depending on variety, plants grow 2 to 12 feet tall, with flower heads from 4 to 12 inches across. The flowers are followed by edible seeds that are much relished by birds. Tall sunflowers should be staked. Plant 1½ feet apart.

IMPATIENS wallerana

☼ ● PARTIAL TO FULL SHADE
💧 REGULAR

Invaluable for providing months of color in sites too shady for most other annuals. Flowers are single or double and come in every color but blue. Dwarf varieties grow 4 to 12 inches high; space these 6 inches apart. Tall kinds reach 2 feet; space 1 foot apart.

PETUNIA hybrida

☼ FULL SUN
💧 REGULAR

Richly colored flowers come in red, pink, blue, purple, yellow, cream, white, and bicolors. There are two main flower types, single and double; single blossoms are simple trumpets, while double ones are ruffled blooms resembling carnations. Plants range from 8 to 27 inches high. Space 7 to 10 inches apart.

Catharanthus roseus

Cosmos bipinnatus

Gomphrena globosa

Helianthus annuus

TAGETES
MARIGOLD

☀ FULL SUN
💧 REGULAR

Robust, fast growing, and virtually trouble free, marigolds come in vibrant shades of yellow, orange, and orange red, as well as white and bicolors. Foliage has a pungent scent. *T. erecta,* called African marigold (though all garden marigolds are actually descended from species native to Mexico), has large blossoms—fully double in most varieties—on plants that grow 20 to 36 inches tall. *T. patula,* the French marigold, bears single or double flowers and grows 6 to 18 inches tall. Space dwarf varieties about 6 inches apart, taller kinds 1 to 2 feet apart. Stake tall marigolds early in the season to prevent them from toppling.

ZINNIA elegans

☀ FULL SUN
💧 REGULAR

Borne on plants 1 to 3 feet tall, colorful daisylike flowers bloom in shades of yellow, orange, red, pink, and purple, as well as white and bicolors. Space 6 to 12 inches apart. Zinnias are susceptible to mildew; to help prevent it, water at ground level rather than sprinkling.

COOL-SEASON ANNUALS

ANTIRRHINUM majus
SNAPDRAGON

☀ FULL SUN
💧 REGULAR

Blooming in bright colors, pastel shades, and white, snapdragons range in size from 6- to 8-inch dwarfs to 3-foot-tall giants. There are several flower forms; besides the familiar "snapping" type with upper and lower "jaws," you'll find snapdragons with double, bell-shaped, and azalea-shaped flowers. Space dwarf plants 9 inches apart, taller kinds 15

Impatiens wallerana

Petunia hybrida

Tagetes patula

Zinnia elegans

inches apart. Snapdragons are prone to rust, so choose rust-resistant varieties. Also avoid overhead watering, which can spread rust spores. (Don't let plants dry out, though; the disease spreads faster in hot, dry conditions.)

CALENDULA officinalis
CALENDULA, POT MARIGOLD
- ☼ FULL SUN
- 💧 MODERATE

Bushy, upright plants with pungently scented foliage reach 1 to 2½ feet tall and bear abundant blossoms reminiscent of double daisies. Flower colors include orange and bright yellow as well as white and more subtle shades of cream, apricot, and soft yellow. The petals are edible, with a slightly tangy flavor. Space plants 12 to 14 inches apart.

LATHYRUS odoratus
SWEET PEA
- ☼ FULL SUN
- 💧 REGULAR

Delightfully fragrant sweet peas bloom in shades of pink, purple, blue, salmon, and red, as well as white, cream, and bicolors. Plant size varies: bush types grow 1 to 3 feet high, while vines can reach 5 feet or taller. Space seeds or plants 6 to 12 inches apart.

Provide a trellis or other support for climbing types as soon as you plant them, since seedlings need support as soon as the tendrils form.

MATTHIOLA incana
STOCK
- ☼ ☼ FULL SUN OR PARTIAL SHADE
- 💧 REGULAR

These old-fashioned favorites bear 1- to 3-foot spikes of clustered single or double flowers with a wonderful spicy-sweet scent. Colors include white, cream, pink, lavender, purple, and red. The soft gray-green leaves are long and narrow. Space plants 9 to 12 inches apart.

Calendula officinalis

Alcea rosea

Lathyrus odoratus

Campanula medium

VIOLA
PANSY, VIOLA
- ☼ ☼ FULL SUN OR PARTIAL SHADE
- 💧 REGULAR

Pansy (*V. wittrockiana*) has 2- to 4-inch flowers in white, blue, mahogany red, rose, yellow, apricot, and purple; the petals are often striped or blotched. Viola (*V. cornuta*) has blossoms about 1½ inches across, in bicolors as well as many clear solid colors. Both pansy and viola grow 8 to 10 inches high; space both 6 to 8 inches apart.

BIENNIALS

Plants called biennials typically complete their life cycle in 2 years. During the first year, they grow from seed into leafy but nonblooming plants. They live through the winter, then bloom, set seed, and die in the following year. This is the life cycle you'll observe if you start seeds. Biennials you buy from a nursery usually bloom the same year, however; the grower has taken care of the first phase of growth for you.

Plant breeders have worked to push biennials into either the annual or perennial category; there are now annual strains of hollyhock (*Alcea*), for example, and some foxgloves (*Digitalis*) are perennials.

To grow biennials, start seed in pots or directly in the garden at the time indicated on the seed packet—usually mid-spring or late summer.

ALCEA rosea
HOLLYHOCK
- ☼ FULL SUN
- 💧 REGULAR

An old-fashioned favorite with 3- to 6-inch-wide, single to double flowers on stems that range from 2½ feet to a towering 9 feet tall. Blossoms appear in summer; colors include yellow, cream, white, pink, red, and purple. Rust can be a serious problem; choose rust-resistant varieties, remove any rust-infected leaves you see, and avoid overhead watering (it can spread rust spores). Plants self-sow freely. Space 1½ feet apart.

Digitalis purpurea

CAMPANULA medium
CANTERBURY BELLS

☼ ☼ FULL SUN OR PARTIAL SHADE

💧 REGULAR

Another choice for an old-fashioned garden, Canterbury bells sends up leafy, 2½- to 4-foot stems bearing loose clusters of bell-shaped flowers 1 to 2 inches across. Blossoms come in late spring or early summer; besides the traditional blue, colors include purple, violet, lavender, pink, and white. Space 15 to 18 inches apart.

DIGITALIS purpurea
FOXGLOVE

☼ LIGHT SHADE

💧 REGULAR

This cottage-garden staple forms clumps of large, furry leaves from which tall flowering spikes (to 4 feet or higher) emerge in spring to early summer. The pendulous, tubular, 2- to 3-inch-long flowers bloom in white, lavender, pink, or purple. Volunteer seedlings often have white or light-colored blossoms. The leaves are a source of digitalis, a valuable medicinal drug (but one that is highly poisonous in the wrong doses). Space 1½ feet apart.

GARDENING IN CONTAINERS

With their rainbow of colors and long bloom season, annuals are naturals for container gardens. Perennials and bulbs offer still more colorful, interesting choices. Shrubs or small trees add structure to a group of containers, while vines can form cool, leafy screens.

Containers come in a dazzling array of shapes, colors, and materials. Whichever you choose, be sure there's at least one hole in the bottom to ensure proper drainage.

SOIL MIXES. Plants in containers need soil that allows roots to grow easily; it should be fast draining yet moisture retentive. Quick drainage means roots won't run the risk of suffocating in soggy soil; good moisture retention saves you from having to water constantly. Regular garden soil, even if it's good loam, is too dense for container use. A better bet is one of the packaged potting mixes sold at nurseries and garden centers.

WATERING. Because they have only a limited amount of soil from which to draw moisture, container-grown plants require more frequent watering than those grown in the ground. In hot or windy weather, some (especially those in hanging baskets) may need watering several times a day; in cool weather, it may be sufficient to water weekly or even less often. Check the soil in the containers and water when the top inch or two is dry.

To water thoroughly, apply water over the entire soil surface until it flows out of the pot's drainage holes. This moistens the entire soil mass.

FERTILIZING. Because the necessary frequent watering leaches nutrients from potting mix, container plants need regular feeding. Apply a liquid fertilizer every 2 weeks; or mix a controlled-release fertilizer into the potting mix before planting.

Containers filled with a variety of plants decorate a patio garden.

PERENNIALS

Perennials—those nonwoody plants that come back year after year—offer almost endless variety in color, texture, shape, and size, making them suitable for virtually any garden location. Many are prized for their flowers; aster and phlox are just two of these. Others, such as ferns and hostas, are valued for their foliage.

Unlike shrubs and trees, perennials do not have permanent woody parts. But while some die down completely at the end of each growing season, then reappear at the start of the next, others spend the winter as low tufts of foliage, ready to grow when weather warms. And a third type is truly evergreen, with foliage nearly unchanged throughout winter.

All perennials have a minimum lifespan of more than 2 years—but beyond this, longevity varies enormously. Some grace the garden for only a few years, while others survive much, much longer (peonies, for example, can live for generations).

Though flowering perennials are often grown in borders, you'll also find them just about everywhere else. They may replace the front lawn or fill a parking strip; they may be used in the vegetable garden to add color and edge planting beds. Some gardeners set them among established shrubs to provide variety and add a touch of color to a predominantly green, leafy planting.

Mixed perennials—including flowering sorts as well as fluffy ornamental grasses—decorate a winding garden path.

A lushly colorful perennial border beautifies the garden and provides flowers for cutting, too.

PLANTING AND CARING FOR PERENNIALS

Most perennials are purchased in 4-inch or 1-gallon containers; mail-order sources often also ship them bare-root. Plant them as directed on pages 36–38.

SOIL, WATER, AND FERTILIZER. In general, these plants prefer soil well amended with organic matter, but a surprising number do well in ordinary or even poor garden soil. Some thrive in full sun; others need some shade, especially in hot-summer climates. Water needs differ, too: some perennials are thirsty, while others succeed with little water. Most perennials appreciate an annual feeding, either in the form of organic amendments worked into the soil in spring or fall or with a complete fertilizer applied in spring. Some, however, are heavy feeders and need regular fertilizing throughout the growing season.

It's also important to find out how wide and high a perennial will ultimately grow. Some reach 7 to 8 feet tall, while others are almost as low as ground covers; and plants that are only a few inches across when brought home from the nursery may eventually form mounds 3 to 4 feet wide. To avoid crowding problems, space plants and choose planting locations with an eye toward plants' mature size.

DEADHEADING AND TRIMMING. Perennials look their best with regular maintenance during the growing season. Deadheading (removing old flowers) keeps the garden looking neat and can prolong bloom for several more weeks.

For many flowering perennials, trimming and pinching also improve appearance. After a spring-flowering plant's bloom period ends, cut back all stems and foliage by one-third; a healthy mound of new growth soon fills in and remains throughout the growing season. To prevent lanky, floppy growth on some summer- and fall-blooming perennials, control growth early in the season. Pinch individual terminal buds (see page 52) to encourage bushier growth; to make plants bushier still, cut back entire branches by a few inches rather than just pinching the top bud.

Even with assiduous pinching and trimming, some perennials will be topheavy when in bloom and will require staking to stay upright. You'll find a variety of stakes at nurseries and garden centers. The most common are simple wood, bamboo, or plastic stakes. Others are circular grids that fit over the growing plants; still others are flexible "fences" or frames that can be positioned where they're needed.

DIVIDING. Gardeners divide perennials for at least two reasons: first, to improve the health and flower production of overgrown, crowded plantings; and second, to gain new divisions to increase a planting. Note that division is usually feasible only for perennials that grow in clumps with an expanding root mass. It is not practical to divide those that grow from a taproot; if you attempt to divide the taproot, you'll probably kill the plant. Such plants are usually increased by root cuttings or from seed.

Though there are exceptions, fall is usually the best time to divide plants that bloom in spring or early summer, while those that bloom in late summer to fall should be divided in spring.

Once divided, a large clump may yield several dozen divisions (or even more), but keep in mind that the smaller the division, the longer it will take to mature and bloom well again. For faster results, divide plants into fewer, larger sections.

To divide most perennials, follow these steps:

Wet the soil thoroughly a day or two before dividing to make the clump easier to dig.

Cut into the soil around the clump with a spading fork or shovel, digging 6 to 12 inches beyond the perimeter of the clump. Then dig under the roots to the depth of the fork or shovel, working around the perimeter until the entire area is loosened.

Remove excess soil from the clump (rinse it off with water from a hose, if necessary) so you can find natural dividing points.

Now begin the actual division. The best tool to use depends on the size of the clump and the type of roots it has. Some perennials have such thick, tough roots that a shovel (or even an ax) may be the only practical dividing tool. Others have mats of small fibrous roots that are easily sliced with a knife or pruning saw. Sometimes hand-held pruners or a trowel will do the job easily; if clumps are very loose, you can even separate by hand.

Cut foliage of large plants back to 4 to 6 inches once you've made the divisions. Keep the divisions' foliage and roots damp while you prepare the planting area; place them in a shady spot if the day is sunny and warm.

Amend the soil with organic matter, whether you are replanting in the same area or in another part of the garden. Many gardeners also work in a dry granular fertilizer high in phosphorus and potassium to promote healthy root development.

Plant divisions and keep them well watered while they're getting established. You can also plant divisions in containers and hold them for planting later or for sharing with fellow gardeners.

DIVIDING SHASTA DAISIES

Lift Shasta daisy (*Chrysanthemum × superbum*) from the ground after loosening soil around and under the clump with a spading fork.

Slice through clump with a trowel, dividing it into four sections. Then break each section by hand into 4- by 4-inch pieces.

Immediately plant divisions in prepared bed.

A SAMPLER OF PERENNIALS

There are probably at least a hundred perennials that will thrive in your garden—but the following sampler gives you a good starting point as you begin to build your collection. The group includes some of the most popular perennials grown today; most are flowering, while some are prized for their foliage. For an explanation of the at-a-glance information introducing each entry, see page 95.

ACHILLEA
YARROW

- ZONES 1–24, 26, 28–45
- FULL SUN
- MODERATE; NEEDS LESS ONCE ESTABLISHED

Among the perennials that flower in summer and early fall, yarrow is among the most carefree and heavy blooming. Enjoy the blossoms outdoors in the garden or indoors as cut flowers; you can even dry them for use in winter bouquets.

The large, flat-topped flower clusters rise on 1½- to 3-foot stalks from clumps of lower-growing foliage. Colors range from white to pastel shades to paprika red, but the familiar yellow yarrows are still favorites. Plants grow well in ordinary soil and with only moderate water; in fact, they may languish if soil is too rich or too moist. Divide when clumps get too crowded.

ANEMONE × hybrida
JAPANESE ANEMONE

- ZONES 3–24, 30–39, 41
- PARTIAL SHADE
- REGULAR

Prized for its late-summer bloom, this graceful plant bears loose sprays of slightly cupped, gold-centered white or pink flowers that resemble wild roses. Blossoms are single or double, 2 to 3 inches across, carried on 2- to 4-foot flower stems that rise from clumps of dark green, softly hairy foliage. Leaves are three to five lobed, up to 6 inches across.

Achillea

Anemone × hybrida

Aster novae-angliae

Foliage clumps are low in early spring, then increase in height as the season progresses. Japanese anemone is especially attractive planted in front of deep green shrubbery, where its flowers stand out dramatically against the dark backdrop.

Japanese anemone prefers good, well-amended soil; it will take claylike soil as long as drainage is good. Plants tolerate some sun in cool-summer climates but need protection from afternoon sun where summers are hot. Where winters are severe, mulch plantings heavily in fall.

Plants establish somewhat slowly but spread freely by rhizomes when mature; you can pull up new shoots to keep plants in bounds. Divide clumps every 5 to 7 years.

ASTER novae-angliae
NEW ENGLAND ASTER

- ZONES 1–24, 31–43
- FULL SUN; PARTIAL SHADE IN HOT-SUMMER CLIMATES
- REGULAR

Asters are on many a gardener's list of favorite fall-blooming perennials. They're easy to grow and add color to the landscape when most other flowers are winding down for the year.

This aster is a stout-stemmed plant 3 to 5 feet tall with hairy leaves to 5 inches long. Pink to deep purple flowers are 2 inches across; two favorite varieties are dark pink 'Alma Potschke' and deep lilac 'Treasure'. Stake plants early in the season to keep stems from flopping over.

Compared to many other asters, New England aster is more tolerant of climatic extremes, taking high humidity and colder winter temperatures. It performs best in rich soil. It prefers regular water and will thrive even in wet soil; if it dries out too much between waterings, it's prone to mildew. Divide clumps every 1 to 3 years.

ASTILBE

- ✿ ZONES 1–7, 14–17, 32–45
- ☼ ● PARTIAL TO FULL SHADE; ACCEPTS SOME SUN IN COOL-SUMMER CLIMATES
- ● REGULAR

Mainstays of the summer shade garden, astilbe provides both bright flower color and attractive foliage. Feathery, plumelike flower clusters in white and a wide range of pink and red shades emerge from loose clumps of toothed, dark green, almost fernlike leaves. Heights vary, but plants typically average 2 to 3 feet tall and wide. By planting varieties with staggered bloom times, you can enjoy flowers from late spring through summer's end.

Astilbe needs rich, moist, well-drained soil. It does best in shade but tolerates sun if temperatures are fairly cool and sufficient water is provided. Survival in the coldest zones (1, 43, 45) depends on good snow cover. During the growing season, apply a complete fertilizer regularly (monthly to bimonthly, depending on soil). Divide clumps when flower production lessens, usually every 3 to 5 years.

CHRYSANTHEMUM × superbum (Leucanthemum × superbum)
SHASTA DAISY

- ✿ ZONES 1–24, 26 (NORTHERN PART), 28–43
- ☼ ◐ FULL SUN; PARTIAL SHADE IN HOT-SUMMER CLIMATES
- ● REGULAR

Botanists have changed this plant's name several times over the years; at one point

Astilbe

Chrysanthemum × superbum

Coreopsis verticillata

it was removed from *Chrysanthemum* and reclassified as *Leucanthemum* (catalogs may still offer it as such). By any name, though, the yellow-centered white daisies look splendid both outdoors in the garden and indoors in bouquets. With routine care, plants will bloom happily from early summer through midfall.

The 3- to 5-inch-wide, single or double flowers are borne individually on leafy stems rising from basal mounds of coarsely toothed, dark green foliage. They're long lasting—in some cultivars, an individual flower may persist up to several weeks. The most popular cultivars grow 2 to 3 feet high and 1½ to 2 feet wide; some of the newer ones are especially heavy blooming.

Shasta daisies prefer fairly rich, moist soil, though some do well in regular garden soil. In all soils, good drainage is important, especially in winter. During the growing season, fertilize regularly to increase the number of emerging flower stalks; cut spent stalks back to the ground after flowers fade. In cold-winter areas, mulch around clumps' bases in fall; don't cover remaining foliage, though. Divide every 2 to 3 years; replant new growth from the edge of each clump and throw away the woody center.

Shasta daisy gall disease causes the root crown to split into many weak, poorly growing plants that quickly die. Dig out affected plants and do not replant new ones in the same spot.

COREOPSIS verticillata
THREADLEAF COREOPSIS

- ✿ ZONES 1–24, 26, 28–45
- ☼ FULL SUN
- ● MODERATE TO LITTLE

Threadleaf coreopsis blooms abundantly all summer long, carrying its daisylike, 1- to 2-inch, yellow flowers above clumps of ferny, feathery foliage. Blossoms are borne so thickly that you can't deadhead individually, so just cut back the multistemmed branches with shears; they'll soon regrow to bloom again.

This plant isn't fussy about soil, but good drainage is important. It is somewhat drought tolerant. Divide clumps every 1 to 3 years—in fall in warm-winter climates, in spring where winters are harsh.

C. v. 'Moonbeam' is a favorite; it forms a fluffy mound to 3 feet tall and wide, covered with pale yellow flowers.

DELPHINIUM elatum

✎ ZONES 1–10, 14–24, 32, 34,
36–41
☀ FULL SUN
💧 REGULAR

Delphinium's majestic bloom spikes are a mainstay of many summer gardens. Flower color covers the full range of blues and purples, and you'll find cool pinks, cream, and white as well. Individual blooms are flat, to 2 inches across, borne in narrow, upright spikes. Leaves are dark green and deeply lobed. The tall-growing cultivars of *D. elatum* are most widely grown; they form 1- to 2-foot-wide clumps and send up 5- to 6-foot flower spikes.

Delphiniums prefer cool, moist summers and chilly but not excessively cold winters. They need rich, porous, nonacid soil; if soil is acid, amend it to neutral before planting (see page 23). Also work in organic matter and a high-phosphorus fertilizer. When new shoots appear in spring, remove all but the two or three strongest and apply a complete fertilizer. Stake flower stalks early. Cut back stalks after bloom, leaving foliage at the bottom; when new stalks emerge, fertilize again to encourage fall bloom.

Even under ideal conditions, delphiniums are usually short lived; dividing them each year in spring may prolong their lives. If grown outside their preferred climate, they're best treated as annuals. Plant in fall in mild-winter zones, and just after frost danger is past where summers are hot.

Besides cultivars of *D. elatum*, tall delphiniums include the Pacific Hybrids, with flower spikes up to 7 feet.

Hybrids of *D.* × *belladonna*, such as 'Bellamosum', are somewhat hardier and less prone to disease than other delphiniums. Don't pinch or disbud these; just let them grow as they will. Their blossom spikes are shorter but more numerous than those of *D. elatum*.

Chinese delphinium (*D. grandiflorum*) is somewhat more forgiving of less-than-ideal conditions than *D. elatum*, though it does have the same soil and climate needs. It's a many-stalked plant that grows just 1½ to 2 feet tall, bearing flowers in blue shades.

ECHINACEA purpurea
PURPLE CONEFLOWER

✎ ZONES 1–24, 26–45
☀ FULL SUN
💧 MODERATE

Striking flowers and a long summer bloom season make this carefree plant a favorite. A North American native, it forms 1½-foot-wide clumps of hairy, rather coarse, deep green leaves that

Delphinium elatum

ABOVE: *Echinacea purpurea*
BELOW: *Geranium endressii* 'Wargrave Pink'

reach about 8 inches long. Borne on stiff, 1½- to 3-foot stalks that never need staking, the 4-inch, daisylike flowers have rosy purple petals that droop slightly from a brownish orange, dome-shaped center; they're popular with butterflies. The bristly cones remain after the petals drop; some gardeners leave them in place to provide food for small birds.

Purple coneflower needs no special treatment, though it appreciates some shade in the hottest regions. It does well in ordinary garden soil. It grows from a rhizomatous taproot and is better left undivided; because it grows slowly, individual plants can be left in place for a long period. To increase your supply of plants, take root cuttings in fall (see page 60). The plant self-sows readily; remove seedlings if you don't want them or if they do not grow or bloom true to the parent.

GERANIUM
CRANESBILL, GERANIUM

✎ ZONES VARY
☀ ◐ FULL SUN OR PARTIAL SHADE;
MUST HAVE AFTERNOON SHADE IN
HOT-SUMMER CLIMATES
💧 REGULAR

Not to be confused with common garden geranium *(Pelargonium)*, the cranesbills include spreading, mounding, and upright plants that make beautiful additions to the summer garden.

Flowers are five petaled, often in shades of rose, blue, and purple; a few varieties have pure pink or white blooms. Beaklike fruits follow the flowers, hence the common name "cranesbill." Leaves are roundish or kidney shaped, shallowly or deeply lobed.

One excellent choice is *G. endressii* (Zones 1–9, 14–24, 31–43), a 1- to 1½-footer that blooms from late spring to fall (to early summer in hotter regions); its variety 'Wargrave Pink', with salmon pink blooms, is most widely grown. Also popular is *G. sanguineum* (Zones 1–9, 14–24, 30–43), a spreading, trailing plant to 1½ feet high, 2 feet across, with deep purple blooms from late spring into summer.

Cranesbills grow best in cool- and mild-summer regions, where they will tolerate full sun or light shade. Where summers are hot, provide afternoon shade. Give moist, well-drained soil. Clumps can be left in place for many years before blooming declines due to crowding; when this happens, divide in early spring.

HELLEBORUS orientalis
LENTEN ROSE
- ☀ ZONES 2–10, 14–24, 31–41
- ☀ ◑ FULL SUN IN WINTER; PARTIAL TO FULL SHADE FOR REST OF YEAR
- ● REGULAR

Lenten rose blooms late in winter, bearing nodding, 2-inch flowers in shades of whitish green, soft purple, or rose, often spotted with purple. The "petals" are actually sepals that shelter the tiny true flowers, which are nestled in the blossom center surrounded by a clump of yellow stamens. These petal-like sepals remain on the plant for several months, long after the true flowers have faded and seeds have set. Leaves are large (to 1 foot across) and dark green, divided into five to 11 tooth-edged leaflets; they're evergreen in mild-winter climates, though you may want to remove tattered foliage during fall cleanup. Both foliage and flower stems emerge from a central point; plants eventually form clumps about 2 feet tall and wide.

Grow Lenten rose in a spot that receives winter sun but is later shaded by deciduous trees or shrubs. It prefers rich, well-amended, neutral to alkaline soil. Don't fertilize more than once or twice a year.

Lenten rose can be divided, but doing so is not recommended, since divided plants take several years to recuperate. However, plants self-sow readily—so to gain additional plants, simply let spent flowers go to seed.

Helleborus orientalis

Nepeta × faassenii

Paeonia lactiflora

NEPETA × faassenii
CATMINT
- ☀ ZONES 1–24, 30, 32–43
- ☀ FULL SUN
- ◔ MODERATE

Catmint blooms from mid- to late spring into summer, when loose spikes of small, clustered flowers form a lavender blue haze above the undulating mounds of soft gray-green, 1-inch leaves. The delicate-looking plants provide a nice contrast to larger, stiffer flowering perennials and annuals; they're an excellent underplanting for roses, too. And in cold-weather climates, they offer an alternative to lavender *(Lavandula)*.

Catmint needs only moderate watering, but will take more if soil is well drained. If dead flower spikes look unsightly after the first flush of bloom, cut them back with hedge shears; this may encourage a second bloom in late summer. If the whole plant looks untidy and floppy after bloom, shear it back by two-thirds. Division is rarely required.

PAEONIA
PEONY
- ☀ ZONES 1–11, 14–16, 32–45
- ☀ ◑ FULL SUN; PARTIAL SHADE IN HOT-SUMMER CLIMATES
- ● REGULAR

Peony flowers are exquisite: large, showy, silky, single or double, available in colors ranging from white and pale cream through pink, red, and even pure yellow. Individual blossoms are as large as 6 to 8 inches across; many are fragrant. Bloom time comes from late spring to early summer; for the longest display, plant varieties with early, midseason, and late bloom. The plant itself is a shrubby, 2- to 4-foot clump of lush dark green foliage, with each 8- to 10-inch leaf divided into elliptical leaflets. In many areas, leaves turn golden yellow in autumn before the plants die back.

The bush-form ("herbaceous") peonies just described are all cultivars of *P. lactiflora;* hundreds are available. Most need winter chill to bloom well. In milder climates, gardeners will usually have better luck with the Japanese cultivars, a popular group that blooms successfully in warm-winter areas.

Peonies are extremely long lived: choose a permanent site where they won't have to compete with other plants, and you'll be rewarded with years of bloom. Give rich, well-drained, neutral to slightly acid soil. Plant the tubers in fall, setting them 2 inches deep in the coldest zones, 1 inch deep in warmer areas (don't plant too deeply; if you do, the peonies won't bloom). Mulch the planting area the first year after the ground has frozen. Plants may not bloom the first year.

PAPAVER orientale
ORIENTAL POPPY
- 🖊 ZONES 1–11, 14–21, 30–45
- ☼ FULL SUN
- 💧⬤ REGULAR TO MODERATE

Oriental poppy blooms in early summer, bearing flamboyant bowl-shaped blossoms on leafy, 2- to 4-foot stalks that rise from a low mound of long, narrow, notch-edged, bristly looking (yet soft-to-the-touch) leaves. The flowers are 4 to 6 inches across. The original color was orange, but today you'll also find red, scarlet, pink, salmon, white, and bicolor blooms. One clump can grow almost 2 feet wide; three planted near each other make a dramatic splash of color at bloom time.

Though Oriental poppy is a favorite in many parts of the country, it needs winter chill for best performance and thrives in cold-winter, cool-summer regions. In these preferred areas, it's easy to grow, flourishing in ordinary garden soil (as long as it's well drained).

Plant Oriental poppy from roots or containers in early fall. Plants will welcome a springtime application of complete fertilizer during their first season.

Oriental poppy grows from a fleshy taproot and is not a good candidate for dividing. The preferred method for increasing a planting is to take root cuttings (see page 60) in summer.

PENSTEMON
PENSTEMON, BEARD TONGUE
- 🖊 ZONES VARY
- ☼ ☽ FULL SUN; LIGHT SHADE IN HOT-SUMMER CLIMATES
- 💧 REGULAR

These bushy, typically upright plants are fairly short lived—but to make up for it, they produce lots of color over a long period. The tubular, 1- to 2-inch-long flowers, popular with hummingbirds, are carried on leafy, semirigid stalks that rise from clumps of narrow, 3-inch-long leaves. Flower colors of penstemon

species are red, orange, and blue, but cultivars have increased the range to include white, soft pinks, salmon, peach, deep rose, lilac, and deep purple. Plants generally grow as wide as they are tall.

Two widely sold species, both offering many cultivars, are *P. barbatus* (Zones 1–24, 31–43), reaching 2 feet tall and blooming from midsummer to fall; and *P. × gloxinioides* (Zones 7–9,

Papaver orientale

Penstemon × gloxinioides

Phlox paniculata

14–24), a 2- to 4-foot-tall summer bloomer.

Grow penstemon in average to sandy or slightly rocky soil; be sure drainage is good. These plants aren't divided, but simply replaced every 3 to 4 years. Don't fertilize them—doing so shortens their already brief lifespan.

PHLOX paniculata
BORDER PHLOX, SUMMER PHLOX
- 🖊 ZONES 1–14, 18–21, 27–43
- ☼ FULL SUN; FLOWERS MAY FADE IN HOT-SUMMER CLIMATES
- 💧 REGULAR

Border phlox is deservedly popular for the showy, dome-shaped clusters of fragrant flowers it produces throughout the summer. Plants reach 2 to 4 feet tall and almost as wide, making a dramatic addition to the border. Leaves are dark green, 3 to 6 inches long; individual flowers are just about an inch across and come in a wide variety of colors.

Given the growing conditions it needs, phlox will reward you with healthy foliage and a long bloom season. Soil must be rich and well drained; dig planting beds deep and amend well with organic matter such as compost or well-rotted manure. Fertilize annually in spring. Deadhead spent blooms, since seedlings will not bloom true to the parent. Divide every 2 to 3 years, replanting only divisions from a clump's edges.

Powdery mildew can cause serious problems in hot, humid areas. To combat it, plant mildew-resistant varieties such as 'Ice Cap'. Cut mildew-infected plants to the ground each fall; then discard the cut-off portions and any debris.

RUDBECKIA fulgida
BLACK-EYED SUSAN
- 🖊 ZONES 1–24, 26–43
- ☼ FULL SUN
- 💧⬤ REGULAR TO MODERATE

Bright colored and easy to grow, black-eyed Susan is covered with 3- to 4-inch-

Rudbeckia fulgida 'Goldsturm'

wide, dark-centered yellow daisies from midsummer until late fall. The flowers are borne on multibranched, 2- to 3-foot stems that rise from a 2-foot-wide foliage clump; leaves are medium green, elliptical in shape, up to 5 inches long. Cut for bouquets or deadhead during the season to prolong bloom, but leave the last blooms of summer in place; the dark centers that remain after petals drop can be used in dried arrangements or left on the plants as food for birds.

Black-eyed Susan grows well in ordinary garden soil, spreading by underground rhizomes to form large clumps (you can remove newly emerging plants if they overreach their boundaries). Divide clumps when they lose vigor and their centers stop growing and blooming (every 4 to 5 years or so).

SALVIA × superba

> ✂ ZONES 2–10, 14–24, 31–41
> ☼ FULL SUN
> ♦ REGULAR

One of the most reliable of the hundreds of salvias grown for the garden, *Salvia × superba* lends vivid purple-blue shades to the garden throughout summer and into fall. The ½-inch flowers are carried on 1½- to 3-foot-tall spikes that rise from clumps of gray-green, 1- to 3-inch, elongated oval leaves with the distinctive sage fragrance common to many salvias. (For the familiar culinary sage, see page 177.)

Among the many available cultivars, two outstanding choices are 'May Night', a compact plant (to 1½ feet high and wide) with deep purple-blue flowers, and 'Blue Hill', also with deep purple-blue flowers but reaching nearly 2½ feet tall and wide.

This salvia grows well in ordinary soil but appreciates soil amended with organic matter. It tolerates some dryness but prefers regular water. To prolong bloom, cut spent flower spikes to the ground. Divide every 4 to 5 years, when clumps become too large or die out in the center.

Salvia × superba

Sedum 'Autumn Joy'

Veronica spicata 'Red Fox'

SEDUM 'Autumn Joy'

> ✂ ZONES 1–24, 29–43
> ☼ ☼ FULL SUN OR PARTIAL SHADE
> ♦ MODERATE TO LITTLE

This plant is a deservedly popular for the year-round interest it brings to the garden. It starts the growing season with fresh green foliage. Dense, dome-shaped, 6-inch-wide clusters of pale pink flowers appear in late summer; in autumn, they turn coppery pink, then rosy rust. The spent flower heads can be left in place for winter decoration and cut back when new growth emerges in spring.

Upright or slightly spreading stems reach 1½ feet tall and are evenly covered with 3-inch, roundish, slightly succulent leaves in pale blue green. Flowers appear at the stem tips.

This plant grows best with full sun and fairly dry soil, but it will also take partial shade and some additional water. Clumps gradually increase in size to 2 feet across; divide them every 2 to 3 years, or center stalks will begin to dry up and fall off when flower clusters emerge.

VERONICA spicata

> ✂ ZONES 1–9; 14–21, 38, 41–43
> ☼ FULL SUN
> ♦ REGULAR

Veronica spicata is just one of the hundreds of *Veronica* species—commonly known as speedwells—offered in nurseries and catalogs. In summer, its rounded clumps of small (to 1½-inch), green, oblong leaves send up candlelike blossom spikes 15 to 20 inches tall, densely packed with tiny (¼- to ½-inch) flowers. Blossoms are tubular, flaring out to four or five lobes. Cultivars include blue-flowered 'Blue Fox', 'Red Fox' (deep rosy red blooms), and 'Icicle' (white blossoms, gray-green leaves).

Give regular water. Well-drained soil is important, especially in Southern gardens. This is one plant that thrives on frequent division; plan to divide clumps every 2 years for best growth and bloom.

FOLIAGE PERENNIALS

Though many perennials are grown for their flowers, a number of others are valued instead for attractive foliage. Leaves may be lacy and fernlike, narrow and grassy, or oversized and boldly dramatic; colors range from silvery white to bronzy red and include every conceivable hue of green. A handful of favorites are described below. Leave room for a few of these beauties in your garden.

Artemisia 'Powis Castle'

ARTEMISIA

- **ZONES 1–24, 29–45**
- **FULL SUN**
- **MODERATE TO LITTLE**

Grown for their silvery, lacy-looking leaves, these artemisias take poor soil (as long as it is well drained) and thrive with little water once established. To keep clumps from flopping, cut old growth back by a third each spring.

A. absinthium 'Lambrook Silver'. WORMWOOD. Borne on erect stalks, the 2- to 5-inch, finely divided, silvery gray leaves have a strong, pleasant fragrance. Plants reach 1½ feet tall.

A. 'Powis Castle'. Covered with foliage so finely divided it looks fluffy, this one resembles a mounding, silvery fern and offers a nice contrast to many plants in both form and color. It soon reaches 4 feet high and wide, so give it plenty of room. In the coldest climates, take cuttings in the fall and replant new plants each spring.

FERNS

- **ZONES VARY**
- **SHADE**
- **WATER NEEDS VARY**

Among the countless ferns sold, you'll find excellent choices for every zone. The two below are widely grown.

Athyrium filix-femina. LADY FERN. Zones 1–9, 14–24, 31–43. Deciduous. An excellent choice for wet, shady corners of the garden; it will also take some sun in cool-summer climates as long as it receives the ample water it prefers. Delicate, lacy, arching fronds rise to 2 to 3 feet; they're broader at the base, narrowing toward the tip. Divide every 3 to 5 years.

Polystichum munitum. SWORD FERN. Zones 2–9, 14–24, 36–38. Evergreen. Extremely easy to grow. Leathery, shiny dark green fronds emerge from the clump's center and reach 2 to 4 feet long. Each plant eventually reaches 2 to 4 feet wide. Needs rich, well-amended soil. Prefers regular water but is not as thirsty as many other ferns once established, making it a good choice for shady but somewhat dry areas. This fern isn't a candidate for division, but the small new plants growing near the base of established clumps can be removed and planted elsewhere.

Polystichum munitum

Hosta varieties

HOSTA

- **ZONES 1–10, 12–21**
- **SHADE**
- **REGULAR**

Hostas are favorites for the shade garden. Hundreds are available in nurseries and from specialty catalogs, from 6-inch dwarfs to 5-foot giants; the range of leaf shapes, textures, and colors is likewise tremendous. Foliage may be heart shaped, lance shaped, oval, or rounded; texture may be smooth or quilted; colors include all green shades, chartreuse, gold, and blue, and many have white, yellow, or cream variegation.

Grow hostas in rich, well-drained soil; never let roots dry out during summer. These plants are carefree in their preferred zones but somewhat difficult to maintain elsewhere. Where slugs and snails are a problem, hostas are a favorite target and almost impossible to protect. In these areas, containers offer the best refuge.

Festuca glauca 'Elijah Blue'

ORNAMENTAL GRASSES

⚘ Zones vary

Exposure needs vary

Water needs vary

Ornamental grasses add a special touch to the garden. The fine, upright foliage of taller deciduous kinds ripples in the slightest breeze. Shorter kinds—both evergreen and deciduous—fill in nicely among other plants, either forming small clumps or spreading over a wider area. Hundreds of choices are available; the two below are manageable in size and easy to grow.

Festuca glauca 'Elijah Blue'. Zones 1–24, 29–45. The best of the blue fescues, this annual grass forms mounding, fine-textured (but somewhat stiff-looking) clumps of a wonderful blue. Each clump is about a foot tall and wide.

This grass grows well in sun or partial shade. It needs only ordinary garden soil and performs well with little water once established. Cut clumps to the ground at the end of winter dormancy; new stems will emerge in the spring.

Pennisetum alopecuroides. FOUNTAIN GRASS. Zones 3–9, 14–24, 31–35, 37, 39. This is one of the smallest of the arching deciduous grasses, typically reaching 3 to 4 feet tall and wide. Bright green leaves emerge in spring. As summer approaches, pinkish flower plumes rise above the foliage

mound; with the onset of fall, leaves turn yellow, then brown.

Give regular water and ordinary to well-amended soil (plants accept acid or alkaline soil). Fountain grass thrives in full sun in cool-summer climates, partial shade in warmer regions. Cut foliage to the ground in winter. Division is rarely needed; do the job only every 5 to 6 years, if at all.

P. orientale, Oriental fountain grass, is similar to *P. alopecuroides* in growth habit and cultural needs. It too has pinkish plumes, but it reaches only 1½ to 2 feet. In cold-winter climates, it is often grown as an annual.

PHORMIUM

NEW ZEALAND FLAX

⚘ Zones 14–28

☀ ◑ Full sun to light shade

●● Regular to little

Fanlike clumps of many swordlike, vertical leaves give these plants their dramatic looks. The largest reach 6 feet tall and wide, but newer cultivars are available in heights as low as 1 foot ('Jack Spratt'), and many are in the 2- to 4-foot range. Some are green; many are bronze or bronzy red; some are striped in green, cream, yellow, and/or red. New Zealand flaxes contrast well with a

wide variety of other plants. They make nice accents around swimming pools; they also tolerate salt air and ocean spray.

P. tenax has stiff foliage; *P. cookianum* has laxer leaves that bend at the tips. Crosses between these two species have resulted in numerous cultivars of specific colors and forms. Those with stiffer foliage take full sun; those with bending leaf tips need light afternoon shade in hot-summer areas.

All do well in ordinary garden soil, but they must have good drainage.

Stachys byzantina

STACHYS byzantina

LAMB'S EARS

⚘ Zones 1–24, 29–43

☀ ◑ Full sun or partial shade

● Moderate

The soft, thick, woolly white-green foliage of lamb's ears is a favorite of many, especially children: it's difficult to pass a planting without stopping to pick a leaf to feel its softness. These 4-inch leaves grow in dense, ground-hugging rosettes; clumps increase by sending out aboveground runners. A mature planting reaches about 1 foot tall and as wide as you let it spread. Lamb's ears is usually grown at the front of a border or along a pathway, where it's easy to see.

Phormium hybrid

BULBS

The many plants known as bulbs bring beauty to the garden in almost every season. The springtime glory of crocus, daffodil, and tulip is closely followed by the summer charm of iris, lily, dahlia, and daylily; more dahlias and crocus follow in autumn. In some climates, bulbs such as crocus and snowdrop bloom even in winter.

All these plants grow from underground structures that serve as storage organs, accumulating a reserve of nutrients to supply energy for growth and bloom in the year to come. Though gardeners typically call all such structures "bulbs," botanists divide them into five types: true bulb, corm, tuber, rhizome, and tuberous root.

TRUE BULB. A true bulb is an underground stem base that contains an embryonic plant complete with leaves, stems, and flower buds, ready to grow when conditions are right. Surrounding this embryonic plant are *scales*—modified leaves that overlap each other in a scalelike manner. At the bottom of the bulb is the *basal plate*, which holds the scales together and produces roots. Many true bulbs, including daffodil *(Narcissus)* and tulip *(Tulipa),* have a protective outer covering called a *tunic.* Lily *(Lilium)* bulbs lack a tunic; they're susceptible to drying and must be handled with care.

An individual bulb may live for many years. New, smaller bulbs, known as *increases* or *offsets,* grow from buds on the basal plate.

CORM. Like a true bulb, a corm is a stem base—but its tissue is solid, without scales. Roots grow from a basal plate at the bottom of the corm; the growth point is at the corm's top. Gladiolus and crocus are two familiar corms.

Each corm lasts for a single year. As it shrinks away after blooming, a new corm forms on top of it; many small increases, called *cormels,* may also be produced around the new corm's basal plate.

TUBER. A tuber, like a corm, is a swollen underground stem base. But it has no basal plate; roots grow both from its base and its sides. Multiple growth points are scattered over its upper surface.

An individual tuber can last for many years. Some (cyclamen, for example) continually enlarge but never produce offsets. Others, such as caladium, form protuberances that can be removed and planted separately.

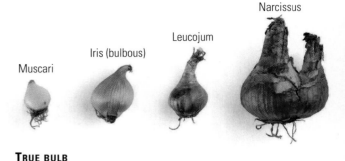

Muscari   Iris (bulbous)   Leucojum   Narcissus

TRUE BULB

Watsonia   Freesia   Crocus

CORM

Begonia   Cyclamen

TUBER

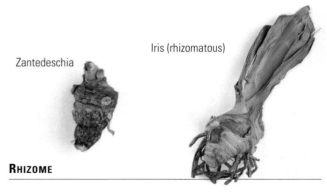

Zantedeschia   Iris (rhizomatous)

RHIZOME

Dahlia

TUBEROUS ROOT

RHIZOME. A rhizome is actually a thickened stem growing partially or entirely below ground. Roots grow directly from its underside. The primary growing point is at one end of the rhizome; additional growing points form along its sides. Bearded iris is probably the best-known rhizomatous plant; others are calla lily (*Zantedeschia*) and canna.

New plants are produced from the growing points, so a planting that starts with a single rhizome can spread horizontally into the surrounding soil.

TUBEROUS ROOT. While the other bulb types are specialized stems, a tuberous root is a true root, thickened to store nutrients. Fibrous roots for uptake of water and nutrients grow from its sides and tip. Tuberous roots grow in a cluster, with the swollen tuberous portions radiating out from a central point. The growth buds are at the bases of old stems rather than on the roots themselves. Dahlia and daylily (*Hemerocallis*) are well-known examples of plants with tuberous roots.

If it has a growth bud, an individual tuberous root can give rise to a separate, new plant.

BUYING BULBS

When you shop, look for plump, firm bulbs that feel heavy for their size. Avoid soft or squashy bulbs; they may have some sort of rot. Also steer clear of lightweight or shriveled bulbs, since these may have lost too much moisture to recover well.

Large bulbs are likely to give the most impressive performance: the biggest tulip (*Tulipa*) and daffodil (*Narcissus*) bulbs, for example, produce larger flowers on taller, thicker stems. But if you're willing to give bulbs a year or two to build themselves up in your garden, you'll get fine results with smaller sizes of most kinds of bulbs—and their lower cost makes them a good buy.

PLANTING BULBS

Like most plants, bulbs need good drainage. If your soil drains very poorly, it's best to plant on a slope or in raised beds.

You can prepare an entire bed for bulbs alone, or intersperse bulbs among existing plants. To plant a bed, remove weeds and other vegetation; then spread 1 to 3 inches of an organic amendment over the soil and sprinkle on a complete fertilizer, following the label directions for amounts. Dig or till in these additions, rake the soil smooth, and you're ready to plant.

In most soils, bulbs should be planted about three times as deep as the bulb is wide. In hot climates or sandy soils, plant slightly deeper; in heavy soils, plant slightly shallower. Most

Tall bearded iris 'Cinderella's Coach'

bulbs can be set quite close together to provide a mass of bloom, but keep in mind that closely spaced bulbs will need dividing sooner than those given more room to grow. For spacing, see the individual descriptions on pages 167–169; or check with the nursery when you buy.

To plant bulbs among other plants, use a trowel or bulb planter to dig a hole for each bulb, making the hole a couple of inches deeper than the recommended planting depth. Put up to a tablespoon of complete fertilizer in the hole and cover it with 2 inches of compost or soil; then set in the bulb and fill in with soil.

After planting, water thoroughly to establish good contact between bulb and soil and to provide moisture to initiate root growth.

CARING FOR BULBS

The right watering and fertilizing schedule can help ensure that your bulbs put on the best possible show.

WATERING. Bulbs need water during their season of active growth. For most kinds, this period begins soon after planting and continues until the foliage dies back (either after flowering has finished or in autumn). If you must supplement rainfall, water deeply enough to penetrate the root zone; the roots grow beneath the bulb. A layer of mulch helps retain moisture. (Bearded iris are an exception; they will rot if mulched.)

FERTILIZING. In addition to applying fertilizer at planting time, give your bulbs a feeding of high-nitrogen fertilizer at the start of the growing season, to enhance the quality of the current season's flowers.

After bloom ends, much of a bulb's stored nutrient supply is gone. If it is to perform well the next year, those nutrients must be replenished. To make sure the bulb has enough food to store, you can do two things. First, *always* leave the foliage on the plant—even if it begins to look unsightly—until it has yellowed and can be pulled off easily. As long as the leaves are green and growing, they continue to manufacture food for the plant and for next year's flowers. Second, apply a complete fertilizer as the flowers fade, using a 10-10-10 formula or a "bulb food" high in phosphorus and potassium. Because phosphorus and potassium must reach the root zone to be fully effective, you'll need to get the fertilizer as close to the roots as you can. In an established planting, scratch the fertilizer lightly into the soil to help it move deeper; then water thoroughly. Or, if there's enough space between bulbs, dig narrow trenches (up to 8 inches deep) close to the plants, taking care not to damage the roots. Scatter fertilizer in the trenches, cover with soil, and water.

DIVIDING BULBS

If an established bulb planting has begun to bloom sparsely, the cause is probably overcrowding—and that means it's time to dig and divide. You'll also need to divide bulbs if you want to make more plantings of a favorite kind. Because each of the five bulb types increases in a different way, techniques for division differ as well.

To divide **true bulbs,** carefully break apart the parent and the increase (smaller bulb) at its base. To divide lily *(Lilium)* bulbs, remove outer scales from the basal plate, dip the ends in rooting hormone, and plant.

Corms renew themselves each growing season by producing a new corm and (sometimes) small cormels on top of the old corm. To divide, separate healthy new corms and any cormels from the old corms.

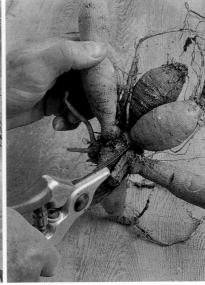

Tubers increase in size and in their number of growing points as they age, but most of them don't form separate increases. To divide, cut a large tuber into two or more sections, making sure each has a growing point.

Rhizomes produce new plants from growth points along their sides. To divide, break the sections apart at the natural divisions between them; be sure each division has at least one growing point.

Tuberous roots form multiple growing points. Some, like daylily *(Hemerocallis),* form separate plants that can be pulled apart; this is usually done in summer or fall, when the plant is growing. Others, like dahlia (above), do not separate as easily. To divide the latter, cut clumps apart so that each root has a growth bud; do the job before planting in early spring.

A SAMPLER OF BULBS

Described here are eleven favorite bulbs. When you make your choices, keep in mind not only flower color and season of bloom, but also your climate and soil. For an explanation of the at-a-glance information introducing each entry, see page 95.

CROCUS
CORM

- ZONES 1–24, 30–45
- ☼ ◑ FULL SUN OR PARTIAL SHADE
- ◗ REGULAR DURING GROWTH AND BLOOM

Most crocuses bloom in late winter or early spring, bearing tubular, 1½- to 3-inch-long flowers in a rainbow of colors. Others, including *C. sativus* (the saffron crocus) and *C. speciosus,* bloom in fall, with flowers rising from bare earth weeks or even days after planting. Plant corms of both spring- and fall-blooming types as soon as they are available in autumn, setting them 2 to 3 inches deep and 3 to 4 inches apart in light, porous soil.

DAHLIA
TUBEROUS ROOT

- ALL ZONES; SEE BELOW
- ☼ ◑ FULL SUN; PARTIAL SHADE WHERE SUMMERS ARE HOT
- ◗ REGULAR DURING GROWTH AND BLOOM

Blooming from summer through fall, dahlias are available in numerous colors and floral forms. Flower diameter ranges from 2 to 12 inches; plant height varies from about a foot to over 7 feet (stake varieties that grow more than 4 feet tall). Plant after the last frost in spring, setting roots 4 to 6 inches deep. Space tall varieties 4 to 5 feet apart, shorter ones 1 to 1½ feet apart.

Though roots can be left in the ground where winter temperatures remain above 20°F/−7° C, gardeners in

Crocus 'Advance'

Dahlia

Galanthus nivalis

most areas prefer to dig them annually. After foliage yellows in fall, cut back stalks to about 4 inches. Dig clumps of roots and let dry in the sun for several hours. Then place in single layers in boxes, cover with dry sand or sawdust, and store in a cool spot over winter. In spring, divide (if needed) and replant.

GALANTHUS nivalis
SNOWDROP
TRUE BULB

- ZONES 1–9, 14–17, 31–45
- ☼ ◑ FULL SUN OR PARTIAL SHADE
- ◗ REGULAR DURING GROWTH AND BLOOM

Snowdrops are among the first bulbs to bloom as winter draws to a close. Plants grow 6 to 8 inches tall, bearing one nodding, bell-shaped white flower on each stalk. Best suited to cold-winter climates. Plant bulbs in fall, setting them 3 to 4 inches deep and 3 inches apart.

GLADIOLUS
CORM

- ZONES 4–9, 12–24, 29–33
- ☼ FULL SUN
- ◗ REGULAR DURING GROWTH AND BLOOM

These long-time favorites have sword-shaped leaves and flaring funnel-shaped flowers borne in slender spikes. The large summer-flowering garden kinds (grandiflora hybrids) grow 3 to 6 feet tall and come in a wide variety of colors. Plant corms in spring after soil has warmed; they'll bloom in 65 to 100 days. If you plant corms at 1- to 2-week intervals over a period of 4 to 6 weeks, you can enjoy an extended flowering season. Set each corm about 4 times deeper than it is thick; space 4 to 6 inches apart.

In the zones listed, corms can overwinter in the ground, though many gardeners prefer to dig them. In colder regions, they must be dug and stored in a frost-free location. Dig after the leaves turn yellow; cut off and discard tops. Arrange corms in a single layer in a dry, dark area and let dry for 2 to 3 weeks. Pull off and discard old corms and roots. Store new corms over winter in onion sacks or nylon stockings hung in a cool, well-ventilated area.

HEMEROCALLIS
DAYLILY
TUBEROUS ROOT

- ALL ZONES
- ☼ ☽ FULL SUN OR LIGHT SHADE
- ◆ REGULAR DURING GROWING SEASON

Tough and trouble free, daylilies are familiar components of perennial borders. Growing in large clumps, the arching, sword-shaped leaves may be evergreen, semievergreen, or deciduous, depending on the type. Modern hybrids grow 1 to 6 feet tall and bloom in spring and summer, producing flowers that vary from 3 to 8 inches wide and come in a wide range of colors. Each flower lasts just one day (hence the common name), but buds open on successive days to prolong the display.

Set out the tuberous roots in fall or early spring, planting them ½ to 1 inch deep and 2 to 2½ feet apart. Set out plants from containers at any time from early spring through midautumn.

Gladiolus

Hemerocallis

Hyacinthus

Iris

HYACINTHUS
DUTCH HYACINTH
TRUE BULB

- ALL ZONES
- ☼ FULL SUN
- ◆ REGULAR DURING GROWTH AND BLOOM

Dutch hyacinth is a spring bloomer with foot-tall spikes densely packed with waxy, bell-like, fragrant flowers in shades of blue, purple, red, pink, buff, and white. It grows best in cold-winter areas, where it lasts from year to year; in these zones, plant in September or October. In mild areas, bulbs will not persist and are best treated as annuals; plant from October to December. Set bulbs 4 to 5 inches deep, 4 to 5 inches apart.

IRIS
RHIZOME

- ⚡ ZONES 1–24, 30–45
- ☼ ☽ FULL SUN OR LIGHT SHADE
- ◆ REGULAR DURING GROWING SEASON

The most widely grown irises are the bearded irises that grow from rhizomes (though there are also beardless rhizomatous irises and bulbous irises). Bearded irises come in a dazzling array of colors and color combinations; plant size varies widely as well. Plant in July or August in cold-winter zones, in September or October where summers are hot. Space rhizomes 1 to 2 feet apart, setting them with their tops just beneath the soil surface and spreading out the roots.

LILIUM
ASIATIC AND ORIENTAL HYBRID LILIES
TRUE BULB

- ALL ZONES
- ☼ ☽ FULL SUN OR PARTIAL SHADE
- ◆ REGULAR; NEVER LET ROOT ZONE DRY OUT

Asiatic Hybrid lilies bloom in early summer on strong, erect stems 1½ to 4½ feet tall. The 4- to 6-inch blossoms come in colors ranging from white through yellow and orange to pink and red. The Oriental Hybrids bloom later, in midsummer to early fall. Their 2- to 6-foot stems bear big (to 9-inch), fragrant flowers with pink or white petals marked with center stripes and speckles.

Plant bulbs as soon as possible after you get them, since they do not store well. If you must delay, store them in a cool place. Before planting, check bulbs carefully; if they look shriveled, place them in moist sand or peat moss until the scales plump up and roots start to form.

Space bulbs 1 foot apart. Cover smaller bulbs with 2 to 3 inches of soil, medium-size ones with 3 to 4 inches, and larger ones with 4 to 6 inches. Viral (mosaic) infection is an incurable problem; to avoid it, buy healthy bulbs from reliable sources. Destroy any lilies that have mottled leaves or are seriously stunted.

MUSCARI armeniacum
GRAPE HYACINTH
TRUE BULB

- ✎ ZONES 2–24, 29–43
- ☼ ◗ FULL SUN OR LIGHT SHADE
- ● REGULAR DURING GROWTH AND BLOOM

Grape hyacinth's narrow, grassy leaves emerge in fall and live through winter's cold and snow. Small, urn-shaped blue flowers, carried in 8-inch spikes, bloom in spring. Plant bulbs in fall, setting them 2 inches deep and 3 inches apart.

NARCISSUS
DAFFODIL, NARCISSUS
TRUE BULB

- ✎ ZONES 1–24, 28–45, EXCEPT AS NOTED
- ☼ FULL SUN
- ● REGULAR DURING GROWTH AND BLOOM

Easy to grow and generous with their spring flowers, daffodils are classified

Lilium Asiatic Hybrids

Muscari armeniacum

Narcissus 'Early Splendor'

Tulipa hybrids   ●

into 12 divisions, based in part on differences in flower form; among these groups are the familiar trumpet daffodils, large- and small-cupped types, and double daffodils. Besides yellow and white, colors include shades of orange, apricot, pink, and cream. Most kinds are hardy in the zones listed; exceptions are the fragrant Tazetta Hybrids, hardy just to 10°F/−12°C, and dainty hoop petticoat daffodil, hardy to about −10°F/−23°C. Plant bulbs twice as deep as they are tall, spacing them about 6 to 8 inches apart.

TULIPA
TULIP
TRUE BULB

- ✎ ZONES 1–24, 28–45
- ☼ FULL SUN
- ● REGULAR DURING GROWTH AND BLOOM

Hybrid tulips come in a multitude of colors, including bright shades, pastels, and even near-black. Flowers very widely in form, too, from the classic egg-shaped blossoms to those that look like lilies or peonies.

Bloom season ranges from mid- to late spring, depending on variety. Most need an extended period of winter chill for best performance, but even in cold-winter areas they may not put on a good show after the first year. To encourage repeat flowering, feed with a nitrogen fertilizer before bloom; be sure to allow foliage to yellow and wither before removing it after bloom. In mild climates, refrigerate tulip bulbs for 6 weeks before planting, and treat the plants as annuals.

Plant bulbs in fall, setting them three times as deep as they are wide; space 4 to 8 inches apart, depending on the ultimate size of the plant.

RIGHT: Framed by flowers, this lush vegetable garden is both attractive and productive.

BELOW: Vegetables planted in wide beds produce bountiful crops.

ROWS, HILLS, AND WIDE BEDS

Most vegetables are traditionally grown in *rows* separated by paths that give you access to the plants and let you till or hoe the soil. This plan works well for tall-growing plants (such as corn) and for those that need support, such as tomatoes and pole beans.

**   *Hills*—a term that refers to a grouping of seeds or plants in a cluster, but not necessarily on a mound—are useful for wide, sprawling plants such as some kinds of squash.**

**   Many vegetables, especially smaller kinds such as beets, carrots, lettuce, and spinach, can be grown more efficiently in *wide beds.* In this arrangement, you prepare a bed about 3 feet wide, then broadcast the seeds over it rather than planting them in rows. Paths on either side allow access to plants, but all in all you'll waste much less space on paths than you would in a row-planting plan—and that gives you more room for vegetables.**

VEGETABLES

Growing your own vegetables is one of the most enjoyable, rewarding sorts of gardening you can do: in return for your efforts, you'll harvest food that's fresh and bursting with flavor. To make your vegetable patch a success, do a little planning before you plant.

If you're new to vegetable gardening, start small. An area of just 100 to 130 square feet can provide a substantial harvest. As you gain experience, you may want to expand the plot.

    List the vegetables your family really enjoys, then consider how much room each kind requires. If space is limited, raise plants that give a good yield for the area they occupy. Beans, tomatoes, and summer squash, for example, can overwhelm you with their bounty from a postage stamp–size plot. At the other extreme are some other kinds of squash, melons, and corn, which require a great deal of space relative to their yield.

'Sierra' lettuce

CHOOSING A LOCATION

Vegetables grow best with at least 6 hours of full sun each day. To avoid both shade and root competition, locate the vegetable patch away from trees and large shrubs. It's also important to choose a spot protected from cold winds in spring and hot, dry winds in summer. Steer clear of "frost pockets"—low-lying areas that may experience frosts later in spring and earlier in fall than other parts of the garden. Watering and other routine tasks are easier on a level site; if only sloping land is available, try to find a south- or southeast-facing slope to take full advantage of the sun.

'Rosy' Batavian lettuce

WORKING WITH THE GROWING SEASON

Once you've chosen a site and decided which vegetables it can accommodate, you'll need to consider climate and length of growing season. These factors, too, will determine your choices. To calculate the length of your growing season, count the number of days between the average last-frost date in spring and the first-frost date in fall (your Cooperative Extension Office or a local nursery can give you these dates).

Last-frost dates let you know when it's safe to set out tender vegetable plants or sow seeds; first-frost dates tell you when you'll probably have to provide protection for tender kinds late in the season. Aim to select vegetables that can mature and bear a good crop in the interval between these two dates. For example, if the seed packet says a certain variety of winter squash requires 120 days from seed to harvest but your growing season lasts only 100 days, look instead for a variety adapted to short growing seasons; or plan to use season-extending techniques, as discussed on page 173.

PLANTING VEGETABLES

Before actually digging your plot, draw a rough plan on paper. Be sure to place tall vegetables to the north, so they won't shade short ones.

Start with careful soil preparation; you'll be repaid with faster growth and a substantially larger harvest. Remove any weeds from the plot and spread the soil with a 3- to 4-inch layer of compost or well-rotted manure. If you're planting a wide bed, scatter a complete fertilizer over the area, following package directions for amounts; if you're planting in rows, apply fertilizer in furrows alongside the rows after planting, as discussed on page 54. Work in amendments and fertilizer by hand or with a rototiller; then rake the area smooth.

If your soil is very poor or does not drain well, you may elect to grow vegetables in raised beds filled with a mixture of compost and good topsoil.

Seedlings started in a cold frame get a jump on the season.

You can start vegetables either by planting seeds outdoors in the garden or by setting out transplants you have started yourself or purchased from a nursery. Vegetables that require a long growing season—peppers and tomatoes, for example—need many weeks of warm temperatures before they produce fruit, and are best set out as transplants. Other vegetables, including broccoli, cabbage, and lettuce, can be seeded directly or transplanted. And some vegetables, especially beans, carrots, corn, and peas, grow better when started from seed sown directly in the garden. For more on sowing seeds and on starting and setting out transplants, see pages 54–57.

CARING FOR YOUR VEGETABLES

For the best possible harvest, keep your vegetables growing steadily—without setbacks—throughout the season. Those started from seed sown directly in the ground usually require thinning, so that each plant will have enough space to develop properly. Thin plants when they're a few inches tall, spacing them as indicated in the descriptions here or on the seed packet.

CHOOSE VEGETABLE SEEDLINGS CAREFULLY

Ideal seedlings are sturdy and stocky, as illustrated in the drawing above. Choose well-established, healthy green plants with at least four true leaves. Pepper and tomato plants should be wider than they are tall. Don't buy seedlings like the ones shown at right and below.

1 Roots growing through drainage hole indicate a root-bound plant.

2 Seedlings produce fruit prematurely when they have been in a small pot too long. They won't be very productive during the rest of the season.

3 Tall, leggy plant has not received the light it needs to thrive.

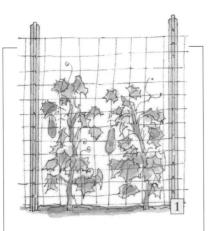

SUPPORTING VEGETABLES

Climbing vegetables (such as pole beans and peas) benefit from support, as do some sprawling sorts, including cucumbers, melons, and tomatoes. Put up the supports at planting time; roots won't have spread yet, so you needn't worry about disturbing them. Train or tie the plants as they grow.

1 Broad-mesh plastic netting attached to hooks in metal fencing stakes can support cucumbers, squash, beans, and peas.

2 Cylinder of welded wire and two stakes support a tomato plant with a minimum of tying. Reach through mesh to harvest.

3 Tepee of bamboo poles tied together at top supports beans planted beside poles.

Provide a steady supply of water from planting until harvest. Transplants need frequent watering until they're growing well; keep the soil moist but not soggy. Rows or beds of seeds and young seedlings likewise need steady moisture, sometimes requiring sprinkling as often as two or three times a day if weather is very hot. As transplants and seedlings grow and their roots reach deeper, you can water less often—but when you do water, be sure to moisten the entire root zone. To water your vegetable garden, you can use sprinklers, furrows, or a drip system; see pages 41–45 for details.

Mulching the garden conserves moisture and suppresses weed growth. An organic mulch such as straw or compost will also improve the soil's structure as it decomposes, making the top few inches looser and more crumbly. However, because organic mulches keep the soil beneath them cool, it's best not to apply them until warm weather arrives. A mulch of black plastic sheeting, on the other hand, helps warm the soil quickly in spring. After preparing the soil for planting, cover it with black plastic; then cut small holes where you want to sow seeds or set out plants. This tactic is especially useful for growing heat-loving crops such as melons and eggplant in regions with cool or short summers.

Black plastic sheeting used as a mulch helps to warm the soil, conserve moisture, and suppress weeds.

For many vegetables, the fertilizer applied at planting time will be sufficient for the entire season. But heavy feeders (such as corn) or those requiring a long growing season, including broccoli, cabbage, and tomatoes, may need one or two follow-up feedings. Lightly scratch dry granular fertilizer into the soil (keep it off plant leaves), then water it in thoroughly; or use a water-soluble fertilizer according to label directions.

Removing weeds is important, since they'll compete with vegetables for water, food, and light. As noted above, a mulch will help prevent weeds from getting started in the first place; those that do appear can usually be eliminated through hand-pulling, hoeing, or cultivating. Whichever approach you choose, be sure to get rid of weeds before they set seed. For more on weed control, see pages 81–88.

Various pests and diseases may occasionally afflict some of your vegetables. To avert or at least minimize the damage, take the following basic steps. (For descriptions of specific pests and diseases and advice on controlling them, see pages 67–80. If you encounter a problem not discussed in this book, contact your Cooperative Extension Office or knowledgeable nursery personnel for help.)

KEEP THE GARDEN HEALTHY. Plants growing in the best possible conditions are better able to resist pests and diseases.

KEEP THE GARDEN CLEAN. Composting or discarding spent plants and tilling the soil (especially in fall) can help you avoid trouble, since a number of insects and diseases overwinter or spend some stage of their lives on plant debris.

PLANT RESISTANT VARIETIES if they're available. Many tomato hybrids, for example, are resistant both to verticillium wilt (see page 80) and to fusarium wilt, another disease caused by a soil-dwelling fungus. (Fusarium wilt enters plants through their roots. Lower leaves may turn yellow or appear scorched; severely infected plants wilt and die.)

MIX DIFFERENT KINDS OF PLANTS. Large expanses of just one sort can encourage equally large populations of pests fond of that plant. Mixed plantings favor more kinds of insects, including those that prey on the troublemakers.

ROTATE THE LOCATION OF CROPS from year to year to prevent the buildup of diseases and insects specific to certain plants in any one part of the garden.

ENCOURAGE NATURAL CONTROLS such as toads, lizards, many birds, and beneficial insects (see pages 63–64, 67–68). Avoid chemical sprays, if possible; they wipe out helpful creatures along with pests, leaving the garden vulnerable to new attack.

PERENNIAL VEGETABLES

A few vegetables are perennials: you plant them once, then harvest crops year after year. Give them their own garden area, so they won't be disturbed when you prepare soil for annual crops. Fertilize and mulch each spring; water as needed during the season.

ASPARAGUS (Zones 1–24, 29–45). Because asparagus takes 3 years from seed to harvest, most people plant 1-year-old crowns, available from nurseries or mail-order catalogs in late winter. Space crowns 1½ feet apart in rows 3 to 6 feet apart.

RHUBARB (Zones 1–11, 14–24, 26–45; best in Zones 1–11, 34–45). Rhubarb sends up new leaves in spring and dies back in autumn. The reddish green leafstalks are the edible part; never eat the leaves, which are poisonous. Plant divisions in late winter or early spring, setting them 3 to 4 feet apart. Let plants grow for two full seasons before harvesting.

Emerging asparagus spears

Rhubarb

SEASON EXTENDERS

Warm-season vegetables may need protection from frost when they are first planted in spring, then again as temperatures begin to dip in fall. In spring, individual plants can be protected with various plastic or paper caps known as hotcaps. Also available is a special plastic hotcap for tomatoes; it consists of water-filled cylinders that trap heat effectively.

Floating row covers made of polyethylene, polyester, or polypropylene are one of the most useful tools for protecting plants from cold temperatures (and from certain insect pests, as well). Sold in rolls, these fabriclike covers can be laid directly over seeded beds or plants or propped on stakes; they serve as miniature greenhouses. They are extremely lightweight, transmit 80 to 95% of the sunlight that strikes them, and allow both water and air to pass through. Burying the cover's edges in the soil will seal out insect pests, though any already on the plants may proliferate (remove covers when plants begin to bloom to admit pollinating insects).

A SAMPLER OF ANNUAL VEGETABLES

Vegetables are designated "warm-season" or "cool-season," depending on the weather they need for best growth. Warm-season vegetables, such as peppers and tomatoes, are summer crops; they require both warm soil and high temperatures to grow and produce fruit. They are killed by frost. Plant them after the last frost in spring.

Cool-season vegetables grow steadily at average temperatures 10° to 15°F/6° to 8°C below those needed by warm-season types. They can be planted in very early spring for early summer harvest or in late summer for harvest in fall and (in mild regions) winter. Many will endure short spells of frost—but in hot weather, they become bitter tasting and often bolt to seed rather than producing edible parts. In areas with short growing seasons (fewer than 100 days) or cool, foggy summers, cool-season vegetables can be grown in summer.

WARM-SEASON VEGETABLES

BEANS, SNAP. Snap beans (also called string or green beans) have tender, fleshy pods. Besides the familiar green sort, you'll find types with yellow or purple pods. You can choose self-supporting (bush) or climbing (pole) varieties. Plant seeds of bush types 2 inches apart, in rows spaced 2 to 3 feet apart; thin seedlings to 4 inches apart. For pole beans, space seeds 4 to 6 inches apart and allow 3 feet between rows; support the plants on a trellis or plant them around a tepee, as shown on page 172. Thin seedlings to 6 inches apart. Begin harvest 50 to 70 days after sowing seeds.

CORN. Most kinds of corn do best in hot-summer areas, but early-maturing hybrid varieties will grow even in regions with cool summers. You must plant corn in a series of parallel rows so that wind can distribute the pollen effectively. Sow seeds directly in the garden, spacing them 4 to 6 inches apart in rows 2½ to 3 feet apart. Thin seedlings to 1 to 1½ feet apart. Harvest 60 to 100 days after sowing.

CUCUMBERS. Cucumber varieties include long green slicers, small kinds for pickling, and yellow, mild-flavored lemon cucumbers. In spring, sow groups of four to six seeds in hills 4 to 6 feet apart; thin seedlings to two or three per hill. Or sow two or three seeds in groups spaced 1½ feet apart at the base of a trellis; then thin seedlings to one per group. Harvest begins 50 to 100 days after sowing; be sure to harvest frequently to keep plants producing.

MELONS. Cantaloupes (also known as muskmelons) are the easiest melons to

A raised bed filled with tomatoes, summer squash, pole beans, and herbs provides a generous summer harvest. Marigolds *(Tagetes)* decorate the bed's perimeter.

grow, because they ripen the fastest. Planting through black plastic (see page 172) speeds harvest. In spring, sow four or five seeds per hill; space hills 4 to 6 feet apart. Thin seedlings to two per hill. Harvest 70 to 115 days after sowing.

PEPPERS. Sweet peppers are available in a range of colors, shapes, and sizes— from bell types to long, slender frying peppers, in hues from green to bright yellow and purple. Hot peppers likewise offer a range of sizes, colors, and pungencies. Start seeds of sweet or hot peppers in flats indoors 6 to 8 weeks before planting time; or buy transplants. Set plants out in spring, spacing them 1½ to 2 feet apart in rows 2½ feet apart. Harvest 60 to 95 days after setting out plants.

SQUASH. There are two basic types of squash. Both are planted in spring, and both are available in vining or space-saving bush varieties. Summer squash (zucchini, crookneck, pattypan) are eaten when the fruit is small and tender; harvest 50 to 60 days after sowing. Winter squash form hard shells; they are harvested in fall (80 to 120 days after sowing) and can be stored for winter use. Sow seeds of bush types 1 foot apart in rows 3 to 5 feet apart; thin seedlings to 2 feet apart. Sow seeds of vining squash in hills spaced about 5 feet apart, placing four or five seeds in each hill; thin to two per hill.

TOMATOES. Easy to grow and prolific, tomatoes are a home-garden favorite. A huge number of varieties is available, varying from tiny cherry types to 2-pound giants; fruit colors include red, yellow, orange, and even pink. Start seeds in flats indoors 6 weeks before planting time; or buy transplants. Set out in the garden in spring, spacing plants 2 to 4 feet apart in rows 3 to 4 feet apart. Bury as much as half to three-quarters of the stem of each plant; roots will form along the buried part and strengthen the plant. Stake plants or place wire cylinders around them for support (as shown on page 172).

COOL-SEASON VEGETABLES

BEETS. Besides basic red beets, nurseries and garden catalogs offer seeds of golden yellow and white varieties. The tender young leaves are edible. Sow in early spring (or in late summer, for a fall crop). Plant seeds 1 inch apart in rows spaced 1½ feet apart, or broadcast them in wide beds; thin seedlings to 2 to 3 inches apart. Harvest 45 to 65 days after sowing.

BROCCOLI. Easy-to-grow broccoli bears over a long season. Start seeds indoors 6 weeks before planting time; or buy transplants. In early spring (or in mid- to late summer, for a fall crop), set out plants 15 to 24 inches apart in rows spaced 2 to 3 feet apart. Or sow seeds

Plant cool-season crops such as lettuce and other greens for harvest in spring or fall.

directly in the garden, spacing them 4 inches apart; thin seedlings to 15 to 24 inches apart. Harvest 50 to 100 days after setting out plants, 90 to 140 days after sowing. Cut the heads before the buds begin to open. After the central head is harvested, side shoots will produce additional smaller heads.

CABBAGE. In addition to the standard green cabbage, you can grow red and curly-leafed Savoy varieties. Start seeds indoors 6 weeks before planting time; or buy transplants. In early spring (or in mid- to late summer, for a fall crop), set plants 15 to 24 inches apart in rows spaced 2 to 4 feet apart. Or sow seeds directly in the garden, spacing them 4 inches apart; thin seedlings to 15 to 24 inches apart. Harvest 50 to 100 days after setting out plants, 90 to 140 days after sowing.

CARROTS. If your garden soil is heavy, plant varieties with short roots. Plant seeds in early spring (or in late summer, for a fall crop). Sow ½ inch apart in rows spaced 1 to 2 feet apart; or broadcast seeds in wide beds. Thin seedlings to 2 to 4 inches apart. Harvest baby carrots 30 to 40 days after sowing, mature carrots 50 to 80 days after sowing.

LETTUCE. Choose among leaf, butterhead, romaine (cos) and crisphead (also known as "iceberg") lettuces. Start seeds in flats indoors about 4 weeks before planting time; or buy transplants. Set out transplants (or sow seed directly in the garden) in early spring; make successive plantings or sowings until daytime temperatures reach 75° to 80°F/24° to 27°C. Plant again in late summer and early autumn for fall crops.

Sow seeds of crisphead lettuce 2 inches apart in rows spaced 1½ to 2 feet apart; thin seedlings to 12 to 14 inches apart. Sow seeds of other lettuces 1 to 2 inches apart in rows spaced 1 to 2 feet apart; thin to 6 to 8 inches apart. Or broadcast seeds of all but crisphead lettuce in wide beds; thin to 6 inches apart. Harvest leaf lettuces 40 to 50 days after sowing, butterhead and romaine in 65 to 85 days, crisphead in 80 to 90 days.

PEAS. Some kinds of peas are for shelling, some have edible pods—and some can be harvested either way. Bush and vining types are available. In early spring (or in early fall, for a fall crop), sow seeds 1 inch apart in rows spaced 2 to 3 feet apart. Thin seedlings to 2 to 4 inches apart. Set up stakes or trellises for vining types at planting time. Harvest 55 to 70 days after sowing.

SPINACH. Spinach bolts quickly into flower if the weather gets too warm or the days too long. For best results, sow seeds in early spring (or in early fall, for a fall crop). Space them 1 inch apart in rows 1 to 2½ feet apart; or broadcast over wide beds. Thin seedlings to 3 to 4 inches apart. Harvest 40 to 50 days after sowing.

HERBS

Fresh herbs bring flavor and fragrance to even the simplest dish. And they're easy to grow, whether planted in their own special plot or interspersed among other plants. Many thrive in containers, too, gracing a deck or patio.

Choose a planting spot that receives 6 to 8 hours of full sun each day. Well-drained soil is essential; if drainage is poor, amend the soil with plenty of organic matter or plant in raised beds. Work in a complete fertilizer before planting, following the label directions for amounts. Herbs aren't heavy feeders, so this will suffice for the entire growing season.

Most perennial herbs are easier to start from purchased transplants than from seed. Nurseries offer many sorts in spring, typically in 2- or 4-inch pots; rosemary and sage are also sold in gallon containers. Annual and biennial herbs such as basil, cilantro, dill, and parsley can be started from seed (see pages 54–57 for more on starting seeds).

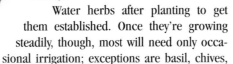

French tarragon

Water herbs after planting to get them established. Once they're growing steadily, though, most will need only occasional irrigation; exceptions are basil, chives, and parsley, which prefer evenly moist soil.

When perennial herbs resume growth in early spring, feed them with a complete fertilizer or spread compost around the base of each plant.

Harvest herbs for drying just as the first flower buds begin to open. The oils in the leaves are most concentrated at this time, and the herbs will maintain their flavor when preserved. Cut sprigs or branches in the morning, after dew has evaporated; tie them together at the cut ends and hang them upside down in a warm, dry, well-ventilated place out of direct sunlight. When the leaves feel crisp, strip them from the stems and store in airtight jars.

You can also dry herbs by removing the leaves from the stems and spreading them on screens placed in a warm, dry, airy place out of direct sunlight. Stir the leaves in the trays every few days. When they feel crisp and crumble easily, store them in airtight jars.

For herbs grown for their seeds, harvest seed heads or pods when they turn brown. Dry them in paper bags until you can shake the seeds loose; then store seeds in airtight jars.

A wagonful of herbs ready to plant in the garden

AN HERB SAMPLER

BASIL. This fragrant annual needs warm weather to grow well. Plants typically reach 1½ to 2 feet tall. Besides varieties with large green leaves, you'll find purple basils and dwarf or small-leafed sorts. You can start from seed or buy transplants. Sow seed indoors in early spring; or sow directly in garden beds after soil has warmed. Thin seedlings or set out plants to grow 1 to 2 feet apart. Pinch off tips and flowers to keep the leaves coming.

CHIVES. A perennial hardy in all zones, chives make a pretty addition to an ornamental garden. Each plant forms a clump of narrow, onion-flavored leaves up to 2 feet high. The rosy purple flowers are also edible. Plants are evergreen in mild climates but go dormant in colder areas. You can pot small divisions to grow indoors on a sunny windowsill. Chives are usually purchased as small plants, but they can also be started from seed. Space plants 1 to 1½ feet apart (or thin seedlings to this distance).

Blooming chives

DILL. The fresh or dried leaves and the seeds of this versatile annual herb are a popular seasoning for many foods—including, of course, dill pickles. The plants grow 3 to 4 feet high, sporting soft, feathery leaves and flat clusters of small yellow flowers. Sow seed directly in garden beds in spring, after all danger of frost is past. Thin seedlings to 1½ feet apart.

MINT. Perennials hardy in Zones 1–24, 26–45, mints spread rapidly by underground stems. Spearmint is the preferred mint for cooking; it has shiny bright green leaves and reaches 1½ to 2 feet tall. Peppermint, great for flavoring tea, grows to 2 feet or taller. Unlike most other herbs, mint thrives not only in sun, but also in partial to full shade. Space plants 1 to 2 feet apart. To keep them from taking over the garden, plant them in containers or install barriers around plantings.

OREGANO. A perennial herb that grows best in Zones 1–24, 30–45, oregano is popular in Italian, Greek, and Spanish cooking. Use its leaves fresh or dried. Many kinds are available; of these, Greek oregano is considered one of the most flavorful. The plants reach 2½ feet tall and spread at a moderate rate by underground stems. Set them out 1½ to 2 feet apart; keep flowers cut back to encourage bushiness.

PARSLEY. A biennial usually grown as an annual, curly-leaf parsley is an attractive edging for herb, vegetable, or flower gardens; in cooking, it's prized for garnishes. Flat-leaf parsley (also called Italian parsley) has a stronger flavor and is favored for seasoning many dishes. Both sorts grow 6 to 12 inches tall. Set out transplants or sow seeds where plants are to grow in the garden in early spring. To speed germination, soak seed in warm water for 24 hours before planting. Space plants 6 to 8 inches apart (or thin seedlings to this distance).

ROSEMARY. A shrubby perennial with aromatic needlelike foliage, rosemary is available in numerous varieties, in heights ranging from 1½ to 4 feet. Most are hardy in Zones 4–24, 26–32, but 'Arp' has survived temperatures as low as −10°F/−23°C. Rosemary is widely used as a landscape plant and also does well in containers; container-grown plants can be brought indoors for the winter in cold regions. Set plants 2 to 3 feet apart.

Harvest of fresh culinary herbs

Dill

Basil

Mint

Parsley

Oregano

SAGE. A perennial adapted to Zones 2–24, 26, 28–41, strong-flavored sage comes not only in the traditional soft gray-green variety, but also in decorative forms with yellow-and-green, purple, or tricolored (gray, white, and purplish pink) foliage. All form dense bushes to 2 feet tall. Start from seed or transplants; set plants 2 feet apart or thin seedlings to this distance.

SWEET MARJORAM. Sweet marjoram is a perennial in Zones 4–24, 29–31; elsewhere, it is treated as an annual or grown in containers and moved indoors for winter. Plants reach 1 to 2 feet tall; the tiny gray-green leaves have a sweet, floral scent and a milder flavor than oregano (to which sweet marjoram is closely related). Start this herb from seed or purchased transplants; space plants 6 to 9 inches apart or thin seedlings to this distance.

TARRAGON, FRENCH TARRAGON. A perennial (Zones 3–24, 29–41) with narrow, anise-flavored leaves of shiny dark green, tarragon dies to the ground in winter but returns the following spring. Plants grow 1 to 2 feet tall; space them 2 feet apart. French tarragon can only be grown from divisions or cuttings. Seed-grown plants belong to a different variety and are inferior in flavor.

THYME, COMMON THYME. Hardy in Zones 1–24, 26, 28–43, this perennial forms a 6- to 12-inch mound of tiny, sweetly pungent leaves. It's a good container plant and an attractive edging for flower, vegetable, or herb gardens. Set plants 1 foot apart. Cut back after flowering to keep plants dense.

WINTER SAVORY. This perennial herb succeeds in Zones 3–11, 14–24, 30–34, 39. It's a mounding, 12- to 15-inch-tall plant with pungent, peppery-tasting dark green leaves (a close relative, summer savory, is an annual with a milder flavor). Seeds of winter savory are slow to germinate, so it's best to buy plants. Space them 6 to 12 inches apart.

RIGHT: Train leafy grapevine over an arbor to create a shady retreat

BELOW, LEFT: Raspberries are easier to pick and prune if grown on a trellis

BELOW, RIGHT: Summer brings tempting harvest of blackberries, blueberries, and raspberries.

BERRIES AND GRAPES

Growing your own berries and grapes gives you a varied harvest of luscious fruit at its vine-ripened best.

SELECTION

Most berries produce a substantial yield from relatively few plants, and most can be integrated attractively into the landscape. Strawberries make a nice edging for a vegetable bed; they're good looking in large containers, too. Blueberries are handsome shrubs with appealing spring flowers and colorful fall foliage. Grapes are classics for cloaking arbors to create a shady hideaway; blackberries and raspberries can be trained to mask a boring or unattractive fence.

For each kind of berry, you'll find a huge selection of varieties, differing widely in their climate preferences. For help in choosing the best kinds for your area, consult a local nursery or your Cooperative Extension Office.

PLANTING

Choose a site in full sun. Keep in mind that, with the exception of strawberries, most berries are fairly long-lived and will occupy the same space for some years. They need well-drained soil to thrive; if your soil is poorly drained, plant in raised beds or mounds. Most kinds of berries and grapes are sold bare-root during the dormant season; see page 36 for planting instructions.

CARE

Given a little attention to watering, fertilizing, and pruning, your berries will reward you with bumper crops of fruit year after year.

WATERING. Water plants thoroughly after you set them out; then water again whenever the top 2 inches of soil are dry. During the growing season, the soil around the roots should be kept moist but not soggy. Applying a mulch such as ground bark or compost will help conserve moisture and keep the soil cool.

FERTILIZING. Most berries prosper with one feeding of a complete fertilizer in early spring. Strawberries have somewhat more exacting requirements; see page 181 for details.

MANAGING PESTS AND DISEASES. A number of problems can affect berries; the individual entries beginning on the right address some of the most serious of these. To minimize pest and disease troubles from the very start, buy certified disease-free stock from a reputable nursery. To identify and control problems not discussed in this book, contact a local nursery or your Cooperative Extension Office.

TRAINING AND PRUNING. Berries that grow on canes and vines—blackberries, raspberries, and grapes—need training when young, Most grow best if tied to a trellis or fence; grapes can also be grown on an arbor or pergola. Yearly pruning encourages better fruit production and keeps the plants in bounds, preventing them from forming jungly, tangled thickets. For details on training and pruning each kind of berry, see *Sunset's Pruning* or consult a nursery or your Cooperative Extension Office.

A SAMPLER OF BERRIES AND GRAPES

Presented here are the basics for growing ever-popular blackberries, blueberries, grapes, raspberries, and strawberries.

BLACKBERRIES

Blackberries grow in two distinct forms; both bear fruit in summer. The canes of both kinds begin growth in one year, then produce a crop in the second year; they then die (to be replaced by new canes).

Blackberry varieties from the midwestern and eastern states tend to be the erect sort: hardy, stiff-caned plants that grow upright to 4 to 6 feet. Both erect blackberries and semierect types (crosses between erect and trailing types) succeed in Zones 1–9, 14–41.

Blackberries commonly grown in the West tend to be trailing. Some of these are so distinctive that they have separate names—boysenberry, loganberry, marionberry, olallieberry. In the South, trailing kinds known as dewberries are often grown. Trailing blackberries are hardy in Zones 4–9, 14–24; some types succeed in Zones 28–32.

Plant erect blackberries 2 to 3 feet apart, allowing 6 to 10 feet between rows. Trailing blackberries need more room; set them 4 to 6 feet apart and allow 9 to 10 feet between rows. After planting, cut back canes of both kinds to 8 to 10 inches long.

In areas with very cold winters, blackberries that are marginally hardy for your area should be mulched heavily over winter. Bury the first-year canes (those that have not yet produced a crop) under a layer of straw, leaves, or cut conifer branches.

PESTS AND DISEASES. Blackberries are susceptible to verticillium wilt, so don't plant them where you have grown potatoes, tomatoes, eggplants, or peppers

Blackberries

in the last 2 years. Prevent problems by buying healthy stock and, if possible, resistant varieties. For more on controlling verticillium wilt, see page 80.

BLUEBERRIES

Besides producing mouthwatering fruit, blueberries are handsome bushes that do well as hedges, borders, and container plants. They perform best in sun but will also succeed in light shade.

Lowbush blueberries (Zones 34, 37–45), native to Maine and Canada's Maritime Provinces, grow from a few inches to 2 feet tall and spread by underground roots. They have been hybridized with highbush varieties to produce half-high blueberries that reach 2 to 4 feet tall; selections of these include 'North Country' and 'Northblue'.

Blueberries

Highbush blueberries include varieties such as 'Bluecrop', 'Patriot', and 'Jersey'. They grow 5 to 6 feet tall (or taller). Most are northern varieties requiring definite winter cold; they succeed in Zones 4–6, 17, 32, 34–43. Southern highbush varieties, including 'Cape Fear' and 'Georgia Gem', are better adapted to warm winters and hot summers. They are good performers in Zones 25, 26, 28, 31, 33.

Rabbiteye blueberries, suitable to Zones 26 (upper portion), 28, 31, and 33, are adapted to hot, humid summers and mild winters. They are often taller than highbush plants.

For better pollination—resulting in larger berries and higher yields—grow at least two varieties of blueberries. Selecting varieties that ripen at different times (early, midseason, and late) will give you fruit from late spring into August.

Blueberries must have highly acidic soil (pH between 3.5 and 5) rich in organic matter (see page 23 for ways to acidify your soil). Space plants 4 to 5 feet apart. An extra-thick (4- to 6-inch) mulch of sawdust, ground bark, or other organic material will help keep the shallow roots moist. Use an acid-forming fertilizer, such as a blend formulated for rhododendrons and azaleas.

Blueberries often produce so many fruit buds that the bushes' growth is stunted and the berries are undersized. To help plants get established, it's a good idea to keep first-year plants from bearing at all by stripping off their buds. On older plants, cut back twig ends during dormancy to the point where flower buds are widely spaced.

PESTS AND DISEASES. Blueberries are usually free from serious problems. Netting will keep birds from getting the berries before you do.

GRAPES

Strong-growing vines of great beauty, grapes provide shade, privacy screens, and delicious fruit for eating fresh, preserving, or wine making.

Grapes fall into three major classes, and there are numerous hybrids between classes as well. *American* grapes are slip-skin grapes of the 'Concord' type. Hardy to well below 0°F/–18°C, they grow in much of the United States, but they don't thrive in the Deep South. There, the grape of choice is the *muscadine,* which bears large fruit in small clusters. Muscadine grapes don't succeed where winter lows dip below 0°F/–18°C. *European* grapes generally need high heat in summer; they're hardy to around 0°F/–18°C. These include table grapes such as

Grapes

'Thompson Seedless' and 'Flame', as well as classic wine grapes.

Some muscadine varieties require cross-pollination. All American and European grapes are self-fertile.

When planting American and European grapes, leave 8 to 10 feet between plants in all directions. Give muscadines even more room—at least 12 feet between plants and 20 feet between rows. After planting, cut the stems of all kinds back to two or three buds to promote deep rooting and the growth of a strong cane for the future trunk.

PESTS AND DISEASES. In some areas, grape leafhopper and grape mealybug infest vines. Check with your Cooperative Extension Office for controls. Powdery mildew is a serious disease of European grapes (most American grapes are immune). For controls, see page 79.

RASPBERRIES

Though most people think of raspberries as red, you'll also find yellow, purple, and black sorts. And while the majority are summer bearing, some kinds of red and yellow raspberries produce their crops in fall. These plants—called everbearing raspberries—bear fruit on the upper third of new canes in the autumn of their first year of growth. The summer of the second year, the same canes bear a second crop on their lower part; then they die (and are replaced by new canes).

Raspberries grow best in regions with fairly cool summers and cold winters (Zones 3–6, 15–17, 36–40, 42, cooler parts of 41 and 43). In hot climates, give them a location receiving afternoon shade.

Space raspberries about 3 feet apart; you can plant them in trenches rather than digging individual holes. Space rows 7 to 9 feet apart. After planting, cut the canes back to about 6 inches.

PESTS AND DISEASES. To control anthracnose and other fungal diseases, spray with lime sulfur during the dor-

Raspberries

mant season and again when flowering begins; this will also help control many insect pests. For more on controlling anthracnose, see page 77.

STRAWBERRIES

Sweet, juicy strawberries are among the easiest fruits for home gardeners to grow—and one of the most productive, too. June-bearing types bear one crop of high-quality berries each year in late spring or early summer. Everbearing (day-neutral) varieties peak in summer and continue to produce into autumn; though they bear for a longer period than June-bearing sorts, they tend to be less vigorous. Within these two types, there are varieties adapted to almost every climate in the United States.

In most parts of the country, strawberries are planted in early spring; where winters are mild, you can also plant in autumn. Plants are usually sold bareroot. Take care that the roots don't dry out. Just before you set plants out, trim roots to 6 inches to make planting easier. Space plants 14 to 18 inches apart in rows 2 to 2½ feet apart.

Most strawberries spread by runners. To get large plants with smaller yields of big berries, pinch off all the runners. For a heavier yield of smaller berries, allow some of the runners to grow and fruit; space them 7 to 10 inches apart in a circle around the mother plant, cutting off extras so the bed doesn't become too crowded.

Fertilize June bearers twice a year—very lightly when growth begins, then more heavily after fruiting. Everbearing types prefer consistent light fertilizing; feed them every 2 weeks. Note that heavy feeding of either type in spring leads to excessive leafy growth, soft fruit, and fruit rot.

Where winters are cold, it's crucial to mulch strawberries to prevent winter damage. In late November, after temperatures have dipped to freezing several times, lay straw loosely over the plants.

Replace plants with new ones as they begin to decline, usually after 3 years.

PESTS AND DISEASES. Strawberries are subject to many troubles, including mites, rose chafers, strawberry root weevils, and verticillium wilt. To help reduce problems, plant only certified disease-free plants; also remove and dispose of diseased foliage and rotten fruit. For more on controlling rose chafers, see page 72. For more on controlling verticillium wilt, see page 80.

Strawberries

PLANTING DEPTH FOR STRAWBERRIES

Plant strawberries so that the crown is just above soil level (a buried crown will rot) and the topmost roots are at least ¼ inch beneath the soil (exposed roots will dry out).

Crown

Correctly planted strawberry

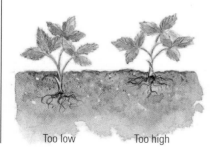
Too low   Too high

FRUIT TREES

There's more than one reason to plant fruit trees. Besides giving you a home-grown harvest of incomparable flavor, they bring interest and beauty to the garden.

SELECTING FRUIT TREES

Which fruit trees are best for you? To answer that question, you'll need to take several factors into account. First, decide how much room you have available. A standard (full-size) apple or cherry tree can reach 40 feet high and 30 to 40 feet wide—too large for many gardens. But a number of choices are available to fit a more limited space. Most kinds of fruit trees are sold not only as standard-size plants but also in semidwarf or dwarf forms, made by grafting a standard type onto a dwarfing rootstock. Semidwarf sorts typically reach one-half to three-fourths normal height; dwarfs grow only 5 to 10 feet tall, depending on the species. Some fruit trees are also available as genetic dwarfs—plants bred to be naturally small (just 4 to 10 feet high). These are well adapted to container culture.

Multiple-variety trees offer another way to grow fruit trees in a limited area. Such trees have three to five varieties of the same or a closely related species grafted onto a single trunk and rootstock.

When choosing fruit trees, also think about your climate. To grow and bloom well, many kinds need a certain amount of cold weather each year; this is known as the chill requirement and is measured in hours needed at temperatures below 45°F/7°C. If you live in a mild-winter region, it's important to choose varieties with a low chill requirement.

TOP: Citrus trees such as this grapefruit grow well in containers. In cold-winter areas, gardeners can move such potted plants to a sheltered location when frosts threaten

BOTTOM: Although this 'Sensation' genetic dwarf peach is small in stature, it bears standard-size fruit.

RIGHT: Spring bloom of 'Black Tartarian' sweet cherry is a glorious prelude to the succulent fruit crop to come.

ESPALIER PATTERNS

| Double U-shaped | Candelabra | Belgian fence | Belgian doublet | Belgian arch | Fan |

ESPALIERED FRUIT TREES

The art of espalier—training plants to grow in a flat plane—is a time-honored way to reap a generous harvest of fruit from a small space. Espalier styles vary. Half a dozen designs are shown above; most kinds of fruit trees can be trained to one or another of these. Citrus trees, however, produce more fruit if grown as an informal espalier—that is, one without a precise pattern. You plant the tree in front of a structure and allow it to branch naturally, then remove any growth that juts out too far. For more on espalier, consult a book on the subject; or see *Sunset's Pruning*.

Cold tolerance is a third factor to consider. Though varieties differ in hardiness, many kinds of apples, sour cherries, and hardy hybrid plums can withstand temperatures as low as −30°F/−34°C, while pears, sweet cherries, and Japanese and European plums tolerate temperatures to −20°F/−29°C. Peaches and apricots may be injured at −15°F/−26°C; most citrus trees are damaged if the temperature falls below 32°F/0°C for any length of time. By taking advantage of your garden's microclimates (see pages 6 and 91), however, you may be able to grow fruit trees beyond their normal hardiness range. Siting trees away from frost pockets can also minimize damage inflicted on blossoms by spring frosts.

Many kinds of fruit trees require cross-pollination for good fruit set. If you live in an area where there are few other fruit trees, check the pollination requirements of those you want to grow. If cross-pollination is needed, you don't necessarily have to plant another tree: you may be able to graft a pollenizer branch onto the chosen tree or even place a bouquet of flowers from another variety in a bucket of water at its base. For more on pollination, see page 16.

PLANTING FRUIT TREES

Fruit trees need full sun to thrive. Most also must have well-drained soil, though apples, pears, and plums are somewhat more tolerant of less-than-ideal conditions. If poor drainage is a serious problem, plant your trees in raised beds.

Deciduous fruit trees are sold bare-root during the dormant season and containerized throughout the growing season. Plant bare-root trees as soon as possible after purchase. For step-by-step instructions for planting both bare-root and containerized plants, turn to pages 36–37.

CARING FOR FRUIT TREES

Though fruit trees often prosper with only minimal care, paying attention to their needs will reward you with a larger, more flavorful crop.

WATERING. Water newly planted trees whenever the top 2 inches of soil are dry. As the plants develop more extensive root systems, you can water less often—but keep in mind that, to produce a juicy crop, all fruit trees must have periodic deep soaking (provided either by rain or by you). Drip systems (see pages 44–45) are well suited to fruit tree culture. Mulching helps conserve moisture.

FERTILIZING. Though commercial growers fertilize regularly, many home growers find that their trees require only minimal feeding. It's best to base your fertilizing schedule on the growth of the tree. If it's growing satisfactorily, its nutrient needs are being met. If its performance is subpar, though, apply a high-nitrogen fertilizer in early spring. Continued poor growth after fertilizing may indicate that your soil is deficient in nutrients other than nitrogen; have a professional soil test done, then follow the laboratory's recommendations.

MANAGING PESTS AND DISEASES. A number of pests and diseases can afflict fruit trees. In the individual entries on pages 186–188, we note some of the most serious problems for each sort of fruit, along with appropriate controls for many. On deciduous fruit trees, using a dormant oil spray during winter prevents many pest problems; the oil smothers the pests as well as any overwintering eggs.

For more detailed information on identifying and controlling fruit tree pests and diseases, consult a local nursery or your Cooperative Extension Office.

TRAINING TO A CENTRAL LEADER

This method produces a straight-trunked, pyramidal tree.

1   Choose the first set of three to five scaffold branches (for simplicity, only two are shown in these illustrations). Do this at planting time if the tree is satisfactorily branched; otherwise, head back the trunk and wait until the first dormant season, when new branches will have grown. Shorten or remove any shoots competing with the leader. Head back the leader to just above buds to get a second tier of branches 1¹⁄₂ to 2¹⁄₂ feet above the first.

2   The next dormant season, choose a higher set of scaffolds. Remove ill-placed branches and head back the leader, if necessary, to get branching at the proper distance above the previous tier. Head back the scaffolds to force branching.

3   For good light penetration—important for growth and ripening of fruit—maintain some open space between tiers and keep the limbs toward the top of the tree shorter than those toward the bottom. Don't allow fruit to set on the leader (this would cause the leader to bend).

TRAINING TO AN OPEN CENTER

Also described as bowl shaped or vase shaped, an open-center tree has no central leader. Instead, several main limbs angle outward from the top portion of a short trunk. A tree trained in this fashion can be kept shorter than it would be if trained to a central leader or modified central leader.

1   At planting, head back the trunk to 2 or 3 feet high (or even lower, if desired). Remove all other shoots.

2   In the first dormant season, choose three to five scaffold branches spiraling around the trunk and having at least 6 inches of vertical space between them. Head back the branches to 2 to 3 feet in length.

3   In the second dormant season, choose two strong lateral branches on each scaffold branch and cut back the scaffolds to the chosen laterals. Head back the laterals to 2 to 3 feet, to force additional branching.

THINNING. Many kinds of trees set too much fruit. If you allow all of it to ripen, the fruits will be small and poor in quality. They'll also be more likely to suffer from pests such as codling moth, since closely set fruit provides a hiding place for undesirables. Certain diseases (apple scab, for example) may be more prevalent as well, due to decreased air circulation.

To encourage a healthier harvest of larger fruits (and to prevent overloaded branches from breaking), thin the crop when the developing fruits are about an inch in diameter. To avoid damaging branches, twist fruit off gently rather than pulling it. Thin apples to 6 to 8 inches apart, apricots to 2 to 3 inches, peaches and nectarines to 6 to 10 inches, and Japanese plums to 4 to 6 inches. Other kinds of plums, prunes, cherries, citrus, and pears usually do not need thinning.

TRAINING AND PRUNING. While they are young, fruit trees need some initial training to establish a strong, well-balanced framework of branches that will be able to support future crops. The three main training methods

THINNING FRUIT

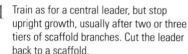

BEFORE

AFTER

are illustrated on the facing page and above. Once they mature, the trees benefit from yearly pruning during dormancy. Preferred training methods for young trees and pruning advice for mature ones are given for each tree in the sampler on pages 186–188.

Regardless of the training method used, initial pruning is the same. If you've planted a 1-year-old unbranched tree (whip), you'll have to force it to develop branches at the desired level—usually fairly close to the ground for easy picking. Heading back the trunk will stimulate lateral buds to grow into branches; cutting back to about 2 to 3 feet high is usually advised. The topmost shoot that develops will become the leader (the central, upward-growing stem).

If you're starting with a branched 2-year-old tree, it may already have a satisfactory leader and scaffold (primary) branches. These branches should be well spaced along the trunk and should radiate in different directions so they don't shade each other. If they're poorly placed, head back the tree as you would a whip and wait for new shoots to develop.

A SAMPLER OF FRUIT TREES

Presented here are profiles of some of the most popular fruit trees for home gardens. All are quite easy to grow.

APPLE

This is the most widely adapted fruit tree, with varieties suitable for almost every climate zone. The fruit ripens from July to early November, depending on climate and variety. Most require between 900 and 1,200 hours of winter chill. In mild-winter regions, choose varieties with a low chill requirement, such as 'Adina', 'Anna', or 'Dorsett Golden'.

With the exception of 'Golden Delicious', all varieties of apples require cross-pollination for good fruit set. Certain varieties (such as 'Gravenstein' and 'Stayman') do not produce fertile pollen and will fertilize neither their own flowers nor those of other apples.

Standard trees reach 40 feet tall and wide but can be kept to 20 feet with pruning. Most gardeners plant dwarf trees—to 5 to 8 feet high and wide—or somewhat larger semidwarf sorts.

TRAINING AND PRUNING. Central-leader training is ideal for smaller and medium-size trees. Train larger trees to a modified central leader to keep fruit within easy reach.

Mature trees need only moderate pruning; remove weak, dead, and poorly placed branches and twigs, especially those growing toward the tree's center.

PESTS AND DISEASES. The chief insect pests are apple maggot, codling moth, and plum curculio, all of which infest the fruit. Codling moth is a problem everywhere, while the other two are found mainly east of the Rockies. Traps help control all three; for more codling moth controls, see page 69. Apple diseases, including apple scab and cedar-apple rust, are prevalent east of the Rockies. To

avoid these, buy resistant varieties. If you do have an infestation, you can help avert future ones by raking up and discarding all fallen leaves and fruit.

APRICOT

Beautiful trees that bear luscious fruit, apricots typically grow best in the Western states (Zones 3–24). In mild-winter areas, choose varieties with a low chill requirement, such as 'Earligold' or 'Royal'. Hardy varieties bred from Manchurian apricot, such as 'Chinese' and 'Goldcot', are worth trying in Zone 2 and adjacent areas of the Great Plains states in Zones 35 and 41. Fruit of most

Apple

Apricot

varieties ripens from late spring into summer. Some apricots need a pollenizer.

Standard trees grow 30 feet high and wide but can be pruned to 15 feet. Semidwarf forms are sold, as are genetic dwarfs reaching 6 to 10 feet high.

TRAINING AND PRUNING. Because apricot trees tend to form too dense a canopy, open-center training is usually recommended. On mature trees, prune out dead, diseased, and broken branches, as well as any that cross through the tree's center or crowd major limbs. Remove older, unproductive branches, cutting back to new branches.

DISEASES. Bacterial canker and brown rot of stone fruit are serious diseases. For information on canker controls, see page 78. To control brown rot, prune trees to improve air circulation; also collect and dispose of diseased fruit. For chemical controls and timetables for treatment, contact your Cooperative Extension Office.

CHERRY

Both sweet and sour cherries are appealing choices for the home garden. Sweet cherries have a high chill requirement, so they don't do well in warm-winter areas; they're also intolerant of extreme heat and intense cold. They perform best in Zones 2, 6, 7, 14, 15, 32, 34, 37, 39. Most need a second variety nearby for pollination; exceptions are 'Glacier', 'Lapins', 'Stella', and 'Sunburst', which are self-fertile. Standard sweet cherry trees are large—up to 40 feet tall and 30 feet wide—and even regular pruning won't keep them much below 25 feet. For smaller trees, look for dwarf and genetic dwarf varieties, which reach only 6 to 10 feet.

Sour cherries, also called pie cherries, are more widely adapted than sweet cherries; they grow well in Zones 1–9, 14–17, 33–43. They are self-fertile. Standard trees grow to about 20 feet tall and wide; dwarf varieties (to 6 to 8 feet high) are also available.

TRAINING AND PRUNING. Both sweet and sour cherries can be trained to a central leader or modified central leader. Sour cherries can be trained to an open center as well. Mature cherry trees need only light pruning, to remove weak and damaged branches and maintain shape.

PESTS AND DISEASES. Scale insects and mites are controlled by dormant oil spray; for more on controlling scale, see page 72. Diseases include blossom blight and brown rot of stone fruit. To control brown rot, prune trees to improve air circulation; also collect and dispose of diseased fruit. For chemical controls and timetables for treatment, contact your Cooperative Extension Office. Use netting to keep birds from eating the cherry crop.

CITRUS

Even without the bonus of delightful fruit, citrus would be popular landscape plants for their attractive form, glossy evergreen foliage, and headily fragrant flowers.

Your region's winter temperatures play an important role in determining what kinds of citrus you can grow. The more common types can be grown outdoors only in the southernmost parts of the United States (Zones 8, 9, 12–27). Lemons, limes, and citrons are generally the most sensitive to freezes; sweet oranges, grapefruit, and most mandarins are intermediate. Kumquats, satsuma mandarins, sour oranges, and calamondins withstand temperatures into the high teens. Hardy citrus, including citrange and 'Changsha' mandarin, are good choices for Zones 7, 28–31 (just outside the typical hardiness range). See pages 90–91 for tips on protecting citrus from occasional frosts (protection is especially important for young trees).

Cherry

Citrus

Peach

Heat requirements also play a role in your choice of citrus. Sweet-fruited varieties need moderate to high heat to form sugars, while sour-fruited types require less heat.

All kinds of citrus trees are self-fertile.

Depending on species and variety, standard trees range from 6 to 30 feet tall and wide; dwarf and semidwarf sorts reach one-half to two-thirds the standard size.

TRAINING AND PRUNING. Train and prune citrus to shape as desired. In freeze-prone areas, don't prune in fall or winter.

PESTS AND DISEASES. Most citrus problems are minor and can be solved by improving growing conditions: give the trees adequate fertilizer, excellent drainage, and enough water to keep soil moist but not soggy. Slugs and snails can be a severe nuisance; for controls, see page 72.

PEACH AND NECTARINE

Beautiful spring blossoms and sweet, juicy fruit make peaches and nectarines favorites for the home garden. The trees look alike and have the same cultural needs; the main difference is that the fruit of peaches is fuzzy skinned, while that of nectarines is smooth.

The many peach and nectarine varieties tend to be adapted to specific regions; one kind or another can be grown in the Southeast, Mid-Atlantic, central and lower Midwest, Southwest, temperate Great Lakes regions, California, and dry-summer areas of the Pacific Northwest and intermountain West. There are extra-hardy selections suitable for parts of the Northeast. To decide on the best peach or nectarine for your area, consult a local nursery or your Cooperative Extension Office.

Most peach and nectarine varieties need 600 to 900 hours of winter chill. In mild-winter areas, choose those with a low chill requirement. Most kinds are self-fertile.

A standard peach or nectarine grows rapidly to 25 feet high and wide, but pruning can keep trees to 10 to 12 feet. A number of genetic dwarf selections are available, ranging in height from 4 to 10 feet.

TRAINING AND PRUNING. Peaches and nectarines are best trained to an open center.

Mature trees need more pruning than other fruit trees do. They produce fruit on 1-year-old branches; severe annual pruning renews the fruiting wood. Each dormant season, remove a quantity of wood equivalent to about two-thirds of the previous year's growth. To do this, prune out any weak or crowding new growth; then head back the remaining branches to staggered lengths, so that fruit will form throughout the crown. Cut back some branches by one-third, others by two-thirds, and the remainder nearly all the way. Keep the center open by removing any vigorous shoots growing through the middle.

PESTS AND DISEASES. Peach tree borer is the most serious pest. It tends to attack stressed trees, so prevention through good growing conditions is the best control. Diseases are usually more of a problem in humid, mild-winter regions than in areas with dry, hot summers and chilly winters. Ailments you may encounter include peach leaf curl and brown rot of stone fruit. For information on peach leaf curl controls, see page 78. To control brown rot, prune trees to improve air circulation; also collect and dispose of diseased fruit. For chemical controls and timetables for treatment, contact your Cooperative Extension Office.

PEAR

Ripening in fall and keeping into winter, pears round out the season for deciduous fruit trees. Clustered white flowers ornament the trees in spring; the leathery, glossy bright green leaves are attractive all summer.

Pears grow best in regions with warm, dry summers and fairly cold winters—Zones 2–9, 14–18, 32–39. Some varieties are adapted to other zones; check with local nurseries or your Cooperative Extension Office for information. To produce good crops, pears need 600 to 900 hours of winter chill. Most require cross-pollination.

Standard pears grow 30 to 40 feet high and about 25 feet wide, but they can be kept smaller—to 15 feet tall and wide—through pruning. Semidwarf pears are about half the size of standards.

Unlike other fruits, pears should be picked when they have reached full size

Pear

Plum

but are still unripe (green and firm). Put them in a cool, dark place to ripen.

TRAINING AND PRUNING. Pears can be trained to a central leader or modified central leader.

Once the framework is established, prune lightly each year to maintain good form and thin out weak, broken, and crowding branches. Remove upright stems growing through the interior of the tree.

PESTS AND DISEASES. Use dormant oil spray to control pear psylla, mites, and other pests. In warm, humid regions east of the Rockies, pears are subject to fireblight; resistant varieties such as 'Moonglow' offer the best chance of success. For more on fireblight, see page 78.

PLUM AND PRUNE

Three main categories of these fruits are grown in the diverse climates of North America. *European* types, such as 'Greengage', are at their best in the

Northeast and the north-central states, but they also produce good crops in the West. (Prunes are European plum varieties with a high sugar content, a trait which makes them suitable for sun-drying.) *Japanese* plums, including 'Santa Rosa' and 'Satsuma', are somewhat less hardy. They're widely grown in the South and West. A third category, the *hardy hybrids,* dominates in regions with severe winters—the Dakotas, Minnesota, and the Canadian prairies. This group includes some small-fruited types known as cherry-plums.

Most European plums don't require a pollenizer. Japanese plums, however, generally produce better crops when cross-pollinated, so plant two varieties. Pollination needs of the hardy hybrids vary; check with local nurseries or your Cooperative Extension Office.

Standard plum trees of all types will attain 30 feet tall and 25 feet wide, but can be kept to 15 feet high and broad with pruning. Dwarf sorts typically reach 8 to 10 feet.

TRAINING AND PRUNING. Plum and prune trees can be trained to a central leader, modified central leader, or open center.

Mature European plums require limited pruning, mainly to thin out annual shoot growth. Japanese and hardy hybrid plums are more vigorous. Each year, prune overly long shoots: head them back to side shoots or remove them completely if they are badly placed or crowded.

PESTS AND DISEASES. The more humid the climate, the more troublesome are plum curculio (which infests the fruit) and the diseases bacterial canker and brown rot of stone fruit. If you have only a few trees, try controlling the curculio with traps. For information on canker controls, see page 78. To control brown rot, prune trees to improve air circulation; also collect and dispose of diseased fruit. For chemical controls and timetables for treatment, contact your Cooperative Extension Office.

INDEX

Our special thanks to the mail-order garden supply companies and manufacturers who contributed tool photographs for this book:

Gardener's Supply Co.
(800) 955-3370; www.gardeners.com

Lee Valley Garden Tools
(800)871-8158; www.leevalley.com

A.M. Leonard
(800) 543-8955, reference BG99; www.amleo.com

Smith & Hawken
(800) 776-3336; www.smith-hawken.com

The Toro Company
www.toro.com

Union Tools, Inc.
(614) 222-4400; www.uniontools.com

PHOTOGRAPHY

William D. Adams: 75 top; **E. M. Ahart:** 125; **Dariel Alexander:** 154 bottom; **Curtis Anderson:** 17 bottom left; **Art Antonelli:** 65; **Scott Atkinson:** 33-3, 33-4, 35-3, 35-4, 37 bottom, 38 top, 42 left, 59 top left, 63 top, 66-3, 82 top left, 82 left silhouettes, 89 bottom, 126 bottom left, 155 all, 177 silhouettes; **Max E. Badgley:** 68 bottom, 72 upper middle, 72 upper bottom, 129 bottom inset; **Ron Boylan:** 81 top; **Marion Brenner:** 32 top left, 99 top, 100 upper middle, 101 upper middle, 103 lower middle, 111 bottom, 147, 152 top, 153 top, 160 middle, 163 bottom; **Gay Bumgarner:** 148 top; **Ralph S. Byther:** 57, 71 upper bottom, 78 middle; **James Carrier:** 17 top left; **James L. Castner:** 73 upper middle, 86 upper middle; **David Cavagnaro:** 1, 39 bottom, 117 center left, 135 upper middle, 141, 156 bottom, 161 upper middle, 162 bottom, 163 top left, 171, 173 left, 176 bottom right, 177 top, 188 bottom; **Van Chaplin/Southern Living:** 123 bottom; **Glenn Christiansen:** 20 bottom, 179 top; **Peter Christiansen:** 84 top, 142 bottom; **Jack K. Clark/Comstock:** 76 right; **Connie Coleman:** 106 top; **R. Cowles:** 129 bottom; **Crandall & Crandall:** 63 center, 66-6a, 129 upper middle, 129 middle inset; **Whitney Cranshaw:** 85 upper bottom; **Rosalind Creasy:** 120 bottom; **Claire Curran:** 109 upper middle, 111 lower middle, 112 middle, 113 upper middle, 113 bottom, 115 bottom, 144 top, 146 top, 151 upper middle right, 152 bottom, 158 top, 168 left, 168 top, 168 bottom; **Alan and Linda Detrick:** 117 right; **Clyde Elmore:** 85 bottom; **Thomas E. Eltzroth:** 77 bottom, 79 top, 79 upper middle, 79 lower middle, 180 bottom, 181 top right; **Derek Fell:** 3 top, 4, 20 top, 22 bottom, 31 right, 69 bottom, 96 top, 100 lower middle, 101 middle, 104 top, 104 lower middle, 104 bottom left, 105 lower middle, 105 bottom, 109 bottom, 112 top, 132 bottom right, 139 bottom, 178 top right, 178 bottom right, 182 bottom left, 186 bottom, 187 bottom; **William E. Ferguson:** 71 upper middle, 72 bottom, 74 upper middle, 74 lower middle; **Charles Marden Fitch:** 71 top; **Flame Engineering, Inc.:** 82 right; **Gardener's Supply Co.:** 27-4, 59 right, 66-2b, 81-1; **David Goldberg:** 33 top, 85 top, 85 middle, 86 lower middle, 87 bottom; **William Hamilton/The Image Bank:** 6 top; **Lynne Harrison:** 145 bottom; **Philip Harvey:** 66-4, 66-5, 109 top, 131; **Margaret Hensel:** 7 top; **Walter H. Hodge/Peter Arnold:** 105 right; **Saxon Holt:** 2 top, 12, 32 bottom left, 45 top left, 51 top, 63 bottom, 96 bottom, 101 top, 101 upper bottom, 101 bottom,102 top, 102 upper middle, 104 lower middle, 105 upper middle, 106 bottom, 111 top, 111 upper middle, 114 top, 115 top, 142 top, 151 lower middle left, 156 lower middle, 159 bottom, 160 bottom, 167 upper middle, 169 upper middle, 176 top right, 186 top, 186 middle; **Sandra Ivany:** 181 bottom; **Arthur Lee Jacobsen/PhotoGarden:** 100 bottom; **A. L. Jones/Visuals Unlimited:** 78 top; **B. Knoop:** 129 top; **Ray Krine/Grant Heilman Photography:** 72 middle; **Michael Landis:** 33-2, 120 top, 123 top, 127 bottom; **Lee Valley Garden Tools:** 42 center, 43 right, 52-3a, 53-5, 124 left bottom, 128 top; **A. M. Leonard:** 35-5, 43 right silhouettes, 52-2, 52-3b, 53-6, 53-7, 53-8, 81-2, 81-3, 124 left top, 124 left upper middle,124 left upper bottom, 126 top left, 127 top; **Janet Loughery:** 48 top; **Ray Maleike:** 28 top; **Allan Mandell:** 113 top, 117 left; **Charles Mann:** 22 top, 25, 27 top, 62, 105 top, 114 bottom, 135 upper middle, 135 lower middle, 137 lower middle, 139 middle, 144 middle, 151 upper middle left, 152 upper middle, 152 lower middle, 153 bottom, 158 middle, 158 bottom, 159 middle, 161 top, 162 top right, 163 right, 167 lower middle, 170 left, 173 bottom right; **John Marshall:** 17 bottom center, 154 top right; **Ells Marugg:** 31 left, 137 upper middle; **Jim McCausland:** 16 right, 89 top; **David McDonald:** 136 lower middle, 136 bottom, 139 top, 188 top; **Jack McDowell:** 110 top, 117 center right; **Charles W. Melton:** 69 upper bottom; **Hugh Palmer:** 167 bottom, 169 bottom; **Jerry Pavia:** 26, 64 center, 99 bottom, 103 upper middle,109 lower middle, 112 bottom, 118, 119, 135 bottom, 136 top, 137 top, 137 bottom, 144 bottom, 145 top, 146 bottom, 157 middle, 157 bottom, 169 lower middle, 172; **Joanne Pavia:** 148 bottom, 150 bottom, 159 top; **Pamela K. Peirce:** 73 upper bottom, 78 upper middle, 85 upper middle, 86 bottom, 87 top, 87 upper bottom, 88, 187 middle; **Norman A. Plate:** 3 bottom, 18, 30 left, 30 right, 32 bottom center, 32 bottom middle, 33-5, 35-6, 41 bottom, 41 top, 43 bottom left, 43 bottom center, 45 upper bottom, 45 lower bottom, 55, 59 bottom left, 84 bottom, 90 bottom, 94, 130, 151 lower middle right, 164, 165, 166, 167 top, 169 right, 170 top right, 174 bottom, 175, 176 left, back cover top left and bottom; **Rob Proctor:** 7 bottom; **Jay Pscheidt:** 77 top; **Ian Reeves:** 33-5, 35-7, 45 silhouettes, 52-1, 66-6b, 81-4; **Paul Resendez/Positive Images:** 99 middle; **E. S. Roth:** 69 top; **Susan A. Roth:** 64 top, 77 middle, 102 lower middle, 103 top, 116 left, 138 top, 145 middle, 151 top right, 157 top, 162 top left, 168 upper middle, 168 lower middle; **Scotts Co.:** 129 middle, 129 top inset; **Richard Shiell:** 74 bottom, 75 bottom, 87 upper middle, 87 middle, 110 bottom; **Malcolm C. Shurtleff:** 80 top; **Steve Sibbett:** 78 upper bottom, 80 bottom, 86 top; **Smith & Hawken:** 66-1, 66-2a, 124 left all; **J. G. Strauch, Jr.:** 143 bottom; **K. Bryan Swezey:** 47 top; **Anthony Tesselaar:** 138 bottom; **The Toro Company:** 126 center, 126 top right; **Michael S. Thompson:** 17 top right, 21, 45 middle left, 46 top, 48 bottom, 50, 53 bottom right, 67 top, 76 left, 90 top,100 top, 103 bottom, 104 bottom right, 105 bottom, 132 top left, 132 bottom left, 136 upper middle, 138 middle, 143 middle, 151 top left, 151 bottom right, 161 lower middle, 161 bottom, 173 top right, 178 left, 182 bottom right, 187 top; **Union Tools, Inc.:** 27-1, 27-2, 27-3, 27- 5, 27-6, 27-7, 33-1, 33-6, 35-1, 35-2, 53-9, 81-5, 81-6, 81-7, 128 bottom; **VISIONS-Holland:** 180 top; **Dominique Vorillon:** 6 bottom; **Lance Walheim:** 28 top; **Darrow M. Watt:** 16 left, 17 top center, 42 right, 46 bottom, 122 middle, 169 top, 170 bottom right, 174 top; **Ron West/Nature Photography:** 24, 68 top, 68 upper middle, 68 lower middle, 69 upper middle, 69 bottom, 70 all, 71 middle, 71 bottom, 72 top, 73 top, 73 lower top, 73 lower middle, 73 bottom, 74 top, 78 bottom, 79 bottom, back cover top right; **Russ Widstrand:** 49, 52-4; **Doug Wilson:** 113 lower middle, 160 top; **Tom Woodward:** 102 bottom, 135 top, 143 top, 150 top, 151 bottom left, 156 top; **Cynthia Woodyard:** 156 upper middle; **Tom Wyatt:** 45 tubing silhouettes, 116 right, 122 bottom, 124 right, 179 bottom, 181 top left, 182 top left; **Ed Young:** 67 bottom.